Du

£3 -

PHILOSOPHY AND LITERATURE

To my parents: Neil and Joyce Rowe

Philosophy and Literature

A Book of Essays

M.W. ROWE
University of York

ASHGATE

Published by
Ashgate Publishing Limited
Gower House
Croft Road
Aldershot
Hampshire GU11 3HR
England

Ashgate Publishing Company
Suite 420
101 Cherry Street
Burlington, VT 05401-4405
USA

Ashgate website: http://www.ashgate.com

British Library Cataloguing in Publication Data
Rowe, M. W.
Philosophy and literature : a book of essays
1. Philosophy 2. Philosophical literature
I. Title
192

Library of Congress Cataloging-in-Publication Data
Rowe, M. W., 1958-
Philosophy and literature : a book of essays / M.W. Rowe.
p. cm.
Includes bibliographical references and index.
ISBN 0-7546-3672-0 (alk. paper)
1. Philosophy. 2. Literature—Philosophy. I. Title.

B66.R68 2004
100—dc22

2004006143

ISBN 0 7546 3672 0

Printed and bound in Great Britain by MPG Books Ltd, Bodmin, Cornwall

Contents

Previous Places of Publication

'Goethe and Wittgenstein': *Philosophy*, 66, 257, July 1991.

'Criticism without Theory': Peter Lewis (ed.), *Wittgenstein, Philosophy, and the Arts* (Aldershot: Ashgate, 2004).

'Wittgenstein's Romantic Inheritance': *Philosophy*, 69, 3, July 1994.

'Arnold and the Socratic Personality': *Prose Studies*, 18, 2, August 1995.

'The Dissolution of Goodness: *Measure for Measure* and Classical Ethics': *The International Journal of the Classical Tradition*, 5, 1, Summer 1998.

'Lamarque and Olsen on Literature and Truth': *The Philosophical Quarterly*, 47, 188, July 1997.

'The Definition of "Art"': *The Philosophical Quarterly*, 41, 164, July 1991.

'Poetry and Abstraction': *The British Journal of Aesthetics*, 47, 1, January 1996.

I am grateful to Cambridge University Press, Ashgate, Frank Cass, Transaction Periodicals Consortium, Blackwells Publishers, and Oxford University Press for permission to reprint these articles.

'Aubade', 'Dockery and Son', and four lines from 'This Be the Verse' are from *Collected Poems* by Philip Larkin, copyright © 1988, 1989 by the estate of Philip Larkin. They are reprinted by permission of Faber and Faber Ltd, and Farrar, Straus and Giroux, LLC. I am grateful to Jeremy Crow and the trustees of Larkin's estate for allowing me to quote the manuscript material in the final essay. The Belvedere Gallery in Vienna is to be thanked for permission to reproduce the picture on the cover. It seemed appropriate – an invitation to view.

Poet, oracle and wit
Like unsuccessful anglers by
The ponds of apperception sit.

Auden, 'The Waters'

Preface

When I wrote these essays, I had no thought that they would one day form a book. My only intention was to illuminate the texts and problems I was writing about, and if the essays are worth anything, then this must still be their primary value. However, they were all written by one person, in a particular set of circumstances, so it is not surprising that certain common themes and ideas should begin to emerge. When the essays are placed back to back, the idea which stands out most clearly is their argument that philosophy and literature have a much greater affinity than is commonly supposed.[1] This therefore is the organizing principle of the book. The idea is more strongly marked in some essays than others, but perhaps this is inevitable when it was not the outcome of conscious intention. I like to think, however, that a book of essays should contain variety as well as unity, and that themes which emerge unbidden are somehow more organic and intertextured than those imposed by the writer's will. This may be an illusion.

In order to show philosophy and literature's kinship, I need to expand what might be called the standard conception of philosophy. It runs as follows. Philosophy is an abstract discipline that uses chains of rational argument – either inductive or deductive – to arrive at theories; and theories are consistent sets of propositional beliefs about the world or some parts of it. No doubt the author of any given theory has a certain history and character, and no doubt the theory has a certain effect on the emotions and perceptions of the reader, but these facts are wholly incidental to the theory's worth, and philosophy is not directly concerned with any of them. Equally, the style and genre in which the theory was first proposed are, as it were, the rhetorical clothing of the theory, but its truth and philosophical importance can be assessed from an accurate paraphrase, possibly in another genre, style or medium altogether.

The opening five essays all attempt to extend this conception. In the second of them, 'Criticism without Theory',[2] I try to show that not all reasoning is inductive or deductive, and not all reasoning should result in propositional truths. I argue that recognizing perceptual and quasi-perceptual patterns is one of the most fundamental forms of understanding, and that the kind of rhetoric designed to prompt others to see these patterns is one of the most fundamental forms of reasoning.[3]

In 'Goethe and Wittgenstein', I apply some of these lessons to philosophy. I argue that philosophical knowledge is not found on the page. Knowledge lies in the mind and senses of the original investigator, and his words are intended to prompt the reader into seeing things in the same way. Whether these prompts work, depends entirely on their style, order and tone. They must be as evocative as a poem, and a paraphrase of the *Philosophical Investigations* no more captures the impact of the original than a paraphrase of *The Prelude* captures that poem's emotional force. There is thus a genuinely internal relationship between genre, style, and philosophical understanding.

In 'Wittgenstein's Romantic Inheritance', I show that the obstacles to clear sight may be deeply rooted in the psyche, and that only a protracted education of the emotions can extirpate them. I argue that Wittgenstein has the same religious conception of inquiry as many German Romantic writers, and this is why their works share so many preoccupations: initial alienation from the ordinary world, the divided self, internal dialogue, the metaphor of the circular journey, the hope of reconciliation with society and the external world, and the wish to achieve inner peace. On this conception, the aim of philosophy is not theory, but clear vision and psychical harmony.

In 'Arnold and the Socratic Personality', I attempt to show that the deepest kind of philosophical influence can sometimes be a matter not of ideas and beliefs but of personality and style. During his period as a social critic, Arnold was not influenced by any Socratic doctrines. However, he did try to turn himself into a Socratic figure by attempting to emulate Socrates' virtues, and by developing a dialogic style which best allowed him to express them. Such an influence goes below the level of belief and into the sensibility itself. I discuss ideas of dialogue and intellectual conduct at greater length than in the previous essay, and I examine the philosophical significance of conversation, friendship, and irony for the first time.

I also explore a pervasive classical influence in 'The Dissolution of Goodness: *Measure for Measure* and Classical Ethics'. One of Shakespeare's insights is to see that a theoretical conception of ethics, based on propositional rules, cannot survive the realities of power. It will divide the self and provide the wrong answer in hard cases, and appetite will eventually sweep all regulation away. Only an ethics founded in practical knowledge, which aims to achieve psychical harmony by educating the appetites, habits, perception, character and emotions, can hope to avoid the denatured coldness of its theoretical rival. In this essay, I try to show that an over-theorized approach to moral philosophy has the same dangers, and the same remedies, as an over-theorized approach to epistemology.

In the first five essays, I argue for a literary and rather psychological view of philosophy: philosophy needs to concern itself with genre, style, perceptions and character. The next three essays belong more obviously to literary aesthetics. In these I argue, conversely, that abstract thought and truth have a role to play in literature as well as philosophy. I have two main targets here. Yeats and Hulme[4] famously said that poetry must have nothing to do with abstraction; and Peter Lamarque and Stein Olsen have argued at length, and influentially, that truth has no part to play in literary value.[5]

If the first five essays carry conviction, then Lamarque and Olsen's position will already have been weakened. First, I hope the discussion of *Measure for Measure* makes clear that the play's important insight into moral knowledge is part of its literary value. Second, Larmarque and Olsen define philosophy in terms of truth and rational argument, and their main motivation for denying that literature is concerned with these things is to distinguish it from philosophy.[6] But if, as I claim, their conception of philosophy is unduly restricted, then the nature of literature and literary value will also have to be thought through afresh. However, in the essay 'Lamarque and Olsen on Literature and Truth', I argue that their account of literary value is untenable in its own right. I show that truth can play a vital part in the assessment of literary merit, although it plays a different role in literature from that which it plays in philosophy.

In the 'The Definition of "Art"', I am also concerned with the role of truth and knowledge in aesthetic appreciation, but here I concentrate on the truths you have to know about a work prior to understanding and appreciating it. I also attempt to show how to distinguish the literary critic's interest in truth from the historian's. In 'Poetry and Abstraction', I discuss objections to the notion that poetry can contain abstract thought. I consider a possible rationale behind these objections and argue that, when it is seen clearly, the rationale actually *justifies* the place of abstract thought. I try to show that although abstract thought in poetry is entirely legitimate, it must – like truth – be treated in a different fashion from the way it is approached in philosophy.

'Poetry and Abstraction' contains a short discussion of Larkin's 'Dockery and Son', and the final essay is an extended commentary on Larkin's 'Aubade'. There are three reasons for including the latter essay here. First, 'Aubade' shows a major poet tackling a philosophical theme, and my commentary is intended to show that the poem exemplifies all the features of correctly handled poetic thought sketched in the previous essay. Second, the essay's final section shows that truth in literature can be a problem for the poet as well as the philosopher. Third, like the piece on *Measure for Measure*, the essay is an extended example of critical reasoning. Unlike the Shakespeare essay, however, it is a line by line commentary, bringing to bear all kinds of considerations, rather than an attempt to explain the work by reference to a single abstract model. There are a number of reasons why this essay seems an appropriate place to end, not least because it speaks of last things and the inability to write.

The essay on 'Aubade' has not been published before, but the preceding eight essays have previously appeared in academic journals and an edited volume. I have reinstated the introductory section of 'Wittgenstein's Romantic Inheritance', originally cut for reasons of space, and repaired a large number of printing errors that appeared in its first incarnation. I have cut the final paragraph of 'The Dissolution of Goodness' because it was more appropriate to the classics journal in which it first appeared than the present context. I have also attempted to brisken the pace of 'Arnold and the Socratic Personality' by removing a few pages originally designed to situate the article in contemporary debate rather than advance the argument. Apart from being placed in a uniform format, the other essays are as they originally appeared, except for a few updated footnotes, factual corrections, and minor rephrasings.

There are a number of people I would like to thank. Michael Tanner at Cambridge showed how it was possible to combine an expert knowledge of philosophy, music and literature. Martin Bell, my DPhil supervisor at York, brought a logician's eye to bear on my written work while happily allowing me to research what I wanted. Peter Lamarque was the instigator of this book and has been its constant supporter, and Paul Coulam at Ashgate has been a most understanding editor. I am also grateful to many people who read and commented on my work over the years: Anita Avramides, Simon Glendinning, Andy Hamilton, Margaret Howatson, Ann Pasternak-Slater, Penelope Pelizzon, Anthony Price, Beth Savickey, the late Flint Schier, David Taylor and David Wiggins. Above all, however, I would like to thank my wife, Marie McGinn, for being such an incisive and supportive critic of my work, and Alan Heaven for his consistent interest and advice. Finally, I am grateful to Pat FitzGerald for her invaluable assistance in preparing the final copy.

Notes

1 I do not wish to claim, of course, that this idea is in any way original, but I hope that the way I make my case, and the details of the argument, are new.

2 Stoppard's *Arcadia* provides reasons for thinking that this form of reasoning underlies and unifies all intellectual activity.

3 I have tried to make the book's order sympathetic to the reader. I have attempted to ensure that the opening is not too abstract, the impact of necessary repetitions is muted, and that each topic flows naturally into the next. From the point of view of explaining the book's argument, however, it is easier to begin with the book's second essay.

4 See W.B. Yeats, *Essays*, p. 362, quoted in L.C. Knights, 'Poetry, Politics and Religion', in *Further Explorations* (London; Chatto and Windus, 1965), p. 73, and T.E. Hulme, 'Romanticism and Classicism', in H. Reed (ed.), *Speculations: Essays on Humanism and the Philosophy of Art* (London; Routledge and Kegan Paul, 1987), p. 134.
5 Peter Lamarque and Stein Haugom Olsen, *Truth, Fiction, and Literature* (Oxford: Oxford University Press, 1994).
6 Lamarque and Olsen, *Truth, Fiction, and Literature*, esp. pp. 321–38 and 368–97.

Chapter 1

Goethe and Wittgenstein

The influence of Goethe on Wittgenstein is just beginning to be appreciated. Hacker and Baker,[1] Westphal,[2] Monk,[3] and Haller[4] have all drawn attention to significant affinities between the two men's work, and the number of explicit citations of Goethe in Wittgenstein's texts supports the idea that we are not dealing simply with a matter of deep lying similarities of aim and method, but of direct and major influence. These scholarly developments are encouraging because they help to place Wittgenstein's work within an important tradition of German letters which goes far beyond his contemporaries and immediate forebears in Vienna; and they show that Wittgenstein's profound interest in literature and music is ceasing to be merely a matter of biographical anecdote, and is being used to illuminate some of the most central areas of his work.

Of course, there are many ideas in Goethe which are not echoed in Wittgenstein: the latter had no belief in the unity of all things, or the divinity of nature, or in reality progressing through dialectics (another stream of German philosophy would develop these ideas). But there are a number of points of contact which are well worth stressing, and in this essay I shall examine two: firstly, that there are a number of very striking similarities between Goethe's conception of science and Wittgenstein's conception of philosophy; secondly, that this shared understanding of aim and method results in a literary form which is common to Goethe's most important scientific treatise – the *Theory of Colours* – and Wittgenstein's *Philosophical Investigations*. By comparing the two, I hope to give at least preliminary answers to two questions raised by Stanley Cavell: 'Why does [Wittgenstein] write [this] way? Why doesn't he just say what he means, and draw instead of insinuate conclusions?'[5]

* * *

Goethe believed that the senses, properly used and developed, showed you the truth about the world, and he vigorously resisted any doctrines, however well entrenched, that tried to show that this fundamental conviction was false. In Germany in the late eighteenth and early nineteenth centuries there were two notable sources of pressure on this belief: the first was the transcendental idealist philosophy initiated by Kant and later developed by Fichte and

Schelling, which, Goethe felt, devalued the objects of the physical world in favour of the metaphysical subject; the second was Newtonian science, which he believed devalued the living multiplicity of nature by ossifying it into mechanisms, dissolving it into mathematical abstraction, and leaving the human subject a prisoner of delusory sensations.[6]

Writing to Schiller after reading one of Schelling's early works, he remarked that he saw no more possibility of transcendental idealists being able to get from mind to bodies than of materialists getting from bodies to mind. Until the philosophers should decide the matter, he continued, he preferred to remain 'in dem philosophischen Naturstande' (in the philosophical state of nature) and to make the best possible use of his 'undivided existence'.[7] He was prepared to concede that the Cartesian divide between subject and object might be an instrument that was useful for one kind of thinking, but it was not a way of conceptualizing the world he could *experience*, and he therefore never felt the need to separate them. He was vehemently opposed to the view that mind and body could be thought of as inner and outer, and that mental activity is something which takes place in the recesses of the mind. Such a belief, he felt, was of a piece with the doctrine that all we can ever experience of nature are appearances, and the poem 'Allerdings' was written in irritated response to yet another expression of this view:

> I have heard this reiterated for sixty years –
> And cursed it on the quiet.
> I tell myself a thousand times:
> Nature gives everything amply and gladly,
> She has neither core
> Nor husk,
> She is everything at once.
> You just ask yourself,
> Whether you are core or husk.[8]

We know from Hacker and Baker's researches that Wittgenstein seriously considered using this verse as a motto to head *Philosophical Investigations*, and the Wittgensteinian elements in the foregoing do not need to be laboured: in the later philosophy, the temptation to divide mind from body, inner from outer, is vigorously resisted; there are no noumena or metaphysical subjects, only ordinary human beings embedded in cultures who respond to and act on their environment.

Goethe was not opposed to conventional science or mathematics but he was opposed to scientism. He disliked the immense prestige these disciplines enjoyed as the final arbiters of what the world did and did not contain, and disavowed any attempt to conceptualize a fluid and dynamic reality in terms of static rules, axioms or definitions. As Humphrey Trevelyan puts it: 'The forces at work, not the finished products, were what enthralled him. For this reason, like Wordsworth, he distrusted "the false secondary power" which classifies, analyses and anatomizes, and strove always to see the living totality.'[9] Nature could not be captured in general terms, but only by bringing intuition ('Anschauung') to bear on particular cases in order to apprehend them in their full individuality. The nature of plant growth, for example, was only to be discovered by sympathetic discernment – apprehending the part, seeing its place in the economy of the whole, returning with renewed insight to the part, and so on – which called on every resource of the investigator's sensibility. In other words, Goethe approached nature with the critical tact of a fellow artist; to understand was not passively to record, but to use imagination in actively seeking and exploring; and self-knowledge and psychical harmony on the part of the investigator were just as necessary for success as thoroughness and precision in the investigation itself.[10]

Unsurprisingly, Goethe reserved his heartiest scorn for the Newtonian treatment of colour. Colour seems the richest and most immediate of sensory phenomena, and yet Newton's mathematical treatment of light in his *Opticks* was regarded as one of the triumphs of modern physics. The detail of Goethe's objections, and the precise nature of his alternative theory need not be investigated here, but the argumentative strategies he employs against Newton in his *Theory of Colours* are well worth considering.

First, he accused Newton of basing his entire theory on a limited number of contrived, highly artificial experiments: very narrow beams of sunlight passing through glass prisms for example. Inevitably, he felt, the erection of a supposedly comprehensive theory on such a narrow base resulted in distortion and partiality: 'Newton ... based his hypothesis on a phenomenon exhibited in a complicated and secondary state; and to this the other cases that forced themselves on the attention were contrived to be referred, when they could not be passed over in silence ...' [F:lii].[11] Second, because of his mathematical background, Newton was interested in system and consistency at the expense of the particular concrete case: '... a great mathematician had investigated the theory of colours and having been mistaken in his observations as an experimentalist, he employed the whole force of his talent to give consistency to his mistake ...' [F:lx]. This could only result in virtually meaningless technical terms, utterly divorced from lived experience ('Bundles and fasces of rays, and like hypothetical notions' [F:401]) and misplaced reification and abstraction ('For hitherto, light has been considered as a kind of abstract principle, existing and acting independently ...' [F:367]).

Goethe wished to discredit such theoretical distortions and artificialities, by placing the phenomenon back in the real world where it belonged, and establishing a much broader base for investigation. In particular, he wished to draw attention to the colour effects everyone experiences (or could experience) in everyday life, and the reader of the *Farbenlehre* is bombarded with a thousand quotidian observations: the sun goes red as it sets, smoke from your neighbour's chimney grows light as it rises, distant mountains look blue, rainbow effects can be seen on spiders' webs in sunlight, washing a dark blue painting can turn it temporarily light blue, tobacco smoke turns roses green. Experienced *en masse*, such observations have the effect of making us see just how limited the kinds of phenomena investigated in laboratories actually are, and draw attention to the quite extraordinary range and complexity of the phenomena we have experienced – but frequently overlooked – in everyday life. Goethe placed far more reliance on the opinions of practical everyday men, who had no inclination to premature theorizing and every reason to observe carefully, than he did in mathematicians and physicists: '[The practical man of affairs] feels the erroneousness of a theory much sooner than the man of letters, in whose eyes words consecrated by authority are at least equivalent to solid coin; the mathematician, whose formula always remains infallible, even though the foundation on which it is constructed may not square with it' [F:lxi]. Consequently, Goethe refers just as often to the untainted observations of dyers, industrialists and painting restorers, as he does to the findings of other scientists.

Here again, the parallels with the later Wittgenstein are striking. Unlike Goethe, he had a very thorough scientific training, but an opposition to the worship of science and scientists was a major motivation behind his philosophical outlook. 'Soapy water science' [CV:49][12] – the attempt to use science to interpret the world for us – was always dismissed with contempt: 'Jeans has written a book called *The Mysterious Universe* and I loathe it and call it misleading ... I might say the title *The Mysterious Universe* includes a kind of idol worship, the idol being science and the scientist' [LC.27]. His attitude towards mathematicians was also ambivalent, feeling that they had an innate tendency to mythologize the nature of proof and necessity: 'There is no religious denomination in which the misuse of metaphysical expressions has been responsible for so much sin as it has in mathematics' [CV: 1].

The idea that the conceptual understanding cannot capture and codify the nature of reality, and that it is essential to understand individual cases in the greatest possible detail is also characteristic of Wittgenstein. In the discussion of family resemblances in *Philosophical Investigations*, for example, he argues that it is not possible to give necessary and sufficient conditions for most of our ordinary concepts, and that a philosopher who imagines he has done so has merely *constructed* a simpler concept which is in some way analogous to ours. Similarly, logicians do not discover a hard logical core underlying our language which makes it usable; and no rule, however detailed, can determine how a practice is to proceed. Wittgenstein is at pains to stress that knowledge, mathematics and language are grounded in *activity*, in ungrounded ways of acting, in an illimitably vast and overlapping series of natural responses. As he says in *On Certainty*: 'Giving grounds, however, justifying … comes to an end; but the end is not certain propositions striking us immediately as true … it is our *acting* which lies at the bottom of the language game' [OC:204]. When, some two hundred sections later, he quotes the famous line from part one of *Faust*: 'In the beginning was the deed' [RPP:I,1236, OC:402], he shows himself aware that his emphasis on life and dynamism places him in the Goethean tradition.

The errors of Newton's *Opticks*, Goethe believed, were caused by concentrating on a narrow range of artificial cases and then prematurely generalizing from them. Wittgenstein brings exactly the same arguments to bear on philosophical error. The philosopher's 'craving for generality and the contemptuous attitude towards the particular case' [BB:18] is frequently caused by 'a one-sided diet: one nourishes one's thinking with only one kind of example' [PI:593] and this 'philosophical disease' can only be cured by *looking* and *seeing* (not simply thinking) at the sheer multiplicity and variety of ordinary practice. Rarefied theoretical discussion is replaced by detailed description of the humdrum affairs of practical life, in an attempt to bring words back from their puzzling metaphysical uses to the ordinary circumstances in which they have their life [PI:116]. In this way, entities which the philosopher feels inclined to reify or 'sublime' are shown not to be puzzling Platonic objects, but words which are perfectly straightforward and unproblematic when their true use and context is established [PI:117].

It is when we reach Goethe's conception of explanation, however, that we arrive at the true centre of his affinity with Wittgenstein. Goethe's central explanatory idea is the *Gestalt*. This is a concrete form or pattern which it is the object of the critic or the scientist to discern amongst a multiplicity of superficially dissimilar instances. Using Goethe's technique (if an expression of someone's being can be called that) of intuitive contemplation, the investigator comes to see – and in some sense or other Goethe meant *literally* see – the form that all the natural phenomena under investigation manifest.[13] As many writers have shown,[14] his method is neither deductive nor inductive, and at first, Goethe himself was evidently puzzled both by the status of his technique and what exactly he was looking for. This can be seen in his quest for the *Urpflanze*: the primal plant of which all others are manifestations. At first, he was sure that this archetypal plant had, or had had, genuine biological existence, and he spent some time in the botanical gardens in Padua looking for it. Later, he came to think that this primal plant was the leaf, and that all the other parts of the plant were metamorphosized leaves; finally, late in life, there is evidence to suppose he acknowledged the *Urpflanze* was an archetype whose origin lay partly within man's self, and that it was a way of grouping or intellectually grasping the totality of plants.[15]

This did not, however, prevent him from claiming, throughout his life, that the *Urpflanze* was something which could be *seen.* This led to a famous incident with the Kantian Schiller, which is recorded in Goethe's diary:

> I explained to him with great vivacity the Metamorphosis of Plants and, with a few characteristic strokes of the pen, conjured up before his eyes a symbolical plant. He listened, and looked at it all with great interest and intelligence; but when I had ended he shook his head saying: This is nothing to do with *experience*, it is an *idea* ... I replied: Well, so much the better; it means that I have ideas without knowing it, and can even *see them with my eyes.*[16]

In the same conversation Schiller further objected, 'How can one equate experience with ideas? For an idea is characterized precisely by the fact that experience can never be fully congruous to it.' A remark which caused Goethe to reflect, '... if he takes for an idea what to me is experience, then there must, after all, prevail some mediation, some relationship between the two'.[17] Erich Heller describes this meeting as 'a dramatic climax in the history of German thought and letters',[18] and it was an incident Wittgenstein knew well. In one of his manuscripts [Vol. VI:256][19] he quotes Schiller's first remark and then transcribes the opening of Goethe's poem 'The Metamorphosis of Plants' addressed to a woman who is initially confused by 'the thousandfold mingled multitude of flowers' but is eventually brought peace by being helped to see the underlying morphological unity.

It should now be evident that Wittgenstein's discussion of *Gestalten*, or 'seeing-as', not only in the second part of the *Investigations* but throughout many volumes of his later writings, keys into a central debate at the heart of German Romantic culture. Wittgenstein's discussion of 'seeing-as' is, amongst other things, an intensely penetrating defence of Goethe's position, since it is concerned to discover the precise nature of the mediation that obtains between ideas and experience.[20] 'Seeing-as' contains elements of thought and elements of experience, but the two are indissolubly fused together and create a category which is *sui generis*:

> Hence the flashing of an aspect on us seems half visual experience, half-thought. [PI:197]

> [Is seeing-as] a special sort of seeing? Is it a case of both seeing and thinking? or an amalgam of the two, as I should almost like to say? [PI:197]

Seeing an aspect, or 'seeing-as', is not only important to Wittgenstein because it is the phenomenon that makes much ethical, critical and psychoanalytic discussion intelligible. Towards the end of his discussion of philosophical method in the *Investigations*, he makes it clear that the purpose of philosophy itself is not to produce theories, but to induce someone to see the world under a new aspect, cleansed of false pictures [PI:115] and the staleness of familiarity:

> The aspects of things that are most important for us are hidden because of their simplicity and familiarity. (One is unable to notice something – because it is always before one's eyes.) The real foundations of his enquiry do not strike a man at all. Unless *that* fact has at some time struck him. – And this means: we fail to be struck by what, once seen, is most striking and most powerful. [PI:129]

Goethe stresses that his science is not concerned with the hidden causes of things, but with patterns in objects which we could see in the visible world if only we learned to look at it correctly: 'For we are not looking for causes here but for conditions under which phenomena appear.'[21] Wittgenstein too, emphasizes that in philosophy we are not looking for anything hidden:

> 126. Philosophy simply puts everything before us, and neither explains nor deduces anything – Since everything lies open to view there is nothing to explain. For what is hidden, for example, is of no interest to us. [PI]

The philosopher, like the Goethean scientist, wants to see the world under a new and more organized aspect, and to do this he constructs intermediate cases, assembles reminders, draws your attention to things, and invents analogies.

Of the latter, Goethe wrote: '… we hope the genius of the analogy may stand by us, as a guardian angel, so that we may not fail to recognize in a single doubtful case a truth which has stood the test in many other instances …'.[22] The extraordinary analogies one can find throughout Wittgenstein's texts are not simply an ornament of his style either, but are integral to his whole conception of method and explanation: 'To resolve philosophical problems one has to compare things which it has never occurred to anyone to compare' [RFM:376]. (Indeed, at one stage of his life he even thought his ability to invent new similes and analogies was his only original contribution to philosophy [CV:19].) At least twice, Wittgenstein compares his own conceptual investigations with Goethe's studies of plants.[23] *The Principles of Linguistic Philosophy*, in which Waismann attempts to summarize several years of conversation with Wittgenstein, contains a particularly important passage. It is worth quoting at length:

> Our thought here marches with certain views of Goethe's which he expressed in the *Metamorphosis of Plants.* We are in the habit, whenever we perceive similarities, of seeking some common origin for them. The urge to follow such phenomena back to their origin in the past expresses itself in a certain style of thinking. This recognizes, so to speak, only a single scheme for such similarities, namely the arrangement as a series in time. (And that is presumably bound up with the uniqueness of the causal schema.) But Goethe's view shows that this is not the only possible form of conception. His conception of the original plant implies no hypothesis about the temporal development of the vegetable kingdom such as that of Darwin. What then is the problem solved by this idea? It is the problem of synoptic presentation. Goethe's aphorism 'All the organs of plants are leaves transformed' offers us a plan in which we may group the organs of plants according to their similarities as if around some natural centre. We see the original form of the leaf changing into similar and cognate forms, into the leaves of the calyx, the leaves of the petal, into the organs that are half petals, half stamens, and so on. We follow the sensuous transformation of the type by linking up the leaf through intermediate forms with the other organs of the plant.
>
> This is precisely what we are doing here. We are collating one form of language with its environment, or transforming it in imagination so as to gain a view of the whole of the space in which the structure of our language has its being.[24]

For Goethe, true understanding of nature is achieved by showing how complex individual phenomena are related to simpler cases, and how these in turn are related to the primary phenomenon, at which point explanation ceases. The *Urphänomen*, as Goethe terms it, is a perceivable example of some class of natural objects or processes which exemplifies the class in its simplest possible form; thus entailing that all other instances of the class are more complex or highly derived. In the case of plants, the primary phenomenon is the *Urpflanze*; for colour phenomena, the mixing of darkness and light. But this understanding, this *seeing*, cannot be established or conveyed in words or symbols: it can only be achieved by each investigator actually *looking* at a whole series of real examples, and when the root to the primary phenomenon is seen then that is the explanation. Goethe had a completely different conception of the role of experiment from the modern scientist. For the scientist, experiment is a means to securing conceptual understanding which can then be handed on to another. For Goethe, experiments work by being placed in a series of similar and otherwise interlinked cases, which do not issue in a theory, but might result in a certain community of vision:[25]

> Everything is gradually arranged under higher rules and laws, which, however, are not to be made intelligible by words and hypotheses to the understanding merely, but at the same time by real phenomena to the senses. We call them [primary] phenomena, because nothing appreciable by the senses lies beyond them, on the contrary, they, are perfectly fit to be considered as a fixed point to which we first ascend step by step, and from which we may, in the like manner, descend to the commonest case of everyday experience. [F:175]

Wittgenstein appears to consider the idea of an *Urphänomen* to be an aberration: 'The "primary phenomenon" (*Urphänomen*) is, e.g., what Freud thought he recognized in simple wish-fulfilment dreams. The primary phenomenon is a preconceived idea that takes possession of us' [RC:III: 230]. But this remark is misleading for two reasons. Firstly, Rudolf Haller makes the excellent point that Wittgenstein's own writings conform to such an explanatory model.[26] For example, the simple language games outlined at the beginning of the *Philosophical Investigations* (e.g., the builder who asks his assistant for slabs [PI:2]), are not supposed to be the kind of exchanges from which full-blown languages actually developed; they are merely objects for comparison, useful didactic models, from which we can gradually ascend to more and more complicated examples. At the end of this process, our own language that 'already lies open to view' will become 'surveyable by ... rearrangement' [PI:92]. Secondly, in *Philosophical Investigations*, Wittgenstein explicitly states that a Goethean conception of explanation should be our ideal. Anscombe translates the first sentence of section 654 as, 'Our mistake is to look for an explanation where we ought to look at what happens as a "proto-phenomenon".' The word here translated as 'proto-phenomenon' is in fact

Goethe's word 'Urphänomene', and the passage would be better translated as, 'Our mistake is to look for an explanation where we ought to look at the facts as "Urphänomene".'[27] In *Remarks on Colour*, Wittgenstein's complaint is not against the idea of an *Urphänomen* as such, but against the way that notion is used in the practice of writers like Freud, where it has hardened into a dogma and become the object of enquiry rather than a useful heuristic device. As he says apropos Spengler, 'The ideal doesn't lose any of its dignity if it's presented as a principle determining the form of one's reflections' [CV:27].[28]

There is also one other very notable Wittgensteinian resonance in the passage from Goethe quoted above – the idea that not only do explanations come to an end, but that they often come to an end sooner than we expect:

> 313. … the temptation is overwhelming to say something further, when everything has already been described – Whence this pressure? What analogy, what wrong interpretation produces it?
>
> 314. Here we come up against a remarkable and characteristic phenomenon in philosophical investigation: the difficulty – I might say – is not that of finding the solution but rather that of recognizing as the solution something that looks as if it were only a preliminary to it. 'We have already said everything. – Not anything that follows from this, no, *this* itself is the solution!'
>
> This is connected, I believe, with our wrongly expecting an explanation, whereas the solution of the difficulty is a description, if we give it the right place in our considerations. If we dwell upon it, and do not try to get beyond it.
>
> The difficulty here is: to stop. [Z]

For Goethe, the greatest methodological temptation is to posit a hidden mechanism behind phenomena which is supposed to account for their behaviour. His work contains several warnings against penetrating phenomena and literally taking leave of the senses, and at one point he likens the Newtonian scientist to a child who thinks that by looking behind a mirror he will at last be able to explain what is seen in it.[29] Wittgenstein evidently took such warnings to heart; not only does he frequently cite the positing of hidden mechanisms as a sign that something has gone philosophically amiss [e.g. BB:3], but in MS.134 he quotes with approval Goethe's maxim, 'Don't look for anything behind the phenomena; they themselves are the theory.'[30] We are only tempted to penetrate phenomena and posit causal mechanisms when a pattern that could have been seen in the real world has been missed. This temptation and its attendant sense of dissatisfaction vanish when a suitable description – one that allows us to see the pattern – has been produced. Nature's secrets are often hidden, but in the way that a man can be hidden in a puzzle picture, not in the way he can be hidden behind a screen.

I hope it is now obvious that Goethe's conception of science and scientific explanation bears the closest possible analogy to Wittgenstein's conception of philosophy and philosophical explanation. Wittgenstein, in fact, went further: he thought Goethe was engaged on a conceptual enquiry which he mistook for a scientific one.[31] In the *Remarks on Colour* [22 and 51] and *Remarks on the Philosophy of Psychology* [I:950] Wittgenstein makes quite clear that he thought Goethe was engaged in a logical endeavour. The latter passage also demonstrates the value of the analogical approach:

> What is it, however, that a conceptual investigation does? Does it belong to the natural history of human concepts? – Well, natural history, we say, describes plants and beasts. But might it not be that plants had been described in full detail, and then for the first time someone realized the analogies in their structure, analogies which had never been seen before? And so, he establishes a new order among these descriptions. He says, e.g., 'compare this part, not with this one, but rather with that' (Goethe wanted to do something of the sort) and in so doing he is not necessarily speaking of *derivation*; none the less the new arrangement *might* also give a new direction to scientific investigation. He is saying 'Look at it like this' – and that may have advantages and consequences of various kinds.[32]

This kind of enquiry results in an almost perceptual understanding of how phenomena are laid out and interrelate, which Wittgenstein called an *Übersicht*,[33] a 'perspicuous representation' [PI:122]. In the introduction to the *Farbenlehre,* Goethe describes this goal:

> During [the] process of observation we remark at first only a vast variety which presses indiscriminately on our view; we are forced to separate, to distinguish, and again to combine; by which means at last a certain order arises which admits of being surveyed with more or less satisfaction.
>
> To accomplish this, only in a certain degree, in any department, requires an unremitting and close application; and we find, for this reason, that men prefer substituting a general theoretical view, or some system of explanation, for the facts themselves … [F:lii]

To accomplish this difficult task, a special kind of literary form is required which makes exceptionally heavy demands on the reader. In many ways it is remarkable how closely *Philosophical Investigations* and the *Farbenlehre* resemble one another, both in terms of the kind of attention the authors explicitly demand of their readers, and also in their literary structure. How far this is due to a similar conception of the enquirer's task and how far to direct influence is hard to assess. Wittgenstein certainly had the *Theory of Colours* open in front of him as he wrote *Remarks on Colour* in 1950, and pungently said to von Wright that it was, 'Partly boring and repelling, but in some ways also very instructive and philosophically interesting',[34] but he has a remark about Goethe's theory in a section of *Culture and Value* [CV:18] written in 1931 which suggests the book was familiar to him long before he started work on the *Investigations.* However, Wittgenstein also says the form of his book is 'connected with the very nature of the investigation' [PI:vii] – so it seems likely that a shared conception of enquiry prompted the literary influence.

Eastlake's English translation of Goethe's book – which omits the polemical and historical material found in the German original – contains 920 numbered sections and a short conclusion, roughly grouped according to subject matter; some are several pages in length, others consist of no more than a short sentence. It is often quite difficult to know how each remark relates to those around it: some seem like short interjections, others form part of a longer argument, some offer summaries, others methodological aphorisms. Such an arrangement and the problems it causes are familiar to readers of the *Investigations*, a book whose first (and more polished) section is divided into 693 numbered remarks, followed by fourteen longer sections which vary from about half a page to thirty-five pages in length, and are themselves divided into shorter paragraphs. As Wittgenstein says in his preface, 'I have written down all these thoughts as *remarks*, short paragraphs, of which there is sometimes a fairly long chain about the same subject, while I sometimes make a sudden change, jumping from one topic to another' [PI:vii].

Both authors also state that they will both make unusually strenuous demands on the reader, both while he is engaged with the text and while he is away from it. The preface to the *Tractatus* begins by announcing that perhaps the book will only be understood by those who have already had similar thoughts, and the penultimate paragraph of the *Investigations*' preface says, 'I should not like my writing to spare other people the trouble of thinking. But, if possible, to stimulate someone to thoughts of his own' [PI:viii]. Goethe too, explains the difficulties his work will pose to the reader (who must be more than a reader):

> Since an analysis like the present requires to be confirmed by ocular demonstration, we beg every reader to make himself acquainted with the

> experiments hitherto adduced, not in a superficial manner, but fairly and thoroughly. We have not placed arbitrary signs before him instead of the appearances themselves; no modes of expression are here proposed for his adoption which may be repeated for ever without the exercise of thought and without leading any one to think; but we invite him to examine intelligible appearances, which must be present to the eye and mind, in order to enable him clearly to trace these appearances in their origin, and explain them to himself and others. [F:242]

One reason why both books encourage the slowest and most considered approach is that they are full of experiments which the reader has to break off and try for – and more specifically on – himself. Wittgenstein's tend to be thought experiments, e.g. 'Make the following experiment: *say* "It's cold here" and *mean* "It's warm here". Can you do it? And what are you doing as you do it? – And is there only one way of doing it?' [PI:510]. Goethe's tend to be real ones: 'Cut in a piece of pasteboard five perfectly similar square openings of about an inch, next each other, exactly in a horizontal line: behind these openings place five coloured glasses in the natural order, orange, yellow, green, blue, violet …' [F:284].

Both the *Tractatus* and the *Investigations* are obscure books but in quite different ways. The *Tractatus* is obscure because we are simply presented with conclusions or answers to questions we have not been told ('1 The world is all that is the case. 1.1 The world is the totality of facts, not of things' (T:1]). and the effort to overcome this obscurity consists in the reader reconstructing the reasoning that gives these assertions meaning and point. In his preface, Wittgenstein says it is not a textbook, and this is usually taken to mean that its difficulty prevents it from being an introduction. This is certainly correct, but it is also true when construed as a remark about *genre.* Mathematics textbooks, for example, consist either of worked questions and answers, or sets of unanswered questions, or some combination of these. No textbook ever consisted of sets of answers alone.

The *Investigations*, on the other hand, is obscure because we do appear to be presented with various reasonings, experiments, considerations, short sections of argument, but we are left to worry out their conclusions, answers and import for ourselves. In a sense, the *Farbenlehre* and the *Investigations* *are* textbooks, workbooks, sets of exercises, because large numbers of experiments and questions are proposed but it is the *reader* who has to answer them. Indeed, one of the most striking facts about the *Investigations* is the sheer *quantity* of questions, most of which either receive no answer at all or an obviously false answer. Such clearly correct conclusions as there are, are no more than simple heuristic devices designed to encourage the reader's continuing struggle, like the sets of exercises in maths textbooks which often give the correct answers to the first two questions in any given set. Such answers are not textbooks' *raison d'être*; their point – like the point of the *Investigations* – is to develop in the reader something non-propositional, a skill or an overview. As Bambrough points out,[35] when Wittgenstein wrote the *Tractatus* he thought that the problems of philosophy could, like the problems of physics, be solved once and for all. As he believed he had solved them, he therefore retired from philosophy and left others to pass on his discoveries. When he wrote the *Investigations* he had come to think that the problems of philosophy, like psychoanalytic problems, were difficulties and temptations which each person had to work through for himself – hence the radical difference in literary form.

It might be thought that Nietzsche is the most obvious source of literary influence on Wittgenstein, but I cannot find much similarity of tone or spirit here. Like Wittgenstein, his fragmented style probably represents a reaction against Schopenhauer's architectonics, and in part it was certainly adopted to make his reader read slowly and well, but here the similarity ends. Nietzsche is genuinely anti-systematic: he is out to disturb and disequilibriate with subterranean excitements, throw us off balance, and break up whatever comforting systems and certainties we may have contrived for ourselves. To do this, he frequently scatters his thoughts in as 'higgledy-piggledy manner'[36] as he could achieve. But Wittgenstein obviously took immense pains to order his thoughts, and to a certain extent the topics in the *Investigations* 'proceed from one subject to another in a natural order and without breaks' [PI:vii] as he originally hoped. The nihilism, excitement and theatricality, not only of Nietzsche's style but of his form, could not be further removed from the *Investigations.*

Von Wright[37] has pointed to the example of Lichtenberg, but here again the parallel is not deep lying. Lichtenberg's aphorisms were not intended for publication, they were simply extracted from his private notebooks after his death. Consequently, they cover a large number of subjects and each aphorism has, except by chance, little to do with the one before or after it. Although they lack Lichtenberg's quirky charm, the remarks collected in *Culture and Value* cover a similar subject matter, and show the same kind of insight and penetration – indeed, in that work, Wittgenstein explicitly praises Lichtenberg's genius [CV:65]. But Wittgenstein did not conceive of publishing *Culture and Value*; like Lichtenberg's aphorisms the material was arranged by editors after his death, and Wittgenstein wrote them for himself with no view of a potential audience. The character of this book is therefore quite different from the works which Wittgenstein intended for publication such as *The Brown Book* or the first part of the *Investigations*. Here the arrangement is carefully thought through and the sense of audience and heuristic purpose very strong (although long stretches of *The Brown Book* strike me as simply too arid, their didactic function all too obvious, to be effective).

Unlike Nietzsche or Lichtenberg, Wittgenstein took immense pains to ensure that the form of his public work should be as coherent as possible; it was clearly something of an agony to him:

> [After] several unsuccessful attempts to weld my results together into such a whole, I realized I should never succeed. The best that I could write would never be more than philosophical remarks; my thoughts were soon crippled if I tried to force them on in any single direction … – And this was, of course, connected with the very nature of the investigation. [PI:vii]

Goethe too, felt that the unorthodox arrangement of his book required mention: 'It will … be gratifying to [the reader] that we have arranged the appearances in a form that admits of being easily surveyed, even though he should not altogether approve of the arrangement itself …' [F:lviii]. (Here it is important to notice that Goethe talks about 'appearances' not chapters or remarks, because he wants us to see through the surveyable structure of his book to a surveyable subject matter.)[38] The care Wittgenstein took over the arrangement of his work is hardly surprising when we remember that, to dissolve a philosophical confusion, a description must not only be correct, but it must hold 'the right place in our considerations' [Z:314], and some early manuscripts show Wittgenstein toying with the idea of using a more elaborate *Tractatus*-style notation system for the *Investigations* to show even more precisely how his remarks relate to one another.[39]

In Goethe and Wittgenstein the literary *surface* is fragmented, but this is precisely because they want the reader to grasp a *synoptic*, organized view of a certain set of phenomena, which cannot be simply stated. The best analogy for their work would be with an art critic trying to make us grasp the unity and organization of a picture. He does not merely want us to know or believe something, he wants us to *see* something. If all the remarks and gestures he makes in trying to make us see the underlying organization were written down, then read in a cursory fashion without the presence of the work they would look a fragmentary and almost incomprehensible mixture: some would be very detailed, some suddenly general, some evaluative, others simply historical and so forth. If we approach Wittgenstein and Goethe in the spirit of this analogy, then their remarks will seem like a series of critical prompts designed to chivvy us into a certain perception of the world. Their remarks, therefore, do not have the isolation, wit and disorder we would expect from a book of aphorisms; nor do they exhibit the *kind* of order and coherence we would expect from more conventional texts with more conventional, quasi-scientific notions of explanation. They do, however, exhibit a deep rhetorical structure which springs from an attempt to educate the eye rather than inform the mind. The way such writing must be approached if its underlying order is to reveal itself, is brilliantly summarized by Heidegger: 'Let me give a little hint on how to listen. The point is not to listen to a series of propositions, but rather to follow a movement of *showing*.'[40]

The analogy with criticism also, I believe, makes sense of some of Wittgenstein's more obscure remarks about philosophical method – an aspect of his work which remained fairly consistent throughout his life. If we continued to think of Coleridge's Shakespeare criticism every time we watched a Shakespeare play then Coleridge would not be the great critic he is. The remarks of the great critic do not compete with or distract us from our enjoyment of a play, they dissolve into our experience of it, structuring, moulding and forming what we see all the more effectively for being invisible; his remarks are forgotten because they have become part of us and our lived understanding of the work. This, I take it, is one reason why Wittgenstein remarks on 'The queer resemblance between a philosophical investigation (perhaps especially in mathematics) and an aesthetic one. (E.g. what is bad about this garment, how it should be, etc.)' [CV:25].

Read in this light, section 6.54 of the *Tractatus* becomes more manageable:

> My propositions serve as elucidations in the following way: anyone who understands me eventually recognizes them as nonsensical, when he has used them – as steps – to climb up beyond them. (He must, so to speak, throw away the ladder after he has climbed up it.) He must transcend these propositions, and then he will see the world aright.

The critic or the philosopher does not use his propositions to convey new information about the world, but to draw attention, to bracket together, to induce community of vision. He tries to convey *by* his prose what cannot be contained *in* his prose, and what he hopes to bring about cannot take place on the page but only in the reader's consciousness. Clearly, on this conception of philosophy, it is no more a body of doctrine than criticism is [T:4.112], and both philosophical and critical propositions are simply a means to an end; the end being to see the world – or some part of it – aright [T:4.112]. By the extremely strict criterion of sense in the *Tractatus*, this use of sentences to prompt aspects of the world to reveal themselves is nonsense, but fortunately this did not prevent Wittgenstein realizing what he was doing and acknowledging its importance.

On this understanding, philosophy and criticism are best taught to small groups by someone who knows his audience, because the ordering, style and emphasis must vary according to their tastes, training, and state of knowledge. We know from innumerable accounts that this was how Wittgenstein liked to conduct his philosophy classes. A *book* of such philosophical activity, however, is a much more risky undertaking than it is on a more conventional understanding of philosophical explanation. The author has to decide in advance on the most rhetorically effective order of his remarks, without knowing exactly on whom they are to be effective; he has to anticipate what the most psychologically appealing temptations are likely to be (this is surely one reason for Wittgenstein's use of the interlocutor); and, to a far greater extent than is usually the case, he is at the mercy of the cursory and unsympathetic reader who is not prepared to harken to Heidegger's hints about listening. Hence, Wittgenstein's writing anticipates, and is haunted by, a fear of failure: 'I make [these remarks] public with doubtful feelings. It is not impossible that it should fall to the lot of this work, in its poverty and in the darkness of this time, to bring light into one brain or another – but, of course, it is not likely' [PI:viii]. Or again, 'A philosopher says "Look at things like this!" – but in the first place that doesn't ensure that people will look at things like that, and in the second place his admonition may come altogether too late; it's possible, moreover, that such an admonition can achieve nothing in any case and that the impetus for such a change in the way things are perceived has to originate somewhere else entirely …' [CV:61].[41]

There is one additional point. An attempt to bring about a *conversion* is bound to have a much lower success rate than an attempt to inform, and our relationship with a writer who tries to convert us is certain to be more close and personal than is the case with conventional philosophical writing. Just as the successes of such a method are few and remarkable, so its failures are many and painful, resulting in a sense of almost personal resentment and animosity. This, I think, goes some way towards explaining the fact – which anybody involved with philosophy can hardly fail to have noticed – that Wittgenstein's work polarizes readers into insiders and outsiders, and that suspicion and contempt are much closer to the surface than, for example, in disputes about Quine.

Let me summarize. Goethe and Wittgenstein both think that theorizing, especially premature theorizing on the basis of artificial and unexamined examples, leads to a profoundly unsatisfactory world-view full of hypostatized entities, hidden mechanisms, distinctions between inner and outer, and appearance and reality. Neither thinks that the world can be codified by the intellect alone, but they do think it can be understood by means of the senses (in an extended sense). They therefore develop a new account of explanation based on the *Gestalt*, and an innovative literary form designed to prompt the reader into seeing. By doing this, they hope to make vivid and immediate what has become stale, abstract and attenuated, and thereby wrest colour and language away from the theoretician, and return them to ordinary men living in the natural world. Enquiry ends when the pattern is seen and we cease to be chafed by the intellectual dissatisfactions created by our theorizing.

When Goethe died, he realized he had failed as a scientist, and that the Newtonian paradigm he abhorred was unshaken by his assaults; apart from some valuable observations about physiological optics and coloured shadows, the immense intellectual effort he put into his 13 scientific volumes appeared to have been wasted. However, I hope we can now see that the Goethean inheritance has informed one of the most original and innovative thinkers this century, and that this can only bear out Matthew Arnold's just and moving estimation:[42] '[Goethe's] profound imperturbable naturalism is absolutely fatal to routine thinking ... and ... no persons are so radically detached from [the old] order, no persons so thoroughly modern, as those who have felt Goethe's influence most deeply.'[43]

Notes

1 G.P. Baker and P.M.S. Hacker, *Meaning and Understanding* (Oxford: Blackwell, 1980), pp. 301–4.
2 J. Westphal, *Colour: Some Philosophical Problems From Wittgenstein* (Oxford: Blackwell, 1987), p. 8.
3 R. Monk, *Ludwig Wittgenstein; The Duty of Genius* (London: Cape, 1990), pp. 303–4, 509–12, 561–3.
4 R. Haller, 'Was Wittgenstein a Neo-Kantian?', p. 53, and 'The Common Behaviour of Mankind', p. 119, both in *Questions on Wittgenstein* (London: Routledge, 1988). In the first paper Haller attacks the once popular alignment of Wittgenstein and Kant.
5 S. Cavell, 'The Availability of Wittgenstein's Later Philosophy', in *Must We Mean What We Say?* (Cambridge: Cambridge University Press, 1976), p. 70. The final section of Cavell's

essay is excellent on the matter of Wittgenstein's literary style, as is R. Bambrough, 'How to Read Wittgenstein', in G. Vesey (ed.), *Understanding Wittgenstein* (London, 1974), pp. 117–32.

6 His attitude towards Fichte and Newton is nicely summarized by two verses in the Walpurgis Night dream sequence from *Faust*, Part 1 (trans. D. Luke, Oxford: Oxford University Press, 1987):

AN IDEALIST
The power of my Fantasy
Today seems much augmented.
I must say, if all this is me,
I'm temporarily demented.
A REALIST
Is substance now no longer sound,
Is something wrong with Matter?
I once stood four-square on the ground:
Today I'm all a-totter.
(Lines, 4, 347–4, 354)

7 Letter to Schiller, 6 January 1798, Quoted in E.M. Wilkinson, 'The Poet as Thinker', in E.M. Wilkinson and L.A. Willoughby (eds), *Goethe: Poet and Thinker* (London: Edward Arnold, 1962), p. 138. In my exposition I have relied heavily on pp. 133–40 of this excellent essay.

8 Quoted in Hacker and Baker, *Meaning and Understanding*, p. 7.

9 Trevelyan, 'Goethe as Thinker', in *Essays on Goethe*, ed. W. Rose (London: Cassell, 1949), p. 122.

10 The following works give a useful account of Goethe's scientific thought. H.B. Nisbet, *Goethe and the Scientific Tradition* (London: Institute of Germanic Studies, 1972); G.A. Wells, *Goethe and the Development of Science 1750–1900* (Alpen aan den Rijn: Sijthoff and Noordhoff, 1978); H. Bortoft, *Goethe's Scientific Consciousness* (Tunbridge Wells: Institute for Cultural Research, 1986); F. Amrine, F.J. Zucker and H. Wheeler (eds), *Goethe and the Sciences: A Reappraisal*, Boston Studies in the Philosophy of Science, vol. 97 (Dordrecht: Reidel, 1987); R.H. Stephenson, *Goethe's Conception of Knowledge and Science* (Edinburgh: Edinburgh University Press, 1995). The best short introduction remains, E. Heller, 'Goethe and the Idea of Scientific Truth' in his *The Disinherited Mind* (London: Bowes and Bowes, 1975), pp. 3–34. Since this chapter was originally published, the connection between Goethe and Wittgenstein has been the object of considerable scholarly attention. See, for example: F. Breithaupt and R. Raatzsch (eds), *Seeing the World's Unity in its Variety: Goethe and Wittgenstein* (Berlin: Peter Lang, 2003).

11 Goethe, *Theory of Colours (Zur Farbenlehre),* trans. C.L. Eastlake (Cambridge, MA: MIT Press, 1970). Hereafter 'F'. Arabic numerals denote section numbers; Roman numerals denote pages of the introduction and prefaces.

12 I use the following abbreviations for Wittgenstein's works. 'LC': *Lectures and Conversations on Aesthetics*, ed. C. Barrett (Oxford: Blackwell, 1978);'PI': *Philosophical Investigations*, ed. G.E.M. Anscombe (Oxford: Blackwell, 1976); 'Z': *Zettel*, ed. G.E.M. Anscombe and G.H. von Wright (Oxford: Blackwell, 1967); 'RC': *Remarks on Colour*, ed. G.E.M. Anscombe (Blackwell, Oxford, 1977); 'RFM': *Remarks on the Foundations of Mathematics*, ed. G.E.M. Anscombe, R. Rhees and G.H. von Wright (Oxford: Blackwell, 1978); 'BB': *Blue Book* (Oxford: Blackwell, 1964); 'CV': *Culture and Value*, ed. G.H. von Wright (Oxford: Blackwell, 1980); 'T', *Tractatus Logico-Philosophicus* (London: Routledge and

Kegan Paul, 1973); 'RPP': *Remarks on the Philosophy of Psychology*, vol. I, ed. G.E.M. Anscombe and G.H. von Wright (Oxford: Blackwell, 1980); 'OC': *On Certainty*, ed. G.E.M. Anscombe and G.H. von Wright (Oxford: Blackwell, 1969). Page numbers are used only in the absence of section numbers.

13 See E.M. Wilkinson, 'Goethe's Conception of Form', in Willoughby and Wilkinson, *Goethe: Poet and Thinker*, pp. 167–84.

14 See W. Hartner, 'Goethe and the Natural Sciences', in Victor Lange (ed.), *Goethe: A Collection of Critical Essays* (New Jersey: Prentice-Hall, 1968), p. 153; Hacker and Baker, *Meaning and Understanding*, pp. 301–4; Wilkinson, 'Goethe's Conception of Form', p. 184; Heller, 'Goethe and the Idea of Scientific Truth', pp. 9–14.

15 See Hartner, 'Goethe and the Natural Sciences', p. 153, and Wilkinson, 'Goethe's Conception', p. 184.

16 Quoted in Heller, 'Goethe and the Idea', p. 7.

17 Heller, 'Goethe and the Idea', pp. 7–8.

18 Heller, 'Goethe and the Idea', p. 6.

19 See Baker and Hacker, *Meaning and Understanding*, p. 302.

20 The relationships between Goethe's concept of a *Gestalt*, the importance of this meeting with Schiller, and how these relate to Wittgenstein's discussion of 'seeing-as' are well brought out in Monk, *Wittgenstein*, pp. 509–12.

21 Goethe, *Die Schriften Zur Naturwissenschaft*, herausgegeben im Auftrage der Deutschen Akademie der Narurforscher (Leopoldina) Weimar, 1947, ff. I, 3, p. 308. Quoted in Nisbet, *Goethe and the Scientific Tradition*, p. 51.

22 Goethe, *Schriften*, I, 10, p. 393. Quoted in Nisbet, *Goethe and the Scientific Tradition*, p. 54.

23 The second passage is RPP:l:950.

24 F. Waisnann, *The Principles of Linguistic Philosophy*, ed. R. Harré (New York: St Martin's Press, 1965), pp. 80–81. The passage is quoted in Monk, *Wittgenstein*, pp. 303–4.

25 I adapt this expression from A. Isenberg, 'Critical Communication' in his *Aesthetics and the Theory of Criticism*, ed. W. Callaghan et al. (Chicago: University of Chicago Press, 1988), p. 167.

26 Haller, *Questions on Wittgenstein*, pp. 118–20.

27 I owe this point and the revised translation to Ray Monk.

28 This passage was brought to my attention by reading Haller, *Questions on Wittgenstein*, p. 120.

29 Remark to Eckermann, 18 February 1829. Quoted in Amrine, etc., *Goethe and the Sciences*, p. viii. See also Bortoft, *Goethe's Scientific Consciousness*, p. 15.

30 Goethe, *Maximen and Reflexionen*, no. 575, ed. Max Hacker (Weimar, 1907). Quoted in Baker and Hacker, *Meaning and Understanding*, p. 285n. Wittgenstein quotes this remark again in RPP:I:889 and I use the translation found there.

31 See Westphal, *Colour*, p. 8.

32 Simon Glendinning drew my attention to this passage.

33 See Baker and Hacker, *Meaning and Understanding*, pp. 301–4.

34 Quoted in Monk, *Wittgenstein*, p. 561.

35 Bambrough, 'How to Read Wittgenstein'.

36 The expression is Michael Tanner's. See his introduction to F. Nietzsche, *Daybreak* (Cambridge: Cambridge University Press, 1982), p. viii.

37 G.H. von Wright, *Wittgenstein* (Oxford: Blackwell, 1982), p. 34.

38 Marie McGinn has emphasized to me that Goethe and Wittgenstein hold fundamentally different ideas about the place of language in their investigations. Both believe that language can be seriously misleading, but whereas Wittgenstein thinks that the phenomena of the world become surveyable to us when we have obtained an overview of our language, Goethe thinks that we can only gain an overview of the phenomena by getting beyond language.

39 See Baker and Hacker, *Meaning and Understanding*, p. 24.

40 M. Heidegger, *On Being and Time* (New York: Harper and Row, 1972). Quoted in Peter Blum (1990), 'Heidegger and Rorty on "The End of Philosophy"', *Metaphilosophy*, 21, 3 (July), p. 223. For Goethe's relation to Heidegger see Bortoft, *Goethe's Scientific Consciousness*, pp. 38–9; for Heidegger's relation to Wittgenstein see S. Mulhall, *On Being in the World: Wittgenstein and Heidegger on Seeing Aspect* (London: Routledge, 1990), pp. 106–22.

41 Quoted in Monk, *Wittgenstein*, p. 516.

42 Matthew Arnold, 'Heinrich Heine' in *Essays in Criticism*, First Series, ed. R.H. Super (Michigan: Michigan University Press, 1962), p. 110.

43 I would like to thank Simon Glendinning, Marie McGinn and Ray Monk, for very useful criticisms of an earlier draft of this chapter.

Chapter 2

Criticism without Theory

Scattered through Wittgenstein's later works are a number of remarks which allow us to develop a general account of critical reasoning.[1] This is not only valuable in itself, but it helps to demonstrate three central claims of his methodology: that one can be held captive by a false picture [PI:155];[2] that one can fail to notice something 'because it was always before one's eyes' [PI:129]; and that there is a standing temptation to offer theoretical solutions to non-theoretical problems [PI:109]. In the present context, this means that abstract accounts of how critics proceed – often given by the critics themselves – are frequently at variance with how they actually proceed. Accordingly, I divide this chapter in two: the first half uses Wittgenstein's remarks to show what happens when critics argue about the value and interpretation of a work of Art; the second shows why, in the light of this, one popular and theoretical account of critical practice cannot possibly be right.

A passage from Cavell makes a useful starting point:

> Why does [the music critic's] assertion 'you have to *hear* it!' mean what it does? Why is its sense conveyed with a word which emphasizes the function of a sense organ, and in the form of an imperative? The combination is itself striking. One cannot be commanded to hear a sound, though one can be commanded to listen to it, or for it. Perhaps the question is: How does it happen that the *achievement* or *result* of using a sense organ comes to be thought of as the *activity* of that organ – as though the aesthetic experience had the form not merely of a continuous effort (e.g., listening) but of a continuous achievement (e.g., hearing).[3]

One way to answer Cavell's questions is to change sense-modality and consider the ambiguous figures used by *Gestalt* psychologists. Jastrow's duck-rabbit (discussed by Wittgenstein at PI:194) is the most famous:

Figure 2.1 Duck-rabbit

In this context, it obviously does make sense to use the achievement-verb (seeing) as well as the effort-verb (looking) in the imperative form. One can be told to see the figure as a duck or as a rabbit, in a way that one cannot be told to see the picture *tout court*. Indeed, Wittgenstein introduces the section of *Philosophical Investigations* in which the figure appears by saying that he intends to distinguish two senses of the word 'see' [PI:193]. One of these ('seeing as') is subject to the will [PI:213]. This is not to say that the imperative 'Now see it as a rabbit!' will always result in a change of experience. Sometimes we encounter people who are blind to one of the ambiguous figure's aspects, and in these cases we try to make the new aspect 'click' by saying, 'Well, here are the ears, here is the mouth', or 'Now you'll have to think of it as looking in this direction'. If this drawing attention, pointing, prompting and highlighting fails to work then we might compare the figure with other pictures of rabbits in similar postures, or sketch in some more details on the figure itself ('This is where its whiskers would be', 'Most of the body would be over here with the tail about here').

Wittgenstein draws attention to the similarity between the dawning of an aspect and aesthetic perception:

> I have a theme played to me several times and each time at a slower tempo. In the end I say, '*Now* it's right' or '*Now* at last it's a march', '*Now* at last it's a dance'. – The same tone of voice expresses the dawning of an aspect. [PI: 206]

> Aspect-blindness will be *akin* to the lack of a 'musical ear'. [PI:214]

We can also see a marked similarity between his descriptions of critical explanation (he calls it 'aesthetic' explanation), and the methods we use in making an aspect dawn on someone:

> What reasons can one give for being satisfied? The reasons are further descriptions. Aesthetics is descriptive. What it does is to *draw one's attention* to certain features, to place these things side by side so as to exhibit these features. To tell a person 'This is the climax' is like saying 'This is the man in the puzzle picture'. Our attention is drawn to a certain feature, and from that point forward we see that feature. [A:38–9]

> Reasons … in aesthetics, are 'of the nature of further descriptions': e.g., you make a person see what Brahms was driving at by showing him lots of pieces by Brahms, or by comparing him with a contemporary author; and all that

> aesthetics does is 'to draw your attention to a thing', to 'place things side by side'. [M:315]

Initially, it is difficult to see how merely describing something, or grouping it together with other cases, could possibly explain anything. It is only when we place these remarks in the context of Wittgenstein's remarks about aspects that we realize such descriptions do not simply describe our experience, they change it. A good interpretation alters how we see the thing interpreted.

Some philosophers have felt uneasy about the analogy between criticism and the prompting of aspects, but this, I suspect, has more to do with the peculiarities of the ubiquitous duck-rabbit than with the basic analogy; and any sense of strain can be removed by considering a variety of different figures. If the duck-rabbit *were* seen as the paradigmatic example of all seeing-as, then we would expect the following to be the case: the ambiguity of a figure would always reside in what was represented; seeing-as would always involve an illusion of depth or three dimensions; in all cases the imagination would add something (the rabbit's body for instance) which was not shown in the picture; the ambiguity would always be binary – either this or that. However, if we consider a line of six dots, for example, which can be grouped in a variety of different ways (1–5, 2–4, 3–3, 4–2, etc.) we can see that these generalizations do not hold. When our imagination regroups the dots, there is no illusion of three dimensions; there is no change in what is represented (because it is not a representational figure); no extra features are added by the perceiver's imagination; and the figure can be grouped in at least five obvious ways. Wittgenstein evidently considered such 'aspects of organization' to be more basic than the representational figures.[4]

The row of dots and the duck-rabbit still share three features which are not present in all cases of seeing-as. Firstly, with most *Gestalt* figures there is a finite number of ways in which they can be seen, but this is not necessarily the case. Consider a group of five dots: four are positioned as if they stood at each corner of a square, the fifth stands in the middle. Now it is obvious that I can see this figure as an upright pyramid seen from above or as an inverted pyramid seen from the same position. It also becomes clear on reflection that I can imagine the central dot as advancing (so that either the pyramid grows taller or the inverted pyramid becomes shallower) or as retreating (so that either the pyramid grows shallower or the inverted pyramid grows deeper). This is an example of what we might call 'aspects of degree' because there are an infinite number of shapes which the figure can represent. Most criticism seems more analogous to discussions of this kind of case than it does to the dramatic switching effect that can be caused by imperatives about the duck/rabbit. At PI:206, Wittgenstein discusses rather exceptional cases where a piece of music suddenly acquires a nameable aspect ('*Now* at last it's a march') but it's clear that most criticism induces not rapid changes of kind, but subtle shiftings of degree – more and less sentimental, for example. Sometimes we will have difficulty in describing our change of experience in words at all.

Secondly, in the case of the dots and the duck-rabbit, the change from one aspect to the next is instantaneous and immediate, but with certain figures the mind finds the new aspect only much more gropingly and by degrees. This is particularly true of those figures which, unlike the dots or the duck-rabbit, strike us as initially chaotic. A black and white picture of a man's head hidden in complex pattern of dots is an example of this: one first finds the eyes, then the beard, then one mistakes the outline of the shoulder and has to go back etc., until gradually the head emerges from its background. This case seems a much better analogy than the duck-rabbit for the experience of finding our feet with an extended and complicated work.[5]

Figure 2.2 Hidden man

Thirdly, there are forms of aspect which are much more abstract than any considered so far. Wittgenstein remarks:

> I should like to say: there are aspects which are mainly determined by thoughts and associations, and others which are 'purely optical', and these make their appearance and alter automatically, almost like after-images [RPP:1, 970]. For example, the principal aspects of the double cross could be said to be 'purely optical' aspects, whereas other ways in which the figure can be seen (e.g., the white cross as the four corners of a piece of paper folded towards the middle) could be said to be 'conceptual aspects' [RPP:II:509]. Sometimes the conceptual is dominant in an aspect. That is to say: Sometimes the experience of an aspect can be expressed only through a conceptual explanation .... [LW: I :582][6]

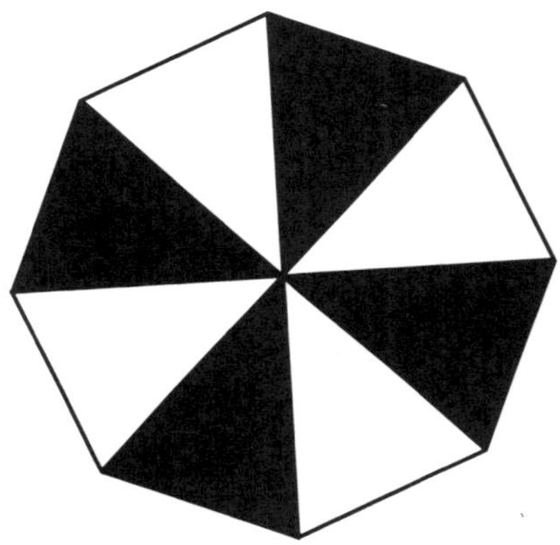

Figure 2.3 Double cross

This leads on to yet more abstract cases where there is no element of visual depiction at all. Wittgenstein clearly thinks that reading an ambiguous sentence like 'Hunting lions can be dangerous' first in one way and then in the other is of a piece with the seeing-as phenomenon. When critics prompt us to see the multiple ambiguity of a sentence, or interpret an entire work according to an abstract intellectual model (seeing Part II of Goethe's *Faust*, for example, as being based on an alchemical metaphor) then we are clearly in the realm of conceptual aspects.

One thing which discussions of ambiguous figures lack, but which holds a central place in critical discourse, is the question of evaluation. But the kind of argument I have been considering can be extended to cover this factor without much difficulty. One obvious suggestion is that the critic tries to make you share his evaluation by persuading you to see the work of art as he does. There is a good example of this procedure at work in Wittgenstein's *Lectures on Aesthetics*:

> I had an experience with the 18th century poet Klopstock. I had found that the way to read him was to stress his metre abnormally. Klopstock put u – u (etc.) in front of his work. When I read his poems in this new way, I said 'ah-ha, now I see why he did this'. What had happened? I had read this kind of stuff before and been moderately bored, but when I read it in this new way, intensely, I smiled and said 'This is grand', etc. But I might not have said anything. [LC: 4]

Here we see Wittgenstein following a critical imperative (which in this case came from the poet but could just as easily have come from another critic) 'When I read his poems in this new way …' etc. The resulting achievement of understanding, of things falling into place, 'I said "Aa-ha, now I know why he did this" …' and finally the reconsideration of his original value judgement, 'I had read this kind of stuff before and been moderately bored, but when I read it in this particular way, intensely, I smiled and said "This is *grand*", etc. …'.

Some commentators[7] have wondered why Wittgenstein is at such pains to play down the role of general commendatory words – 'fine', 'good', 'beautiful' – in critical discussion. One reason is that he wants to emphasize that critical discussion does not issue in a proposition ('This is good' or whatever) but in an experience which *may* be described in a proposition. A discussion about aspects has not had its intended effect if you simply *know that* or *believe* (perhaps because reliable people keep telling you) that this figure can be seen as a rabbit as well as a duck; you have to *see it* as a rabbit. Similarly, a critical argument has not been successful if you merely believe the Klopstock poem is grand, you have to come to know its grandeur by *hearing* it as grand. Faced with a very ingenious interpretation of a play, we can frequently acknowledge the interpretation's intellectual coherence while feeling that it does not quite marry up with our experience of the play in performance: the two never coalesce or become a unity.

Philosophers and critics sometimes tend to model rational argument on inductive and deductive reasoning, sometimes, in their more confident moments, even going so far as to exclude all other forms of enquiry from the realms of meaningful language. But critical language cannot be understood if only such restricted resources are allowed. Inductive and deductive reasoning deal with the relationship between propositions, and the train of reasoning comes to an end with a proved or probable proposition. Critical reasoning, on the other hand, deals with immediate experience, knowledge by acquaintance, and if it changes that experience in the appropriate way then it has been successful.

The critic is concerned to tell you *how to see*: to point out patterns, to draw your attention to features that allow patterns to emerge, and to render coherent what looks arbitrary, disordered and inexplicable. Besides redescribing the work, or issuing imperatives ('Don't look *at* it, look *into* it!') he can do this in three ways: he can literally point out certain features of the work so that they become highlighted in our experience of it; he can compare it with other works so that points of similarity and dissimilarity are enhanced; or he can describe it in terms of a model or an analogy. Sometimes these models can be as simple as a straightforward paraphrase. Faced with opening of a poem like e.e. cummings' initially incomprehensible 'ygUDuh' one can be quite grateful for a broad critical hint:

YgUDuh

ydoan
yunnuhstan

ydoan o
yunnuhstan dem
yguduh[8]

When we are told that the opening line can be paraphrased as 'You've got to' then we gradually discover comprehensibility spreading throughout the entire poem. Our experience here is very similar to the visual experience undergone when we attempt to find the man's head in the cluster of dots. Similarly, the utterly basic matter of grouping together parts of a long and complicated work into subsections can be genuinely enlightening. Writing of Wordsworth's 'Immortality Ode', Trilling remarks:

> [The] poem is divided into two main parts. The first part, consisting of four stanzas, states an optical phenomenon and asks a question about it. The second part, consisting of seven stanzas, answers that question and is itself divided into two parts, of which the first is despairing, the second hopeful.[9]

Even two such evaluatively neutral actions as my hinted paraphrase and Trilling's grouping have evaluative consequences: I think it is generally found that what is incomprehensible is boring, and the discovery of structure and meaning can only increase our interest in the work we are reading.

Some descriptions can have more obvious evaluative consequences. Two people have recently remarked to me that they disliked Ian McEwan's novel, *The Comfort of Strangers*,[10] because they felt it was a story about the discomforts and disorientations of being abroad which the author tried to make significant by adding a particularly nasty murder at the end. This description of the book suggests to me that they have been misled by the title. It is better to read it as a tale about an impeccably liberal couple, who, disorientated by their alien circumstances, are attracted and obscurely excited by the presence of an old fashioned, right-winger who knows nothing about the restraint of instincts however unsavoury – indeed he considers it his right to indulge them. When the couple surrender to his fascination, then the murder follows as an inevitable consequence of flirting with the primitive forces of the Id. Perhaps a more effective way of making this point – one which would allow the point to make itself – is to recommend that the novel be read in the context of *Heart of Darkness*, *Equus*, *Lord of the Flies* and other twentieth-century works which examine the conflict between liberal values and the powers of the unconscious.

Frequently, the critic will draw our attention to patterns that the casual reader is likely to miss. Thus, writing on the 'Immortality Ode', Cleanth Brooks remarks:

> With stanza III the emphasis is shifted from sight to sound. It is a very cunning touch. The poet has lamented the passing of a glory from the earth. But he can, he suggests, at least *hear* the mirth of the blessed creatures for whom the earth still wears that glory. Stanza III is dominated by sound: the birds' songs, the trumpets of the cataracts, echoes, the winds – presumably their sound – one can't *see* them. Even the gambolling of the lambs is associated with a strong auditory image – 'As to the tabor's sound.' Hearing these sounds, the poet tries to enter into the gaiety of the season. He asks the shepherd boy to shout, and goes on to say in stanza IV: 'Ye blessed Creatures, I have heard the call / Ye each to the other make …'. The effect is that of a blind man trying to enter the joyful dawn world.[11]

If you have not read the poem, then Brooks' point is likely to seem so much dull information. But if you have read it, and had not noticed this subtle sensory change, then his remarks should strike you with the force of recognition: 'Of course!', you think, 'How could I have missed it?' Now that his point has been made, it is most unlikely that you will ever be able to read the poem again without observing the change from sight to hearing – it will leap at you from the page. Indeed, trying to forget it will be like attempting to re-solve Wittgenstein's puzzle picture by pretending you haven't noticed where the man is hidden.

Sometimes a critic has an insight which can remove the thick glaze of familiarity from a well-known text. Consider the opening lines of *Macbeth*: 'When shall we three meet again? / In thunder, lightning, or in rain?' Frank Kermode comments:

> The play, uniquely concerned with prophecy, begins with a question about the future: 'When shall we three meet again?' The speaker adds, without much apparent sense: 'In thunder, lightning, or in rain?' But these are three conditions which flourish, so to say, in the same hedgerow; they do not differ so completely as to be presentable as mutually exclusive alternatives.[12]

Until I had read these remarks I had seen neither the connection between central theme of the play and the opening line, nor the peculiar nature of the 'alternatives' offered in the next, nor the extraordinary sequence of triple questions and double answers which, as he goes on to point out, the first act contains.[13] Insights of this calibre, it seems to me, cause the same sense of delight that is caused by good jokes; and like good jokes they point out unseen but obvious connections between things with which we are thoroughly familiar.

Macbeth also offers a good example of the *Gestalt* switches that criticism can sometimes bring about. For Bradley, the central character has

> … the imagination of a poet, – an imagination on the one hand extremely sensitive to impressions of a certain kind, and, on the other, productive of violent disturbance both of mind and body, through it he is kept in contact with supernatural impressions and is liable to supernatural fears.[14]

For Mary McCarthy, on the other hand, Macbeth is merely, 'A commonplace man who talks in commonplaces, a golfer … a bourgeois type: a murderous Babbit, let us say. … [He] has no faith which requires imagination. He is literal-minded; that, in a word, is his tragedy.' His belief in the supernatural suggests 'heavy credulousness' of a piece with his 'prosing about the weather', and '[his] main concern throughout the play is that most selfish of all concerns: to get a good night's sleep'.[15] The evidence tells either way, and it seems entirely a matter of directorial preference which interpretation is followed.

I shall now give one extended example of a much more ambitious kind of criticism: a critic trying to interpret an entire *oeuvre* according to an abstract model. It is naturally quite difficult to think of a large scale interpretation, together with the evidence that supports it, which can be illustrated within a reasonable compass, but the following tongue-in-cheek passage from David Lodge's novel *Changing Places* gives a good impression of the kind of rhetorical strategies involved. The scene is a tutorial with Professor Morris Zapp, and the topic is 'Eros and Agape in the Later Novels of Jane Austen':

> Morris felt in the mood for a little display of high-powered exposition. Agape, he explained, was a feast through which the early Christians expressed their love for one another, it symbolized non-sexual, non-individualized love, it was represented in Jane Austen's novels by social events that confirmed the solidarity of middle-class agrarian capitalist communities or welcomed new members into those communities – balls and dinner parties and sight-seeing expeditions and so on. Eros was of course sexual love and was represented by Jane Austen by courtship scenes, *tête-à-têtes*, walking in pairs – any encounter between the heroine and the man she loved, or thought she loved. Readers of Jane Austen, he emphasized, gesturing freely with his cigar, should not be misled by the absence of overt reference to physical sexuality in her fiction into supposing she was indifferent or hostile to it. On the contrary, she invariably came down on the side of Eros against Agape – on the side, that is, of the private communion of lovers over against the public communion of social events and gatherings which invariably caused pain and distress (think for instance of the disastrous nature of group expeditions, to Sotherton in *Mansfield Park*, to Box Hill in *Emma*, to Lyme Regis in *Persuasion*). Getting into his stride, Morris demonstrated that Mr Elton was obviously implied to be impotent because there was no lead in the pencil that Harriet Smith took from him; and the moment in *Persuasion* when Captain Wentworth lifted the little brat Walter off Anne Elliot's shoulders … He snatched up the text and read with feeling: '"… she found herself in the state of being released from him … Before she realized that Captain Wentworth had done it … he was resolutely borne away … *Her sensations on the discovery made her perfectly speechless. She could not even thank him. She could only hang over Charles with the most disordered feelings*." How about that?' he concluded reverently. 'If that isn't an *orgasm*, what is it?' He looked up into three flabbergasted faces.[16]

How does Zapp succeed in shaking his students from their dogmatic slumbers about Jane Austen? He begins by explaining the nature of Agape and Eros. The model is then fitted to the novels by means of the equation: Agape = large social gatherings, Eros = courtship scenes, etc. After dealing with an obvious objection he then explains the meaning of Agape and Eros again. This cannot be to *inform* the listeners as they have only just been told, but to keep the model *vivid* and *before their minds*. In attempting to massage listeners' perceptions into the appropriate mould one has to skip lightly from the general view to detail and then back again. If there is too much text they will forget the model and if there is too much model they will forget the text; both must be perceived *as a unity*. Zapp then goes on to argue that Austen shows her suspicion of Agape by invariably making group expeditions disastrous, and, to support this idea, he homes in on particular scenes in particular books for the first time. To show Austen's dealings with Eros, he now *describes* an incident (concerning Mr. Elton's pencil) rather than simply applying an adjective to it, and the exposition draws to its close with the triumphant detail of a quotation. Finally, he ends with a question. As a teacher, he knows that his pupils will be most impressed by conclusions they reach themselves. Having supplied the basic prompt, he therefore sits back to watch his theoretical outline perform the reordering of their perceptions.

The technique of comparing, prompting, emphasizing and goading with a view to changing someone's experience is not confined to criticism of the arts. As John Casey points out in *The Language of Criticism*,[17] it is the way we reason about the ends of morality. A good example of this procedure can be found near the beginning of Jane Austen's *Emma*, where Emma Woodhouse tries to disenchant Harriet Smith with Mr Martin:

> He is very plain, undoubtedly – remarkably plain: – but that is nothing, compared with his utter want of gentility. I had no right to expect much, and I did not expect much; but I had no idea he would be so very clownish, so totally without air. I had imagined him, I confess, a degree or two nearer gentility.

His rusticity, boorishness, and bad manners are itemized in minute detail ('The older a person grows ... the more glaring and disgusting any loudness or coarseness or awkwardness becomes') and these are thrown further into dramatic relief by telling comparisons with the elegant and accomplished Messrs Knightly, Weston and Elton:

> I think, Harriet, since your acquaintance with us, you have been repeatedly in the company of some, such very real gentlemen, that you must yourself be struck with the difference with Mr. Martin. At Hartfield, you have had specimens of well educated, well bred men. I should be surprized if, after seeing them, you could be in company with Mr. Martin again without perceiving him to be a very inferior creature – and rather wondering at yourself at ever having thought him at all agreeable before...What say you to Mr. Weston and Mr. Elton? Compare Mr. Martin with either of *them*. Compare their manner of carrying themselves; of walking; of speaking; of being silent. You must see the difference.[18]

Harriet admits that Mr Martin is not particularly handsome or accomplished, but the purpose of Emma's bombardment is to transmute these unstable beliefs into hard and fast attitudes – to make her experience him as intolerably crude and unbearably common, someone in sum, with whom she could not bring herself to associate.

Even talk of *Gestalt* switches does not seem out of place in discussing this kind of experience (from Harold Nicholson's story 'Lambert Orme'):

> [Sligger Urquhart] seemed to have no particular feeling for Lambert, either for or against: he pouted for a moment, and then said that he had found him 'absurdly childish'. I do not suppose that that remark was intended to be very penetrating: I only know that it penetrated me like a lance. The angle from which I had begun to regard Lambert Orme was shifted suddenly: it ceased to be an ascending angle and became in the space of a few seconds a descending angle: I had begun … to look up to Lambert: I now, quite suddenly and in every way, found myself looking down.[19]

Here, Nicholson locates a noticeable peculiarity of critical reasoning – its ability to operate at a deeper, less wholly rational level of the psyche than the kinds of thought normally discussed by analytic philosophers. Our perceptual *Lebenswelt* is already structured, interpreted and imbued with value – with our wants, beliefs, memories, myths and theories. To adjust this whole interpretative set by means of critical reasoning is to make it seem, not as if the world remained the same but our theories about it altered, but that the world itself had fundamentally changed its nature. Critical reasoning appears to by-pass our ordinary, rational defences, and blights a pleasure irrevocably by means of an eccentric comparison, or makes us begin to enjoy something in spite of our determination not to. This is well brought out in a trivial but telling example from John Wisdom, the one analytic philosopher who made Wittgenstein's remarks on explanation absolutely central to his conception of philosophy:

> [Someone] is trying on a hat. She is studying it in the mirror. There's a pause and then a friend says 'My dear, the Taj Mahal'. Instantly the look of indecision leaves the face in the mirror. … And … this happens in spite of the fact that the hat could be seen perfectly clearly and completely before the words 'Taj Mahal' were uttered. … And yet nothing will undo the work of that far-fetched allusion. The hat has become a monument and too magnificent by half.[20]

There is, of course, the closest possible relationship between aesthetic and ethical criticism. When discussing a novel we frequently consider the ethical justifications for a character's behaviour, or the author's intentions in writing the work, and these can influence our estimate of the novel's aesthetic value.

In addition, a critic who finds that his points about a work are not persuading his opponent will frequently start to apply his rhetoric to other works his interlocutor finds significant. If setting the work in this larger context still fails to place it in a new *Gestalt*, then it is natural that this should lead to criticism of the opponent's values in general – his tastes, his values, his life-style, his ethics. Most influential critics or schools of criticism grow out of or develop a larger ethical purpose. Consider Leavis's disparagement of Bloomsbury and the world of Sunday newspaper reviewing; Arnold's contempt for the smug, practical-minded Englishman of his day; Trilling's unease at the hegemony of unreflective liberal values; Deconstruction's promise to subvert and undermine comfy bourgeois certainties. There *is* arguing about taste, because our artistic taste is not detached from the rest of our personality; it reflects and expresses our whole ethical character. Convincing us to modify one of our value-judgements (i.e., persuading us to see part of the world slightly differently) can have ramifications through the entire system.

Wittgenstein's identification and description of critical reasoning seems to me to be one of his most central contributions to philosophy. This is for three main reasons.

Firstly, Wittgenstein discovered the kind of non-inductive, non-deductive reasoning used in interpretative or evaluative contexts. What is so remarkable about this is that all of us encounter it all the time in writing, reading and talking, and yet nobody prior to Wittgenstein realized how different it is from the methods used in the sciences. It is an absolutely paradigmatic case of something that could not be noticed because we were too close to it. Most books on critical theory which are not directly influenced by Wittgenstein, even such distinguished examples as Richards' *Principles of Literary Criticism* or Ellis's *The Theory of Literary Criticism*,[21] tell one absolutely nothing about the persuasive techniques and strategies which must be used by critics.

Secondly, there is a very influential view of ethics according to which one's initial choice of ends is a *donnée* that is beyond the reach of rational criticism.[22] On this view, one could only criticize the means employed and the consistency with which the basic principles were adhered to. In Broad's phrase, ethics becomes a subject where 'we twit one another with inconsistency'.[23] However, Wittgenstein's observations show how people's wants, tastes, desires, goals and aspirations can be subject to rational criticism. This both makes ethics a far richer and more nutritious subject, and also shows the role that works of art can play in forming our conceptions of how life should be lived. Literature not only explores possible forms of life, but it provides models with which reality and aspirations can be implicitly or explicitly compared.

Thirdly, it makes sense of all those kinds of thought and talk where we are not giving one another information or drawing inferences from it. Most thought is not of the goal-directed propositional kind, heading inexorably towards conclusions and wedded to 'that'-clauses, but ruminating, turning over, dwelling on, entertaining, recalling, mulling over, reflecting. The aim of this activity is to sift out and play down what is inessential, and highlight or foreground what is of central relevance to our experience. This alters the mental set with which we meet any new situation and determines what we notice or attend to or observe. This kind of thought is not something over and above perception; it imbues our perception and becomes part of it.

Similarly, most talk consists not of passing information down the line, but of pointing out, observing, drawing attention to, reminding, reflecting. When we gossip about people, for example, we use the most heterogeneous mix of descriptive and evaluative terms, analogies and parallel cases, parodies, detailed instances and general principles with which to emphasize to ourselves and others the salient points of the person under discussion. If the exchange has been fruitful, then we may not have learnt any new information, but our impression of the subject will be sharper, clearer and firmer in outline than before we entered the conversation. In the same way, a really effective insult or sneer highlights a person or situation's least admirable features by bracketing it off, grouping it with other cases. 'Ah', says the father as his adolescent son and girlfriend enter the room, 'love's young dream' – and this remark can make *them* feel awkward, clichéd, 'placed' and miserable. The power of a devastating parody, a grotesque cartoon image, or well-placed insult is that they 'stick': they become a filter through which we see ourselves and through which others see us, and any reasoned rebuttal, redress or explanation must always come too late.

* * *

I have now given a general Wittgensteinian account of the aims and methods of criticism. In this section, I turn to examining one widely held false picture of the 'logic' of evaluative discourse.

Here is a simple and typical pattern of argument:

A. I thought that was extraordinarily good.
B. Why?
A. There was something exhilarating about it.
B. What?

A. Oh those string scales, the high, screaming woodwind, the off-beat chords on the brass, the insistent timpani rhythms …

The difficulty many philosophers have seen in such schemata is this: how is it possible to move from the purely descriptive 'string scales' to the evaluative terms 'good' and 'exhilarating'? Because philosophers spend most of their time thinking about logic and mathematics they usually reply, 'By means of principles'. Daniel Taylor's exposition of this position in his book *Explanation and Meaning* can stand as a representative example:

> To refer to any property *p* as a reason for judging a work good is to imply that one holds as a principle that any similar work possessing this property is equally commendable.
>
> Consequently when someone calls a novel a good novel because it has *p*, he is committed to the principle that any *p* novel is good. Should we discover another novel which this man concedes to have *p*, yet refuses to judge as good, he stands convicted of inconsistency …
>
> If *p* is a success property p (imaginative, elegant, balanced) … to assert a work to be *p* will be to evaluate it as possessing a particular merit or demerit … Such an evaluation will in turn require an explanation or justification in terms of further properties *q*, presumably (factual properties, e.g., the characters and their relationships) *and further principles* (my italics).[24]

On this account, the act of evaluating something becomes a matter of drawing *inferences*. I have a major premise ('All texts which have X are good'), I then discover the text I am reading to have X, and I draw the inference, 'This text is good'. The model is widely held, and not only amongst philosophers. In the 'Polemical Introduction' to his *Anatomy of Criticism*, Northrop Frye remarks that 'comparative estimates of value are really inferences, most valid when silent ones …', and goes on to claim that:

> I have proceeded deductively [although] … the deductiveness does not extend further than tactical method, and so far as I know there is no principle in this book which is claimed as a perfect major premise, without exceptions or negative instances. Such expressions as 'normally', 'usually', 'regularity', or 'as a rule' are thickly strewn throughout.[25]

'A perfect major premise', without qualifications, as a basis for deductions, is implied to be the ideal to which true criticism should aspire.

If we examine this model of evaluative discourse in detail, however, we discover it to be unworkable. Taylor's account is quite detailed and I shall therefore use him as my main stalking horse.

In the quoted passage, we can see that *p* can either be a 'factual term' or a 'success term' and I shall begin by considering the latter. Let my final judgement be 'good' and let the property denoted by *p* be 'exhilarating'. For Taylor, we can only move from 'exhilarating' to 'good' by means of principles, and the question arises, 'What kind of principles could justify the move from one to the other?' This does not appear to present much of a difficulty since, like most general aesthetic terms, 'exhilarating' serves both to describe and to evaluate something. Being exhilarating – unless very special circumstances obtain – is one way of being good. As Hume remarks:

> There are certain terms in every language which import blame, and, others praise, and all men who use the same tongue must agree in their application of them. Every voice is united in applauding elegance, propriety, simplicity, spirit in writing, and in blaming fustian, affectation, coldness and false brilliancy.[26]

There is a logical relation between 'exhilarating' and 'good' which would only disappear if the word 'exhilarating' changed its meaning. This is not to imply that the word 'exhilarating' may not be applied to a work in a generally unfavourable summing up, but that 'exhilarating' will not *support* the evaluation: a work will be bad *in spite* of being exhilarating; it will be bad overall *but* exhilarating in parts. Another way to neutralize the evaluative element in the word is to add a more powerful pejorative modifier – 'cheaply exhilarating' perhaps.

In view of these considerations it is odd that Taylor should say, 'To refer to any property *p* as a reason for judging a work of art good is to imply that *one holds as a principle* that any work possessing this property is equally commendable', especially when he goes on to acknowledge that if *p* is a success property then to assert it of a work 'will itself be to evaluate it'. If this principle of mine is something over and above the logical point which Hume describes, then it is very hard to see why it should be necessary, as the language itself allows for this transition. If the principle is just the feature of evaluative terms that Hume discusses, then describing it in this way is about as natural as saying that 'All bachelors are men' is one of my principles. The statement 'exhilarating implies good' is not just something I happen to approve of or hold to be true at the moment. If not buying a certain country's produce is one of my principles, it is quite conceivable that I should one day forego this principle, or that others in my community should never have held it. But 'exhilarating implies good' is a logical truth which speakers of English cannot ignore, and which will only become false if some or all of its constituent words change their meaning.

The oddity of Taylor's position becomes fully obvious when he says that a man who judges a *p*-novel to be bad will 'stand accused of inconsistency' if he judges a further *p*-novel to be good. Consider a damning verdict for a moment: a man who thinks a book is awful because it is boring and vacuous. (Taylor's *p*-terms, I take it, are evaluative terms which can either praise or disparage.) If a man judges one novel to be bad because it is boring and vacuous, and then goes on to claim that another novel is good because it is boring and vacuous, then he *will* be inconsistent, but this is not what is peculiar about his second remark, since we would not understand him if he judged only one novel which he considered boring and vacuous to be good. 'Boring and vacuous but what ...?', we would want to ask, 'relaxing perhaps?' If he said that the work did not have any more detailed good qualities at all (it wasn't merely that he couldn't articulate them) and he liked the novel *because* it was boring and vacuous, then I think we'd have to stop talking to him, try and explain how these critical predicates function, dismiss his judgement as affected, ironized or perverse, change the subject because this one's getting embarrassing.

The real difficulties with Taylor's account, however, arise when we come to consider the step from 'string scales' to 'exhilarating' or 'good', or from Taylor's 'factual' to his 'success' terms. Can we deduce 'good' or 'exhilarating' from 'string scales' as we can deduce 'good' from 'exhilarating'? Clearly not: one can easily imagine exhilarating pieces of music that do not contain any string scales, and pieces full of string scales that are neither exhilarating nor good. The principle that will allow us to move from factual to success terms cannot be quasi-logical or analytic. Perhaps some general value statement based on inductive evidence, or some critical axiom derived *a priori* from reflection on the human mind, will yet allow us to move from the factual to the evaluative. But neither of these suggestions can be right either. If someone judges a work of art according to a principle, whether based on induction or *a priori* reflection, we are entitled to ask this person how he knows it to be a good or correct principle. The only way you can demonstrate the worth of a principle is by showing that all or most of the works which conform to it are good ones, and this requires the ability to judge works of art without the benefit of this or any other principle. Norms of this kind either lead to an infinite regress or they beg the question at issue. It is anyway quite absurd to suppose that if you think badly of a piece of music, you will be disposed to alter your evaluation simply because somebody says you found every other piece containing ascending scales interesting and worthwhile.

To diagnose exactly what has gone wrong with this deductive model, let us return again to the duck/rabbit. Consider the following two snatches of conversation:

A. See it as a rabbit.
B. I can't.
A. These lines here are the ears.

A. It's beautiful.
B. Why?
A. These curves here, the pastel tones.

Clearly, there are no laws or norms linking 'lines' to 'ears' and 'ears' to 'rabbit' because most lines don't represent ears and most pictured ears don't belong to pictured rabbits, but this does not produce a 'line/representation problem' of how one is justified in moving from 'lines' to 'rabbit'. What both of these schemata have in common is that the conversations are both rendered rational, not by covering laws or general precepts, but by *the visual context* in which they are conducted, and it is because the visual contexts required to make them intelligible are inevitably lacking in philosophical articles that they have been found so problematic. If the point of a discussion is not merely to make someone believe but to make them *see* something as a rabbit or *see* something as beautiful it is a necessary precondition that they *can see* – in the most straightforward sense – the object in question. If I ask you what a picture I have not seen represents, and you reply cryptically, 'It contains ears', then I won't find this helpful. If, however, I am trying to make sense of a puzzle drawing and you point to some lines and say 'ears' then this may be all I need to see the rabbit.

Similarly, there are no laws linking 'curves' to 'beautiful', and if you simply say that vase I cannot see has curves then I will have no idea whether it has any aesthetic merits or not. On the other hand, if I am looking at a vase with a slightly mystified expression and you draw my attention to the way the curves grow shallower towards the rim, then that may be all I need to find the beauty which you see in it. It should now be clear that A's reasons are not universalizable. He is not implying that the presence of curves suggests or guarantees beauty, he is only committed to the claim that appreciation of *those* curves in *that* context will lead to a just evaluation of *that* vase. A's remarks are not minor premises of some kind which hint at the existence of a concealed major premise (e.g. 'All curves are beautiful') but *prompts* to help B's imagination structure his visual experience.

Although A separates out in propositional form various aspects of his experience in order to help B share that experience, A did not start with the 'facts' listed at the bottom of the schema and then work upwards. He did not first apprehend the lines and then *infer* (using deductive, inductive, strongly criteriological principles, etc.) the existence of the ears, then the rabbit. Nor did he first see the curves and the pastel tones and then infer that the vase must be extraordinarily beautiful. Apart from the obvious craziness of such a suggestion, it would make it quite intelligible for a man who had not seen the vase to say, 'Ah, well if it has curves then it must be beautiful', or for a man who could see the vase to say, 'I can see it in front of me, but I've no idea whether it's attractive or not because I can't remember whether the principle is "Most curved and pastel coloured objects are beautiful" or "All curved objects are beautiful" or …' Now with cognitive claims we do persuade somebody to agree with our judgement by presenting him with the reasons which we have already run through to establish our own judgement. Consider this snatch of conversation:

C. The answer's four.
D. Why?
C. You subtract the six from the ten.
D. Ah.

It is sometimes asserted that critics begin with their conclusions, but the word 'conclusion' is extremely misleading in this context as we can see by comparing this mathematical dialogue with the critical conversation already discussed. C *does* present his conclusion first, and then persuade D to see it by rehearsing a pattern of argument he has been through at least once already. But while a critic like A *has reasons* for his judgement, he did not arrive at his judgement *by reasoning* – he simply looked.

It would always be possible to ask C to check his own working, in which case we can imagine him saying to himself at the end of the calculation 'ten minus six is four', but the only way A can check his evaluation is to imagine looking (or actually look) at the vase again. You will not catch him saying to himself, 'These curves here, the pastel tones'. A lightning calculator may invariably arrive at correct solutions without knowingly inferring or calculating, but in this case propositional reasoning must have occurred otherwise his constantly correct solutions would be inexplicable. In the critical case reasoning only occurs in the face of puzzlement or opposition: in the normal case no reasoning occurs and none is needed.

In the examples I have considered so far, B disagrees with A's valuation, and his 'why?' – question could be paraphrased as, 'I don't see it. What can you say that would make me alter my evaluation?' But a similar question could be heard to mean, 'Yes, I agree, but how is this effect achieved?' It is important to realize that the kind of argument used to resolve puzzlement or opposition on the *ground* of an evaluation is different in kind from the form of argument employed where two people disagree over the evaluation itself.

The first difference to observe is this. A and B may both agree that a picture is excellent, but A thinks its excellence is due solely to its vivid coloration, while B thinks that the epic proportions of its physical size is all important while its coloration is irrelevant. C and D both think that the painting is awful, but C thinks its garishness is entirely to blame, while D thinks its awfulness is solely attributable to its comically grandiose scale.[27] Now it is quite possible that A and B might be able to decide which one of them is correct by means of experiment. In a critical dispute, this kind of disagreement will usually be resolved by means of a thought-experiment, but the distinction between disputes over quality and disputes over grounds for quality can be made clearer by considering a real one. Thus A could present B with a much reduced but otherwise perfect reproduction of the picture with the words, 'Doesn't your evaluation remain the same?', while B could show A a monochrome but life-size photograph with much the same question. C and D could adopt similar means to resolve their dispute. These experiments *could* be inconclusive in various ways. They might conclude that they like the work for genuinely different reasons (it is not that one or both of them are in error), or they might decide that both the vividness and the epic size are important. However, it is conceivable that these experiments could be decisive. But it is not possible even to begin to imagine what kind of experimental procedures C might adopt to show A that the painting is garish not vivid, or what experiment B could use to convince D that the picture is of noble and epic proportions rather than comically overblown. The only method to adopt here is critical reasoning of the emphasizing, exhorting, comparing, persuading kind: 'Don't you see how marvellously he …', 'Are you honestly saying that this bit …?', 'But think of it as …', etc.

Secondly, borderline cases apart, you cannot be unsure as to whether a work rivets your attention, leaves you cold or repels you altogether. Of course, you might refuse to say whether you thought a work good or bad for at least three reasons. Firstly, you might be unsure that you understand a work correctly, and hence not wish to risk committing yourself. Secondly, you may be asked to evaluate a work where your response swings from one extreme to the other and never achieves any stability. (In my own case, this occurs with the Liszt piano sonata). Thirdly, faced with a very long and uneven work an overall assessment may require considerable reflection. However, these complications apart, you cannot be absolutely baffled by a work's quality as you can imagine a person liking a work very much and yet be completely at sea as to *why* he likes it. This person could indeed resort to the kind of experimental procedures described above in order to decide whether it is the colour or the size which so appeals to him. (There may, of course, be no *one* factor which explains its attraction: it may be that colour in that position used to depict that subject matter …, etc., which exercises the appeal.) Because – barring the special cases of self-deception and interference from non-aesthetic factors – you cannot be puzzled as to whether you are attracted or repelled by a work at any given moment, and because you cannot disagree with yourself as to whether a work is wonderfully vivid or hideously garish, one person will never direct critical demands and exhortations towards himself.

Reasoning of the exhorting, persuading variety is always directed towards another person in order to change his experience of a work. If successful, it will lead him to revise his general evaluation ('boring' to 'impressive' perhaps) and the aspect under which he sees the work (what he saw as garish he now sees as vivid). Reasoning of the more experimental variety is directed either at one's own or somebody else's grounds for a general evaluation, and it is intended to help understand that experience not to change it – except insofar as an understood experience is a new experience. Seeing the correct explanation will be a matter of recognition: in one sense the reason demanded is implicit in the experience as one has knowledge by acquaintance of the feature referred to, but one did not know that it was this feature which played such a major part in inducing the experience.

When A tried to persuade B to see the object as beautiful by mentioning the curves and the colours, his remarks had a rhetorical not a logical order – they did not map out the way he had travelled. Clearly, A apprehended the curves, the colour and its general attractiveness *as a unity*, and no one of these elements had priority in his experience. If someone says that he finds a work overwhelmingly good whereas I find it execrable then this indicates both that there will be disagreement (and therefore reasoning) and some idea of what form this reasoning will take. I can then pass on to his general reasons, 'exhilarating', etc., and finally ask him which sections or aspects of the work make him want to apply the concept. In all probability he will then mention detailed, 'factual' points about string scales, off-beat brass chords, etc. If the conversation were to start at the factual end with him saying 'Those string scales' then, unless it were said in a particular tone of voice, the remark would tell me precisely nothing, as those may well be the very scales I would want to point to as being notably hackneyed and *faux*-sprightly.

Thus the question, 'How did I come to pass from "curves" or "string scales" to "beautiful" or "extraordinarily good"?' is doubly misconceived. Firstly, I did not and could not pass from one to the other; I saw the object and my response to it was natural and immediate. The strength of my attraction to a work will not only determine which general evaluative terms are employed, but will affect the concepts employed all the way down the evaluative/descriptive continuum. If I like a work I may describe it as unified, intense and complex, if I dislike it then I may describe it as monotonous, convoluted and over-heated. It is only when we arrive at the purely descriptive, 'in G major', 'ABBA rhyme-scheme' that we should expect accord between praisers and disparagers. Secondly, in critical discussion it is normal to begin with the purely evaluative terms and then pass to the purely factual by way of the evaluative-cum-descriptive (mixed terms). Having reached this point, our predicates may well start moving back up the evaluative scale 'drawing attention rhetorically to the features of what we are talking about, insisting how different it is from this, how like to that, passing insensibly from the purely factual through the semi-factual, semi-critical, to the critical predicate at issue. Only this mixture is critical proof and the name of it is rhetoric.'[28] Critical discussion will move up and down the evaluative/factual scale until agreement, weariness, disgust or lack of time put an end to the discussion.

Thus we can see that critical discussion can only take place within an affective response: the primitive feelings of attraction, revulsion or boredom are the *sine qua non* of evaluative discussion, and the purpose of critical debate is not to by-pass and eliminate them, but to change or understand them. As Wittgenstein puts it: 'Aesthetic discussion is something that goes on inside the range of likes and dislikes. It goes on before any question of taste arises' [A: 38]. The task of deciding what sort of explanation can be given of this basic aesthetic response, and then actually to propose such an explanation, are two of Aesthetics' most pressing tasks.[29]

Notes

1 I know of three sustained attempts to defend a position similar to the one articulated in this paper. They are Arnold Isenberg, 'Critical Communication', in his *Aesthetics and the Theory of Criticism*, ed. Callaghan, Cauman et al. (Chicago: Chicago University Press, 1973), pp. 156–71; John Casey, *The Language of Criticism* (London: Methuen, 1968); John Reichert, *Making Sense of Literature* (Chicago: Chicago University Press, 1977). The last two derive their inspiration from Wittgenstein; Isenberg appears to have arrived at similar conclusions independently.

2 I use the following abbreviations for Wittgenstein's works. A: *Wittgenstein's Lectures, Cambridge 1932–1935*, ed. A. Ambrose (Oxford: Blackwell, 1979); LC: *Lectures and Conversations on Aesthetics, Psychology and Religious Belief*, ed. C. Barrett (Oxford: Blackwell, 1978); M: 'Wittgenstein's Lectures in 1930–33', ed. G.E. Moore, in H. Osborne (ed.), *Aesthetics* (Oxford: Oxford University Press, 1979); PI: *Philosophical Investigations*, ed. G.E.M. Anscombe (Oxford: Blackwell, 1976); RPP: *Remarks on the Philosophy of Psychology*, vol. 1, ed. G.E.M. Anscombe and G.H. von Wright (Oxford: Blackwell, 1980). Page numbers are given only in the absence of section numbers.

3 Stanley Cavell, 'Music Discomposed', in his *Must We Mean What We Say?* (Cambridge: Cambridge University Press, 1969), p. 191.

4 In this section I am indebted to Malcolm Budd's discussion of aspects in *Wittgenstein's Philosophy of Psychology* (London: Routledge, 1989), especially pp. 77–86.

5 The illustration is based on one used by P.B. Porter (1954), *American Journal of Psychology*, 67, p. 550. See also M.L. Johnson Abercrombie, *The Anatomy of Judgment* (London: Hutchinson, 1960), p. 24.

6 This passage is taken from Budd, *Wittgenstein's Philosophy of Psychology*, pp. 81–2.

7 See Michael Tanner 'Wittgenstein and Aesthetics', *Oxford Review*, 3 (1966), pp. 14–17.

8 e.e.cummings, *Collected Poems* (New York: Harcourt, Brace, 1953), p. 393.

9 Lionel Trilling, 'The Immortality Ode', in his *The Liberal Imagination* (Oxford: Oxford University Press, 1978), pp. 125–6.

10 Ian McEwan, *The Comfort of Strangers* (London: Cape, 1981).

11 Cleanth Brooks, 'Wordsworth and the Paradox of Imagination', in M.H. Abrams (ed.), *Wordsworth: A Collection of Critical Essays* (Englewood Cliffs, NJ: Prentice-Hall, 1972), pp. 176–7.

12 Frank Kermode, *The Sense of an Ending: Studies in the Theory of Fiction* (London: Oxford University Press, 1968), p. 83.

13 Kermode, *The Sense of an Ending*, p. 85.

14 A.C. Bradley, *Shakespearean Tragedy* (London: Macmillan, 1985), p. 295.

15 Mary McCarthy, 'General Macbeth', in her *The Writing on the Wall* (Harmondsworth: Penguin, 1973), pp. 9–13.

16 David Lodge, *Changing Places* (Harmondsworth: Penguin, 1978), pp. 214–15.

17 Casey, *The Language of Criticism*, pp. 52–7.

18 Jane Austen, *Emma* (London: Oxford University Press, 1973), pp. 26–7.

19 Harold Nicholson, 'Lambert Orme', in his *Some People* (Oxford: Oxford University Press, 1983), p. 47.

20 John Wisdom, 'Philosophy and Psycho-analysis', in his *Philosophy and Psycho-analysis* (Oxford: Blackwell, 1969), p. 278.

21 I.A. Richards, *Principles of Literary Criticism* (London: Routledge and Kegan Paul, 1955); J.M. Ellis, *The Theory of Literary Criticism: A Logical Analysis* (Berkeley: University of California Press, 1974).

22 Aristotle appears to hold such a position in the *Nicomachean Ethics*: 'We deliberate not about ends but about means', Bk 3, 112b5–26, in J. Barnes (ed.), *Ethics* (Harmondsworth: Penguin, 1976), p. 119. The interpretation of this passage, however, is the subject of much scholarly debate.

23 This phrase was reported in a lecture given by Renford Bambrough in Cambridge in about 1980. I have not been able to trace the source of the remark: it may have been made orally.

24 Daniel Taylor, *Explanation and Meaning* (Cambridge: Cambridge University Press, 1970), pp. 93–5. For influential accounts of critical reasoning that bear close affinities to Taylor's, see Monroe C. Beardsley, *Aesthetics: Problems in the Philosophy of Criticism* (New York: Harcourt, Brace, 1958), pp. 454–556; and William G. Lycan and Peter K. Machamer, 'A Theory of Critical Reasons', in B. Tilghman (ed.), *Language and Aesthetics* (Lawrence: Kansas University Press,1973), pp. 87–112. Beardsley's theory is usefully discussed in Frank Sibley, 'General Criteria and Reasons in Aesthetics', in John Fisher (ed.), *Essays in Aesthetics: Perspectives on the Work of Monroe Beardsley* (Philadelphia: Temple University Press, 1983), pp. 3–20; and George Dickie (1988), *Evaluating Art* (Philadelphia: Temple University Press, 1988), pp. 53–80. For an interesting discussion of critical principles see, Wayne C. Booth, 'The Peculiar "Logic" of Evaluative Criticism', in his *The Company We Keep: An Ethics of Fiction* (Berkeley: University of California Press, 1988), pp. 51–60, where a similar position to Taylor's is ascribed to Gabriel Josipovici.

25 Northrop Frye, 'Polemical Introduction' to *The Anatomy of Criticism* (Princeton, NJ: Princeton University Press, 1957), p. 25.

26 David Hume, 'Of the Standard of Taste', in W. Kennick (ed.), *Art and Philosophy* (New York: St Martin's Press, 1979), p. 486.

27 I take the handy pairing of 'vivid' and 'garish' from Michael Tanner, 'Objectivity and Aesthetics', *Proceedings of the Aristotelian Society, Supplementary Volume*, XLII, 1968, p. 69.

28 John Wisdom, 'Note on the New Edition of Professor Ayer's *Language, Truth and Logic*', in his *Philosophy and Psycho-analysis*, p. 246.

29 For some hints as to how the line of thought in this paper might be developed see: M.W. Rowe, 'The Objectivity of Aesthetic Judgements', *British Journal of Aesthetics*, 39 (1999), pp. 40–52; 'How do Criticism and Aesthetic Theory Fit Together?', *British Journal of Aesthetics*, special issue, *Aesthetics in Britain*, 40, (2000), pp. 115–32; and 'Wittgenstein, I.A. Richards, and Psychological Aesthetics', *Wittgenstein-Jahrbuch 2001/2002*, pp. 173–90.

Chapter 3

Wittgenstein's Romantic Inheritance

In this essay, I want to explore the implications of an important but little discussed passage in Wittgenstein's *Culture and Value*:

> I often wonder whether my cultural ideal is a new one, i.e. contemporary, or whether it derives from Schumann's time. It does at least strike me as continuing that ideal, though not in the same way it was continued at the time. That is to say, the second half of the Nineteenth century has been missed out. This I ought to say is a purely instinctive development and not the result of reflection. [CV:12][1]

Prima facie, this is surprising, because when Wittgenstein actually drew up a list of his influences, the first half of the nineteenth century is very poorly represented, while the late nineteenth and early twentieth century virtually predominate:

> I don't believe I ever *invented* a line of thinking, I have always taken one over from somebody else. I have simply straightaway seized on it with enthusiasm for my work of clarification. This is how Boltzman, Hertz, Schopenhauer, Frege, Russell, Kraus, Loos, Weininger, Spengler, Sraffa have influenced me. Can one take the case of Breuer and Freud as an example of Jewish reproductiveness? [CV:19]

Here, there is only one name – Schopenhauer – which belongs to the early nineteenth century, and there are good reasons both for supposing that he is extremely untypical of German philosophy at the time, and that his influence on Wittgenstein's later philosophy is negligible.[2] However, the tension between the first and second passage, and the second passage's worry about originality, can be resolved by considering the following distinction:

> I believe that my originality (if that is the right word) is an originality belonging to the soil rather than the seed. (Perhaps I have no seed of my own). Sow a seed in my soil and it will grow differently than it would in any other soil.

> Freud's originality too was like this, I think. I have always believed – without knowing why – that the real germ of psycho-analysis came from Breuer, not Freud. Of course Breuer's seed-grain can only have been quite tiny. [CV:36]

The second invocation of the Freud/Breuer case suggests that he is talking about the same phenomenon as in the first passage. It thus seems reasonable to suppose that the influences of late nineteenth-century figures like Frege and Hertz, are the 'result of reflection' and are represented by the seeds in the passage quoted above. The soil, on the other hand, represents Wittgenstein's whole disposition and direction of mind: a sensibility which finds itself powerfully and instinctively attracted to the ideals and aspirations of the early nineteenth century. This explains why his list of influences omits any reference to the early nineteenth century apart from Schopenhauer. A careful reading makes clear that the list is not designed to enumerate every thinker whose work affected him, but is rather intended to illustrate a certain *kind* of influence, viz., where Wittgenstein took over the seed of an idea, 'a line of thinking', from another man. Consequently, if we look for the influences on the soil, his disposition of mind, on this list we shall find them absent. This is important not only because sensibility lies at a level deeper than belief, but because Wittgenstein realises that it is in his early nineteenth-century sensibility, rather than in the predominantly late nineteenth- and early twentieth-century ideas it takes as its objects, that his true originality lies.

The fact that Wittgenstein describes his cultural ideal as 'purely instinctive' does not mean that he was simply born with it or that it had no cultural context. The Christian influences on his work make a useful comparison here; indeed, as I shall show in the next section, it is intimately connected with the Romantic influence. No one could doubt the extent of this influence, and yet the confessional writers who meant so much to Wittgenstein from quite early in life – St Augustine, Tolstoy, Kierkegaard – are not mentioned on the list of influences either. These too seem to matters of soil rather than seed (he once remarked to Drury, 'I am not a religious man but I cannot help seeing every problem from a religious point of view'[3]) but there can be no doubt that such an attitude grew out of a certain historical tradition. In fact, this kind of influence, which invisibly permeates our sensibility from the very cultural air we breathe, appears to be precisely what Nietzsche has in mind when he remarks in *The Anti-Christ*: '[This kind of influence] is not tradition, it is *inheritance*: only as inheritance does it have the effect of a natural quality.'[4]

The precise denotation of 'Schumann's time', however, requires some caution. Romanticism in music appears much later than it did in literature.

It would not be contentious to claim that Romanticism in German literature made its first appearance in Goethe's *Werther* in 1774, whereas Weber's *Der Freischütz*, which plays an equivalent role in music, was not performed until 1821. Even if one wants to stretch a point, and claim that Romanticism in music initially manifests itself with the first performance of Beethoven's *Eroica* in 1804, this is still some 30 years behind literature. Schumann was born in 1810 and the writers who had the greatest influence on him – E.T.A. Hoffmann (1776–1822) and Jean Paul Richter (1763–1825) – were born three and a half and four decades earlier; although it should be noted that most of the latter's work was written between 1792 and 1809. Consequently, when Nietzsche searched for literary counterparts to Schumann's outlook, and described him as 'half Werther, half Jean Paul'[5] he was identifying him with literature written between 20 and 50 years before Schumann's career *began*. Thus, if we want to capture his cultural ideal conceptually, we shall have to look much earlier than the actual dates of his career (about 1829–54) would seem to indicate – back at least to the 1790s.

How can influences on the soil be uncovered? One strategy would simply be to look for references to the names, concepts and ideas of early Romantic writers in Wittgenstein's work, but this would suggest reflection rather than instinct, and the comparative paucity of allusions to early nineteenth-century writers in Wittgenstein's major texts hardly gestures at the depth of influence suggested by the phrase 'my cultural ideal'. Another more fruitful line of approach, would be to take up an aphorism Wittgenstein discusses in *Culture and Value* – 'Le style c'est l'homme même' [CV:78] – and consider how much the form and imagery of Wittgenstein's writing owes to the influence of the Romantics. After all, the form in which one writes is chosen prior to any ideas being written down, and will in large measure dictate both the nature and reception of those ideas; and whereas a man's beliefs can change frequently, the nature of his metaphors and analogies seems a much more personal, permanent and deep-rooted affair. As Wittgenstein remarks: 'It is sometimes said that a man's philosophy is a matter of temperament, and there is something in this. A preference for a certain sort of similes could be a matter of temperament and it underlies far more disagreements than you might think' [CV:20].

In this chapter, therefore, I want to argue that the later Wittgenstein's approach to philosophical problems, his conception of explanation, his style of writing, and the form of *Philosophical Investigations*, have their origin in German literature and philosophy written in the three decades following 1790. These Romantics forms and styles are themselves metamorphosed versions of approaches which have their origin in Christian devotional literature.

Accordingly, in the first section, I begin by noting some striking similarities between the Christian confessional tradition and the style of the *Investigations*. In the second section, I show how these elements of the confessional tradition were altered, adapted and secularized by German Romantic philosophers, and demonstrate that the *Investigations* is an heir to this refracted inheritance rather than a direct continuation of the Christian tradition itself. Finally, in the third section, I examine Goethe's *Wilhelm Meister's Apprenticeship*, and demonstrate its affinities with the form and preoccupations of the *Investigations*. My hope is that when the *Investigations* is placed in its cultural context, many features which seem eccentric or wilful become natural and intelligible.

I

In the first chapter of his book *Natural Supernaturalism*, M.H. Abrams outlines what he calls the 'Biblical plot' whose various vicissitudes and transformations he will chart through the succeeding centuries. Its nodal points are: creation, paradise, temptation, sin, fall, redemption, and finally the attainment of 'new heaven and new earth' (Isaiah 65: 17–25).[6] Originally, this story evolved as a way of interpreting the entire history of mankind but, as Abrams points out, even as early as Paul's account of his own conversion the Biblical plot becomes internalized into the psycho-biography of the believer. A particularly clear case is the *Confessions* of St Augustine. Here we read of Augustine's beginnings as an innocent child of a pious mother (creation and paradise); his ensnarement into a life of wickedness and debauchery (temptation, sin and fall); his rescue by Christ through the agencies of St Anthony, St Ambrose and Simplicianus (redemption); and, finally, the possibility and expectation of eternal union with God (new heaven and new earth). For many later Christians (the poet Edmund Spenser, for example) the Biblical plot held a double significance: it referred explicitly both to the history of mankind and to the inner life of the believer.

Wittgenstein described the *Confessions* as 'the most serious book ever written',[7] and it is mentioned at five important points in the *Investigations*. More significantly, the confessional mode permeates the very texture of the work. A confession is not – except incidentally – a work of reasoning, but of memory, self-scrutiny and interpretation; and this is precisely the kind of thought we find in Wittgenstein's book. As Cavell puts it:

> In confessing you do not explain or justify, but describe how it is with you. And confession, unlike dogma, is not to be believed but tested, and accepted

> or rejected. Nor is it the occasion for accusation, except of yourself, and, by implication, those who find themselves in you. There is exhortation ... not to belief, but to self scrutiny. And that is why there is virtually nothing in the *Investigations* which we should ordinarily call reasoning.[8]

From the perlocutionary point of view, the purpose of confession is not to convey belief or seek assent but to bring about conversion to a particular way of viewing the world. 'Belief', says Cavell, 'is not enough. Either the suggestion penetrates past assessment and becomes part of the sensibility from which assessment proceeds, or it is philosophically useless. In asking for more than belief it invites discipleship, which runs its own risks in terms of dishonesty and hostility.'[9]

The natural medium for confession, as Cavell notes, is dialogue. The reason for this is that a confession is the history of an inwardly riven soul. 'My inner self was ... divided against itself', says Augustine at one point:[10] '[There] are two wills in it ... it is a disease of the mind.'[11] Consequently, in the *Confessions* we not only discover the kind of debate which goes on between one person and another but also – that mark of the modern – Arnold's 'dialogue of the mind with itself'.[12] The two voices are the voice of temptation and the voice of conscience, and their relative strengths vary throughout the work. Near the beginning, Augustine yields to temptation without compunction; in the central sections he is torn apart; towards the end of the autobiographical section the voice of conscience has gained the upper hand (although maintenance of this victory still requires perpetual vigilance and strength of will); ideally, in the future, he would like not to hear the voice of temptation at all. The earlier self is included but transcended in the later self, and the two voices are transmuted into 'what I was once' and 'what I am now'.[13]

The *Investigations* also records an inner struggle which is characterized in the language of religious disputation: 'a battle against the bewitchment of our intelligence by means of language' [PI:109] against 'superstition' (not 'mistakes', as he remarks at PI:110.) There is thus a continual conflict between what one half of the self would like to say, and what the more philosophically perspicuous self, with its eye on the object, can see is really the case. It is this which issues in the inner dialogue between what Cavell calls 'the voice of temptation' and the 'voice of correctness'[14] (although some have felt 'correction' to be more accurate):

> [The book] contains what serious confessions must: the full acknowledgement of temptation ('I want to say ...' 'I feel like saying ...'; 'Here the urge is

> strong ...') and a willingness to correct them and give them up ('In the everyday use ...'; 'I impose a requirement which does not meet my real need.') ...[15]

In the *Investigations*, Wittgenstein is at the same stage as Augustine was when he wrote the *Confessions*. Many of the temptations he examines are those to which he yielded in the *Tractatus*, whereas now he can understand and therefore resist them. Thus in the *Investigations* too, the voice of temptation is in many cases the voice of 'what I was once'; the voice of correction, 'what I am now'.

By comparing Bunyan's spiritual autobiography – *Grace Abounding* – with his later *Pilgrim's Progress*, we can see that Christian allegory frequently takes over and generalizes many features of the confessional form. In the later work, Bunyan uses dialogue so extensively that he feels it necessary to defend his practice in the verse apology which precedes the main text: 'I find that men (as high as trees) will write / Dialogue-wise; yet no man doth them slight / For writing so ....'[16] Here too, despite appearances, the dialogue is internal: although the conversations appear to take place between one person and another, all the characters Pilgrim encounters are personifications of his own temptations, and all the events occur in the context of the narrator's dream.

Augustine's travels (to Madaura, Carthage, Rome, Milan, Cassiciacum) are both caused by, and act as an analogue to, his quest for spiritual truth. Similarly, in Christian allegory it is usual for the Christian soul to be portrayed as a traveller, pilgrim or wayfarer who will only find rest and enlightenment after long and arduous journeyings. Typically, at the beginning of the work, the wayfarer has become disheartened and lost amidst an inhospitable landscape. Dante's *Inferno*, for example, opens: 'In the middle of life's journey I found myself in a darkling wood, where the traces of straight path were lost';[17] and Bunyan's *Pilgrim's Progress* begins, 'As I walked through the wilderness of this world, I lighted on a certain place where was a Den, and laid me down in that place to sleep ....'[18]

The root metaphor which underlies the whole of Wittgenstein's work is also that of a journey; specifically, a journey which explores our language.[19] The landscape described is usually rural, but it is not the hostile wilderness of Christian allegory. Although occasionally mountainous, it has green valleys, paths criss-cross in every direction, and the danger lies less in losing the track altogether than in taking the wrong turning:

> 203: Language is a labyrinth of paths. You approach from *one* side and you know your way about; you approach the same place from another side and no longer know your way about.

> 426: In the actual use of expressions we make detours, we go by side-roads. We see the straight highway before us, but of course we cannot use it, because it is permanently closed.
> 123: A philosophical problem has the form: 'I don't know my way about.'
> 525: (A multitude of familiar paths lead off … in every direction.)
> The relationship between these concepts form a landscape which language presents us with in countless fragments; piecing them together is *too hard* for me. I can make only a very imperfect job of it. [CV:78]

Like Bunyan and Dante, Wittgenstein presents himself as both a solitary and a walker in order to demonstrate that only his own native resources can be called upon.[20] Taken in one sense the wayfarer is an emblematic figure who represents each individual who wishes to make, or must make, this solitary journey (hence, in Christian allegory, the wayfarer is frequently 'Pilgrim', 'Christian', 'Everyman'); in another, he is an explorer who has scouted the terrain and discovered its complexities. Although each of us has to make this journey alone, the philosopher who has gone ahead can at least warn, exhort and advise those who follow:

> I am showing my pupils details of an immense landscape which they cannot possibly know their way around [CV:56].

> Language sets everyone the same traps; it is an immense network of easily accessible wrong turnings. And so we watch one man after another walking down the same paths and we know in advance where he will branch off, where walk straight on without noticing the side turning, etc. etc. What I have to do then is erect signposts at all the junctions where there are wrong turnings so as to help people past the danger points. [CV:18e]

Although Augustine eloquently records the effect conversion had on his vision and understanding of nature,[21] his ultimate goal remains other-worldly, and he eagerly anticipates the joys and splendours of heaven. Some interpretations of the biblical plot, however, taking their inspiration from texts like Luke 17:21 ('… for behold, the kingdom of God is within you') psychologize the story still further. For puritans like Gerrard Winstanley writing in the 1640s, and others in the north European Protestant tradition, all Biblical figures – Adam, Cain, Abel, Moses, etc. – are 'to be seen within you'; and orthodox theology, which treats them, along with heaven and earth, as externally real, is but 'a Doctrine of sickly and weak spirit, who hath lost his understanding'. Likewise, the second coming and apocalypse are regarded solely as symbolic presentations of events which actually take place in the believer's soul: 'Now the second *Adam* Christ, hath taken the kingdom of my body, and rules in it; *He makes it a new heaven and a new earth wherein dwells Righteousnesse.*'[22] On this interpretation, the goal of heaven is actually *this* world, but experienced by 'our redeemed and glorified senses'.[23]

The extent to which Wittgenstein was a believing Christian is disputed: Gasking, Jackson[24] and von Wright[25] assert that he was not; but Wittgenstein's sister Gretl said '[Ludwig] *was* a Christian to my reckoning',[26] and Russell reports that at one stage Wittgenstein seriously thought about becoming a monk.[27] What is clear, however, is that Wittgenstein was powerfully attracted to Christianity at certain points in his life (especially during and just after the First World War) and that when he was attracted, it was always towards an inner-light Protestantism which cared little for verifiable quasi-scientific or historical doctrines, and everything for Christian practice and a transformed life:

> Christianity is not a doctrine, not, I mean, a theory about what has happened and what will happen to the human soul, but a description of something that actually takes place in human life. For 'consciousness of sin' is a real event and so are despair and salvation through faith. Those who speak of such things (Bunyan for instance) are simply describing what has happened to them, whatever gloss anyone may want to put on it. [CV:28e]

> I believe that one of the things that Christianity says is that sound doctrines are all useless. That you have to change your *life* ....[CV:53e]

In orthodox Christianity, the biblical plot is conceived of as a linear development through time, and when it is allegorized it becomes a linear movement from one place to another (better) place. In *Pilgrim's Progress*, for instance, Christian starts off at the edge of the wide field, falls into the Slough of Despond, passes through the Valley of the Shadow of Death, and eventually arrives at the Celestial City. There is, however, another way of interpreting the biblical plot which finds its archetype in the story of the prodigal son.[28] The son's journey, of course, is not ultimately a journey from one place to another, but is circular in form and arrives back at its point of starting, although this point of starting is now transformed by the experiences undergone on the way. This is the most natural way for an inner-light Protestant to allegorize his experience, since he has not won through to a *new* world but simply to a redeemed, clarified and glorified vision of the world from which he began. This is also the form of Christianity which is most amenable to the Romantic transformation of the Biblical plot which I shall discuss in the next section.

II

For German Romantics in the 30 years after 1790, the central philosophical problem was how to heal the division between the world of nature and the experience of the subject. This had been caused in the first instance, they believed, by bringing analytic thought to bear on our relationship with the world; and, in the second, by the rise of physical science which divided the world into private Cartesian subjects on the one hand, and an alien, dead world of matter on the other. The only solution appeared to be to reconceptualize the relationship between man and nature, and let a higher more subtle philosophy repair the damage that analytical crudities had inflicted. As Schelling puts it, analytic thought is 'a spiritual sickness of mankind … an evil', and without the 'original separation … we would have no need to philosophize'; true philosophy sets out 'to annul and sublimate that separation forever'.[29] This division between man and nature led to two others: 'a strange disorder' in which 'we are in inner dispute with ourselves', and a deep sense of alienation from the society surrounding them. Their deepest wish was to see the original dichotomy, and the other two which arose from it, healed: 'To end that eternal conflict between our self and the world' wrote Hölderlin in the preface to *Hyperion*, 'to restore the peace which passeth all understanding … is the goal of all our striving ….'[30]

Hölderlin, Schelling and Hegel became friends when they attended the same theological seminary at Tübingen in the late 1780s and early 1790s. Because of their theological background, it was natural for them to conceive of this problem in terms of fall and redemption. On this model, our original unity with nature is regarded as Eden; our disastrous attempts at analytic thought as original sin; and our rivenness from self, nature and society as our fallen condition, from which only a higher and more exalted philosophy can redeem us. It was equally natural that when they looked for a suitable literary genre that could give satisfactory expression to their outlook they lighted on the Christian spiritual autobiography as their model and archetype. Abrams points out that many of the features already noted in Augustine's *Confessions* – the subjective narrative form, internal dialogue, the gradual progress towards self-transcendence – are also to be found in a work like Hegel's *Phenomenology of Spirit*:

> [It] turns out to have been a concealed first person narrative … and one that is told explicitly, in the mode of a double consciousness. For the spirit at the end of the process narrated in the *Phenomenology* has experienced a rebirth into

> a new identity … And from the vantage of this new and enlightened self … the spirit proceeds to remember and represent itself to itself as it was during its own earlier stages of development …[31]

These approaches and attitudes link up significantly with the form and outlook manifest in the *Investigations*. Wittgenstein's suspicion of science and the view of mind to which it almost invariably leads is characteristically Romantic: 'I suppose the paradigm of all science is mechanics, e.g. Newtonian Mechanics' [LC:29]; 'It isn't absurd to believe that the age of science and technology is the beginning of the end for humanity; that … there is nothing good or desirable about scientific knowledge and that mankind, in seeking it, is falling into a trap. It is by no means obvious that this is not how things are' [CV:56e]; 'It is humiliating to have to appear like an empty tube which is simply inflated by a mind' [CV:11]. We also find Schelling's idea that the false picture of man and nature generated by science and analytic philosophy is a 'sickness' (although an inevitable sickness) without which we would have no need for higher, more clear-sighted philosophical activity: 'A main cause of philosophical *disease* – a one-sided diet … of example[s]' [PI:593]; 'What a mathematician is inclined to say about [objectivity] … is … something for philosophical *treatment*' [PI: 254]; 'The philosopher's treatment of a question is like the treatment of an *illness*' [PI:255] (my italics).

Wittgenstein was quite conscious that the confessional nature of the *Investigations* urged him towards a two-voiced, dialogic structure: 'Nearly all my writings', he noted while revising the book, 'are private conversations with myself. Things that I say to myself *tête-à-tête*' [CV:77]. As in Hegel, the narrating self is fragmented into opponents and interlocutors who are sometimes 'I' ('I should like to say: "I experience the because"' [PI:177]), sometimes 'we' ('We feel as if we had to *penetrate* phenomena …' [PI:90]), sometimes 'you' ('Thus you were inclined to use such expressions as …' [PI:188]) but which are ultimately all aspects of Wittgenstein and the reader who finds himself in Wittgenstein. A similar structure is found in the *Phenomenology*: '[The protagonist of the story], the spirit, is also his own antagonist, who appears in a correlative multitude of altering disguises, so that one actor plays all the roles in the drama; as Hegel says of one stage of the evolution, 'the I is the *we*, and the *we* is the I'.[32] Significantly, as in Hölderlin, the end of philosophy in the *Investigations* is not theory or even understanding but *peace*, an end to inner rivenness and dialogue: 'The real discovery is the one that makes me capable of stopping doing philosophy when I want to – The one that gives philosophy *peace* [my italics] so that it is no longer tormented by questions which bring *itself* in question ...' [PI:133]; 'Thoughts that are at peace. That's what someone who philosophizes yearns for' [CV:43].

In the works of men like Russell and Carnap, philosophy is conceived of in quasi-scientific terms: it consists of theories based on evidence; it makes, or ought to make, progress; it can sometimes be a communal enterprise; it tells us about the objective universe. Such a mode of thought is remote from the confessional tradition where the aim is to clarify and understand one's past life, to achieve self-knowledge, and where the struggle to acknowledge and understand is subjective and – ultimately – solitary. In the latter tradition, the basic data on which the intelligence operates is *memory*. A work like Augustine's *Confessions* is obviously a work of recollection and autobiography, and the most sustained philosophical discussion in that work, appropriately enough, takes memory for its topic.[33]

The central importance of memory is inherited in the philosophy of Hegel and Wittgenstein. In Wittgenstein, philosophical method is a matter of prompting and reminding in order to allow someone to recall what he really says and does: 'The work of the philosopher consists in assembling *reminders* for a particular purpose' [PI:127] (my italics); 'Something that we know when no one asks us, but no longer know when we are supposed to give an account of it, is something we need to remind ourselves of ...' [PI:89]. The purpose of this process is firstly to reveal what the real philosophical data are, and secondly to achieve a well-grounded 'perspicuous overview' of our language and therefore our world. In Hegel too, memory is the means to self-knowledge and self-transcendence:

> Recollection, the *inwardizing* of [previous] experience, has preserved [outer experience] and is the inner being, and in fact the higher form of the substance. So although this spirit starts afresh and apparently from its own resources to bring itself to maturity, it is none the less on a higher level that it starts.[34]

In the German Romantics, this quest to retrieve and organize what, in some sense, we already know, is often allegorized. It is imagined as a journey which arrives back at its starting point, a starting point which has been transformed by the experience of the way; and the inner-light Protestant's scheme of salvation is secularized into an account of maturation and self-education. In these philosophers, as in much devotional literature, the significance of the journey is twofold: it represents the development of the individual spirit, and simultaneously it represents the stages through which the human race as a whole has passed. It is in this doubled form that the circular journey metaphor is most frequently encountered. Here are two examples from Hegel and Fichte respectively:

> 'To become true knowledge' the spirit 'has to work its way through a long journey' [*Weg*]; and 'every individual must also pass through the contents of the educational stages of the general spirit but ... as stages of a way that has been prepared and evened for him ... It is a circle that returns into itself, that pre-supposes its beginning and reaches its end only in its beginning.'[35]

> But the collective journey [*Weg*], which ... mankind pursues here below, is no other than a way back to the point upon which it stood at the very beginning, and has no other goal than to return to its origin.[36]

The end point is the 'beginning from which we set out' but at a higher level' because the spirit 'is at home (*bei sich*) with itself in its otherness as such'.[37]

This conception of inquiry is appealing to outlooks which are suspicious of progress in any straightforward sense, and prefer to stress wisdom and the understanding of what is already to hand. This option was very much alive amongst Wittgenstein's intellectual contemporaries and mentors in Vienna. In his poem 'Zwei Laufer' ('Two Runners'), Karl Kraus contrasts those who find no use for tradition and believe in unending progress with those for whom 'the origin is the goal' and who have already arrived at where they wished to go.[38] Wittgenstein, of course, was of a similar mind. He draws attention to the dissimilarity between his own aim of clarity for its own sake and the dominant belief in progress and construction [CV:7], and stresses that his own conception of philosophy is a wandering journey which frequently discovers its end in its beginning: 'For the place I really have to get to is a place I must already be at now' [CV:7]; in some moods this almost made the journey seem unnecessary, 'If you want to get deep down you do not need to travel far; indeed, you don't have to leave your most immediate and familiar surroundings' [CV:50]. More famously, in the preface to the *Investigations*, he writes:

> [The] very nature of the investigation ... compels us to travel over a wide field of thought criss-cross in every direction. – The philosophical remarks in this book are, as it were, a number of sketches of a landscape which were made in the course of these long and involved journeyings. [PI: vii]

The point of these wanderings is not to penetrate through to a higher reality or to arrive at a theoretical understanding of phenomena. On the contrary, the purpose of the journey is to see the place we began from – the ordinary humdrum world of everyday experience – clearly for the first time; and this is difficult to do precisely because it is so familiar:

> How hard I find it to see what is *right in front of my eyes.* [CV:39]
>
> The aspects of things which are most important for us are hidden because of their simplicity and familiarity. (One is unable to notice something – because it is always before one's eyes.) ... [We] fail to be struck by what, once seen, is most striking and powerful. [PI:129]
>
> ... We are not contributing curiosities ... but observations which no one has doubted, but which have escaped remark only because they are always before our eyes. [PI:415]

At the outset of inquiry we are beset by doubts and difficulties we are unable to solve because we are too familiar with the data on which solutions are based. Initially, the purpose of Wittgenstein's metaphorical journey is to make us aware of our starting-point's position by setting it in relation to other places. This makes our home environment seem strange enough for us to be able to see it clearly for the first time. Ultimately, the journey's purpose to induce a cognitive state whereby the starting point is both clearly perceived (so that our initial difficulties vanish), and yet we are utterly familiar and at one with it; a condition accurately captured in the complexities of Hegel's phrase, '[The Spirit is] at home with itself in its otherness as such'. This conception of philosophical method is only a step away from Wittgenstein's conception of Christianity: both describe, they do not theorize; and both aim not for a transcendental goal but a cleared and clarified vision of the ordinary world from which we set out. When David Pears quotes T.S. Eliot's lines, 'And the end of all our exploring / Will be to arrive where we started / And know the place for the first time', as an epigraph to his study of Wittgenstein, three divergent lines of the same tradition – the Christian, the Romantic, and the Wittgensteinian – converge again.[39]

Whatever Wittgenstein's general attitude towards Christianity, the *Investigations* is insistently secular in spirit. Paradoxically, the views of scientifically-minded, atheist metaphysicians like Russell are implicitly bracketed together with those of orthodox Christians. The reason for this is that neither is satisfied with a transformed and clarified picture of the here and now, but both hanker after a higher or deeper 'beyond'. This leads Wittgenstein to mock the metaphysician's superstitions in strikingly religious language:

'Thought is surrounded by a halo' [PI:97]; 'We might give thanks to the Deity for our agreement' [PI:234]; '"For surely," I tell myself, "I was being *guided*" – Only then does the idea of the ethereal, intangible influence arise' [PI:175]; 'subliming our whole account of logic' [PI:94]; 'We are not *striving after* an ideal' [PI:98]; 'This order is *super*-order' [PI:97]; 'For us, of course, these forms of expressions are like pontificals ... [but] we lack the effective power that would give these vestments meaning and purpose' [PI:426].

Like the Romantic philosopher, Wittgenstein is only interested in communicating his vision of the natural world, and for this reason sees himself not as metaphysician or theologian but as an *artist*: 'Things are placed right in front of your eves not covered by any veil – this is where religion and art part company' [CV:6]. This idea constantly permeates the imagery in which he describes his own task. In the preface to the *Investigations*, he describes his work as really only 'an album' of 'sketches' [PI:vii]; 'Everything that comes my way becomes a picture ...' [CV:31]; 'And after all a painter is basically what I am, often a very bad painter too' [CV:82]. Sometimes the art changes: 'My style is like bad musical composition' [CV:39]; 'I think I summed up my attitude to philosophy when I said: philosophy ought really to be written only as *poetic composition*' [CV:24]. Throughout, aesthetic and philosophical problems are grouped together: 'I may find scientific questions interesting, but they never really grip me. Only *conceptual* and *aesthetic* questions do that' [CV:79]; 'The queer resemblance between a philosophical investigation ... and an aesthetic one ...' [CV:25]. For this reason he scorns, 'People ... [who] think that scientists exist to instruct them, poets, musicians etc. to give them pleasure. The idea *that these have something to teach them* – that does not occur to them' [CV:36].

There are thus several striking similarities between Wittgenstein's form and imagery and the work of the German Romantic philosophers, but I would not wish to claim that he actually read their work.[40] However, he did read a great deal of German Romantic literature, and it seems highly probable that he absorbed the atmosphere of German philosophy through literature. As Abrams has observed, this was possible because '[at] no other place and time have literature and technical philosophy been so closely interinvolved as in Germany in the period beginning with Kant'.[41] Schelling and Hegel both wrote poetry; Goethe and Schiller wrote philosophy; and those in other countries who came under their influence (Coleridge for instance) became equally involved with both. Not surprisingly, therefore, one can find the same underlying problems, preoccupations and metaphors in the two disciplines. In addition, as I showed in the first section, Wittgenstein was deeply interested in devotional literature.

It seems highly likely that an interest in the same fundamental set of problems, and a similar disposition of mind, led him and the German Romantics to modify their joint inheritance of the Christian confessional tradition in similar ways. In the next section, however, I want to turn to a writer who influenced both the Romantic philosophers and Wittgenstein intimately and directly – Goethe – and to a text which Wittgenstein knew well and referred to in his philosophical work.[42]

III

The metaphor of the wandering, often ultimately circular journey is most obvious in the late eighteenth- and early nineteenth-century novel of cultural education and self-discovery – the *Bildungsroman*. This finds its paradigmatic expression in Goethe's *Wilhelm Meister*,[43] and below, I shall briefly outline those features of the plot which I intend to discuss.

At the beginning of the novel, Wilhelm is presented as a soul detached from the external world. He is entirely preoccupied with his childhood love of the puppet theatre, and he quite overlooks the boredom of Marianne, his lover, as he delivers a narration on his activities that lasts for the best part of six chapters: 'Marianne, overcome by sleep, had put her head on her lover's shoulder. He held her tight while he continued his narration' [WM:13]. 'It is to be hoped', comments the authorial voice dryly, 'that in the future our hero will find more attentive listeners for his favorite stories' [WM:15] (see also WM:11).

The affair with Marianne ends and Wilhelm destroys the drafts of his early poems. Forced to take up an uncongenial life of business, he becomes a divided and riven self: `My dear Wilhelm', says his brother, Werner, 'I have often regretted your strenuous attempts to banish from your mind what you feel so strongly … If I am not mistaken, you might try, better to achieve some reconciliation with yourself…' [WM:46]. Wilhelm is sent on a business trip by his brother, and, largely neglecting his task, gives in to his theatrical ambitions and joins a wandering band of actors. As in Christian allegory, his unscheduled wanderings around the country are a symbol of striving after inner harmony. This latter task is helped and paralleled by the roles he takes up as an actor; a clergyman remarks in Book II, '[Extemporization] is the very best way to take people out of themselves and, by way of a detour, return them to themselves' [WM:67]. Significantly, his first experience of Shakespeare is also one in which he loses all sense of division from the world, and therefore within himself: '[He] was seized ... by the torrent of a great genius which swept toward a limitless ocean in which he completely, lost and forgot his own self' [WM:105].

By this stage he has been told, and was ready to be told, that his earlier obsession with the puppet theatre was juvenile:

> Let's suppose that Fate has destined someone to become a good actor ... but unfortunately chance has it that as a child this young man became so addicted to the absurdities of the puppet theatre that he finds stupidity not only tolerable but even interesting, and cannot regard these childish impressions, which never fade and continue to attract, from the proper perspective. [WM:68]

In spite of the severity of this judgement, Wilhelm still has a propensity to 'go on dreaming as before' [WM:81], and to build 'castle[s] in the air' [WM:121]. By Book IV, even though he has acquired a profound grasp of literature, his understanding of human beings is still grossly defective. Aurelie, the sister of the company's director and main actor, tells him:

> You are able to penetrate into the very depths of the poet's mind and to appreciate the subtlest nuances in its presentation. [Yet] nothing comes into you from the outside world. I have rarely met anyone who knew so little of the people with whom he lives – indeed fundamentally misjudges them. [WM: 153]

Amongst other manifestations of this fault are a tendency to 'deduce everything from the ideas he had already formed' [WM:163], and an inability to write about 'external things which, as he now noticed, had not in any way distracted his attention' [WM:159]. He is prevented from achieving 'harmony within himself' [WM:171] because he had 'abandoned his own natural way of thinking' and '... placed too much trust in the experience of others and attached too much value to what other people derived from their own convictions' [WM:171].

Having given his theatrical ambitions full rein, he comes to see only too clearly that he will never be a great actor, and that much of his insensitivity has been due to being blinded by his own obsessions. On leaving the company, he comes to realize that 'people much concerned with their own inner life are apt to neglect external circumstances ... for the first time [he became] aware that he needed external means to promote effective activity' [WM:300]; a thought which is elaborated by the Beautiful Soul's uncle:

> [One] should not pursue the cultivation of one's moral life in isolation and seclusion. We are more likely to find that a person intent on moral advancement will have every cause to cultivate his senses as well as his mind, so as not to run the risk of losing his foothold on those moral heights, slipping into the seductive allurements of uncontrolled fancy and debasing his nobler nature by idle frivolities, if not worse. [WM:248]

At the end of his apprenticeship, Wilhelm's experience of the ordinary world is transformed. When his moral vision was fogged by theatrical daydreams, he was sunk in self-division and oblivious to others and the external world. Now, he is fully alive to both, and seems to perceive them 'through a new organ':

> Felix [Wilhelm's son] ran out into the garden and Wilhelm followed in a state of exhilaration. It was the most beautiful morning, everything around him looked lovelier than ever, he was sublimely happy, … Wilhelm was observing nature through a new organ, and the child's curiosity and desire to learn made him aware of how feeble his interest had been in things outside himself and how little he knew, how few things he was familiar with. On this day, the happiest in his entire life, his own education seemed also to be beginning anew …. [WM:305]

Thus he arrives at the same point as the Spirit at the end of the *Phenomenology*: '… now reborn of the Spirit's knowledge– is the new existence, a new world and a new shape of Spirit. In the immediacy of this new existence the Spirit has to start afresh to bring itself to maturity … It is none the less on a higher level that it starts.'[44]

Clearly, *Wilhelm Meister* is a fine example of a circular journey, which transforms its place of starting, but this similarity can lead us to notice several other affinities with the Romantic philosophers and, ultimately, the *Investigations*. To begin with, we have the confessional form itself. '… All my published works are but fragments of one confession',[45] Goethe tells us in *Dichtung und Wahrheit*, and *Wilhelm Meister* is obviously based on Goethe's own search for identity, his affairs, indiscretions, early attempts at writing, and extensive experience of the theatre. Consequently, the central interest of the novel lies in its 'interiority' (to use Moretti's word[46]), and attention focuses on the protagonist's inner divisions and sense of struggle. Because of this, the main intellectual weight of the novel is borne by dialogue. This takes place between Wilhelm and his brother Werner (Wilhelm's 'alter-ego' as Moretti observes[47]), other characters, and, most of all, with himself (e.g., WM:

34). As in Schelling, this inner schism is a 'sickness' which induces morbid introspection and prevents the subject acting effectively on the world.

The cause of internal dialogue is our natural propensity towards the construction of false pictures and fantasies. These ensure that we cannot gain proper access to the real world because we are continually torn between the claims of one fantasy and reality, or between one fantasy and another. *Wilhelm Meister* is the history of one man's struggle to work through an all-consuming and ultimately debilitating illusion: an addiction to the make-believe world of acting and the conviction that he is intended to be a great actor. Wilhelm's obsession with acting results in a series of day-dreams and inner fantasies which make him cut-off and impercipient, and his education is devoted to letting him work through these illusions by allowing him to see that they are no more than illusions. Eventually, Wilhelm ceases to be in emotional thrall to his fantasies, comes to realize that they are simply 'castles in the air', and regains contact with nature and society.

Wittgenstein thought that the traditional problems of metaphysics are entirely generated by a series of alluring false pictures [PI:115], illusions [PI:111]), and false similes [PI:112] that distort our vision and render us unobservant. These pictures are often firmly rooted in the surface grammar of our language and can only be extirpated with immense difficulty. The task of philosophy is to explore the temptations that lead us to hold these false pictures since they will lose their power to captivate us once they are revealed for what they are. By this means, therefore, we shall gain access to a cleared and clarified vision of phenomena. Accordingly, Wittgenstein employs metaphors strikingly similar to Goethe's 'castles in the air' when he defends his purely destructive attitude towards the constructions of traditional metaphysics. In an early version of the *Investigations* he describes them as 'edifices of mist'.[48] In the final draft he remarks: 'Where does our investigation get its importance from since it seems to destroy everything interesting, that is, all that is great and important? ... What we are destroying is nothing but houses of cards ...' [PI:118].

One reason for the construction of false pictures is that we spend too much time *thinking* how things must be without actually *looking* at how they are. A tendency like Wilhelm's to 'deduce everything from ideas he had already formed' is also castigated by Wittgenstein: '... [A] preconceived idea to which reality *must* correspond. (The dogmatism into which we fall so easily in doing philosophy)' [PI:131]. Similarly, a failure like Wilhelm's to pay proper attention to external things is precisely the target of Wittgenstein's methodological exhortation: 'Don't say: "There must be something common, or they would not be called 'games'" – but *look and see* whether there is anything common to all ... To repeat: don't think, but look!' [PI:66]. As we might expect, Goethe – like Wittgenstein – has little time for the claims of introspection, and thinks that only close attention to the public realm will produce anything of value: 'Know thyself', wrote Goethe, '[is] a ruse of conspiring priests to confuse men by unattainable demands and tempt them away from acting on the real world to a false inner contemplation. Man knows himself in so far as he knows the world, which he only perceives in himself and himself in it.'[49]

The greatest problem created by false pictures is that they subvert the subject's natural relationship with other people. In Wilhelm's case they render him completely blind to the needs and interests of others; he is simply incapable of reading them correctly. The Cartesian *Weltbild*, to which Wittgenstein stands opposed, makes the problem of the Other more serious still: the mind comes to be pushed out of the public realm altogether so that it becomes hidden behind or within the body. (The body is a tube which is simply inflated by the mind, to use Wittgenstein's earlier analogy.) This picture, of course, gives rise to the problem of other minds, since it makes our convictions about the mental states of others seem based on the thinnest possible evidence. All the foundational beliefs on which our relationship with our community depend seem called into question, and our natural and intuitive convictions about the way other people think and feel come to be tainted with suspicion and scepticism.

Consequently, for Wittgenstein, the philosopher at the beginning of his investigation has ceased to be 'bei sich' with his community, he can no longer find his feet with them: 'When we do philosophy we are like savages, primitive people, who hear the expressions of civilized men, put a false interpretation on them, and draw the queerest conclusions from it' [PI:194]. Alienated responses are caused primarily by alienated language; words float free from the context in which they have their life and meaning. The philosopher, therefore, has to be shown the long linguistic route back to earned acceptance of his natural responses by being reminded of the simple social situations from which his words acquired their significance. Theory has convinced him, for example, that he only ever observes pain behaviour and not pain, and that he is the only one who can feel *this* [PI:295, 298]. The task of Wittgenstein's therapy is to remind him that his knowledge of others is based on attitudes not beliefs [PI:223, p. 178]. This can only be done by relating to him 'the natural history of human beings' [PI:415]; by reminding him how he would actually react in real cases of injury; and by allowing him to recall the kind of circumstances in which he actually uses the word 'pain' and its cognates. With luck, these promptings will bring his alienated words 'back from their metaphysical to their everyday use' [PI:116], back from 'holiday' [PI:38], to the language-game which is their 'original home' [PI:116].

A firm grip on the actual, an appreciation of the very texture of ordinary life, is not the starting point but the goal of Goethe's work.[50] The novel is the genre in which the quotidian details of everyday life are most at home, and it is therefore peculiarly well fitted to express this philosophy. As Moretti remarks, *à propos* the *Bildungsroman*: 'the novel exists not as a critique, but as a culture of everyday life. Far from devaluing it, the novel organizes and "refines" this form of existence, making it ever more alive and interesting', it therefore has an 'obligation to use the common language'.[51] In the same way, arriving at a clear-eyed conception of the ordinary and everyday by overcoming false pictures suggested by surface grammar, is the aim of Wittgenstein's later philosophy; indeed, to suppose that words like 'being' or 'reality' refer to something grander or higher than what we ordinarily mean by them is itself one of the most tempting of philosophical illusions. Accordingly, he defends ordinary language against philosophers who attempt to degrade and diminish it by implicitly comparing it with illusory and inappropriate standards of purity: '... [If] the words "language", "experience", "world", have a use, it must be as humble a one as that of the words "table", "lamp", "door"' [PI:97] (see also PI:98 and 120). The ordinary is the goal of all our striving; the standard by which philosophy itself is to be judged:

> When philosophers use a word – 'knowledge', 'being' ... – and try and grasp the *essence* of the thing, one must always ask oneself: is the word ever actually used in this way in the language game which is its original home? - What *we* do is bring words back from their metaphysical to their everyday use. [PI:116]

The desired general movement in Goethe, as in Hegel, is always *outwards*: from the private, subjective and internal towards the public, objective and communal.[52] The same movement, although now transposed from the ethical to the metaphysical level, is to be found in the *Investigations*. One of the most important of Wittgenstein's polemical targets is a false picture of the inner which grossly and unworkably inflates its importance. Introspection can yield nothing of value even when its 'gaze' is turned on 'objects' which seem almost uncontentiously subjective and inner: Wittgenstein argues, for example, that it can tell you nothing interesting about the nature of pain, or thought, or the self (e.g., PI:262, 274, 413). The starting point for any such investigation must not be a glance inwards, but a scrupulous examination of our shared public language.

He has even less sympathy with the Empiricist tradition, running from Locke to Russell, which tended to analyse meaning, necessity, believing, and intending in terms of private objects, mental images, sensations, and feelings of necessity. In Wittgenstein's work, this kind of phenomenology is demoted in importance, and the real explanatory weight is shown to be taken by public rules, practices, institutions, conventions and objectively verifiable actions. (Games and financial transactions are a favourite source of analogy.) Other subjectivist trends in modern philosophy are rejected equally firmly. He disavows the Positivist idea that physical objects are logical constructions out of sense-data, just as he rejects a scientific realism which leaves the subject trapped within a veil of secondary qualities. Wittgenstein's later philosophy is resolutely anthropological and naturalistic, and insists that the epistemological investigation must start with the world of public objects; the language of how things *seem* is secondary and derived (e.g., PI:379–84).

The scrupulous honesty and observation of confession rather than the argument of a treatise or a critique are what is needed to clear away ossified opinion and fantasy and re-establish contact with society and nature. However, the purpose of confession in Goethe is not simply to make contact with the details of the natural world, but to organize that detail into surveyable and meaningful patterns. To make sense of one's life therefore, one might not only be able to burn through dishonesty and self-deception but achieve a perspicuous overview of the events revealed. It is precisely this overview which Wilhelm feels, at several low points in his life, he is unable to achieve:

> I lost myself in deep meditation and after this discovery I was more restless than before. And after I had learnt something it seemed as though I knew nothing, and I was right: for I did not see the connection of things [Zusammenhang] and yet everything is a question of that. [WM:7]
>
> … He could grasp nothing of what surrounded him, nor leave it alone; everything reminded him of everything. He overlooked the whole ring of his life; only alas, it had broken in pieces in front of him, and he never seemed to want to write again. [WM:349–50][53]

Even though we are told, 'everything is a question of that', it is easy to overlook the force that the expression 'see the connection of things' has for Goethe. It is, in fact, the foundation of his whole epistemology. In his scientific work, he makes quite clear that he is not interested in a conceptual or quasi-mathematical theory of the world of nature (*à la* Newton), but only in a clarified, nuanced and graduated *vision* of phenomena.[54] In the introduction to the *Farbenlehre* (Theory of Colours), for example, he writes:

> During [the] process of observation we remark at first only – a vast variety which presses indiscriminately on our view; we are forced to separate, to distinguish and again to combine: by which means at last a certain order arises which admits of being surveyed with more or less satisfaction.
>
> To accomplish this, only in a certain degree, in any department, requires an unremitting and close application; and we find, for this reason, that men prefer substituting a general theoretical view, or some system of explanation, for the facts themselves.[55]

Thus we can see that observing the connections between things, seeing them in unified and coherent patterns, is the underlying explanatory idea in both his literary and scientific work. The way one understands a life, and the way one understands the world, are the same.

A corresponding connection between life and work, confession and explanation, is found in Wittgenstein. In a letter written to Engelmann in 1920, Wittgenstein remarks:

> … I took down a kind of 'confession', in which I tried to recall the series of events in my life in as much detail as is possible in the space of an hour. With each event I tried to make clear to myself how I should have behaved. *By means of such a general over-view* [*Übersicht*] *the confused picture was much simplified* [my italics]. The next day on the basis of this newly gained insight, I revised my plans and intentions for the future.[56]

Philosophy, for Wittgenstein, is no more than a natural extension of this process: 'No one *can* speak the truth; if he has still not mastered himself' [CV:35]: 'Working, in philosophy … is really more of a working on oneself, one's own interpretation. On one's own way of seeing things' [CV:16]. This use of confessional techniques in philosophy aims to achieve not a theory or a hypothesis but (Goethe's very words) an 'Übersichtliche Darstellung':

> A main source of our failure to understand is that we do not *command a clear view* of the use of our words. – Our grammar is lacking in this sort of perspicacity. A perspicuous representation produces just that understanding which consists in 'seeing connexions'. Hence the importance of finding and inventing intermediate cases.

> The concept of a perspicuous representation is of fundamental significance for us. It earmarks the form of account we give, the way we look at things …. [PI:122]

The rich, personal, quasi-perceptual quality of such an overview entails that it cannot simply be translated into propositional truths and then passed on to another; it has to be earned by a hard-won transformation, otherwise its significance will be missed or it will be thought oppressive. The Society of the Tower – the secret society which oversaw Wilhelm's education – did not force the nature of truth on Wilhelm, they left him to discover it for himself or merely prompted him when they felt he was ready. In order to overcome his natural tendencies to daydreaming and impercipience, Wilhelm had first to be weaned off puppetry, then human actors, and only at that point was he capable of focusing on the ordinary human beings around him. 'The duty of a teacher', says the priest summing up the Society's attitude, 'is not to preserve man from error, but to guide him in error, in fact to let him drink it in, in full draughts …' [WM:302]; and Goethe himself reflects: 'One can see how human beings like to reach their ends only by their own means, how much trouble it takes to make them understand what is self-evident …' [WM:189]. Here, I think, we not only hear the accent of Wittgenstein's remarks about the difficulty of seeing what is in front of you, but also the reflections on teaching he appended to his comments on Frazer's *The Golden Bough*: 'one must start out with error and convert it to truth. That is, one must reveal the source of error, otherwise hearing the truth won't do any good. The truth cannot force its way in when something else is occupying its place. To convince someone of the truth, it is not enough to state it, but one must find the path from error to truth' [GB:61].

In the scientific tradition of philosophy (Russell, Carnap, Quine) philosophical knowledge is a web of interesting true propositions sustained by argument. On this understanding, a biographical interest in a philosopher is at best something supplementary to his philosophy, and at worst a trivial taste for gossip and anecdotes. In the confessional tradition, on the other hand, personal vision, inner transformation, is all. This cannot be summarized or handed on to another, and language can only be used to try to prompt the reader into shared understanding.[57] If we accept this, then it becomes quite natural for us to be interested in the lives of such philosophers, in exactly the same way that we are interested in the lives of poets, painters and saints. Anything which might enable us to catch on, to sympathize, to induce community of vision is philosophically valuable; and, as Wittgenstein emphasized in his

Lectures on Aesthetics, this will frequently be information about the writer's background and culture [LC:8 and 32]. It is therefore a mistake to regret that Wittgenstein's personality and style of thinking appear to have such a strong hold on those who met and read him, or that his life should exert such an enormous fascination.[58] Far from distracting us from his philosophy, these interests are continuous with it and help us to locate its true centre. Indeed, as I have tried to show, the spirit of the confessional autobiography underlies the pages of the *Investigations* itself.[59]

Notes

1 I use the following abbreviations for Wittgenstein's works: BB: *The Blue Book* (Oxford: Blackwell, 1964); CV: *Culture and Value*, ed. G.H. von Wright (Oxford: Blackwell, 1980); GB: *Remarks on Frazer's The Golden Bough* in *Wittgenstein. Sources and Perspectives*, ed. Luckhardt (Brighton: Harvester, 1979), pp. 61–81; LC: *Lectures and Conversations on Aesthetics*, ed. C. Barrett (Oxford: Blackwell, 1978); OC: *On Certainty*, ed. G.E.M Anscombe and G.H. von Wright (Oxford: Blackwell, 1969); PI: *Philosophical Investigations*, ed. G.E.M Anscombe (Oxford: Blackwell, 1976). Page numbers are given only in the absence of section numbers.

2 See Wittgenstein's remark at CV:36.

3 The remark is quoted in Norman Malcolm, *Wittgenstein: A Memoir* (Oxford: Blackwell, 1984), p. 83.

4 Nietzsche, *The Anti-Christ* (Harmondsworth: Penguin, 1978), p. 157. Appropriately enough, Nietzsche is here talking about a kind of thought which he thinks is particularly characteristic of Christians and Jews: the instinctive rejection of all 'concepts, symbols, attitudes' except those used by priests.

5 Nietzsche, *Beyond Good and Evil* (Harmondsworth: Penguin, 1976), p. 158.

6 M.H. Abrams, *Natural Supernaturalism: Tradition and Revolution in Romantic Literature* (London: Norton, 1973), pp. 32–7. I have relied heavily on this extraordinarily erudite and brilliant book.

7 Quoted in R. Monk, *Ludwig Wittgenstein: The Duty of Genius* (London: Cape, 1990), p. 282.

8 Stanley Cavell, 'The Availability of Wittgenstein's Philosophy' in his *Must We Mean What We Say? A Book of Essays* (Cambridge: Cambridge University Press, 1976), p. 71.

9 Cavell, 'The Availability', p. 71.

10 Saint Augustine, *Confessions*, ed. R.S. Pine-Coffin (Harmondsworth: Penguin, 1971), p. 170.

11 Augustine, *Confessions*, p.172

12 Matthew Arnold, 'Preface to the First Edition of Poems (1853)', in *Arnold: The Complete Poems*, ed. K. and M. Allott (London: Longman: 1987), p. 654.

13 Augustine, *Confessions*, p. 208.

14 Cavell, 'The Availability', p. 71.

15 Cavell, 'The Availability', p. 71.

16 H. Elvert Lewis (ed.), *Bunyan, The Pilgrim's Progress* (London: Dent, 1927), p. 5.

17 Dante, *Inferno*, Canto 1, lines 1–3. I use the translation found in Lewis, *Bunyan, The Pilgrim's Progress*, p. ix.
18 Lewis, *Bunyan, The Pilgrim's Progress*, p. 7.
19 The journey metaphor in Wittgenstein is noted by Austin E. Quigley, 'Wittgenstein's Philosophizing', *New Literary History*, 19, No. 2 (Winter, 1988), p. 210.
20 I have emphasized the element of internal dialogue in confession, but I would not wish to underestimate the importance of external dialogue as well. Inner transformation is obviously something which happens to the individual alone, but an important role in it can be played by those who argue, prompt and listen. I am grateful to Beth Savickey for pressing this point.
21 Augustine, *Confessions*, pp. 256–7.
22 Gerrard Winstanley, *The New Law of Righteousness*, in G.H. Sabine (ed.), *The Works of Gerrard Winstanley* (Ithaca, New York, 1941), pp. 215, 567–8, 173–4. Quoted in Abrams, *Natural Supernaturalism*, pp. 32–3.
23 Abrams, *Natural Supernaturalism*, p. 33.
24 D.A.T. Gasking and A.C. Jackson, 'Wittgenstein as Teacher', in K.T. Fann (ed.), *Ludwig Wittgenstein: The Man and His Philosophy* (Brighton: Harvester, 1978), p. 27.
25 G.H. von Wright, *A Biographical Sketch*, in Fann, *Ludwig Wittgenstein*, p. 53.
26 Monk, *Ludwig Wittgenstein: The Duty of Genius* (London: Cape, 1990), p. 171.
27 Letter from Bertrand Russell to Lady Ottoline Morrell, 20 December 1919. Quoted in B. McGuinness, *Wittgenstein: A Life: Young Ludwig* (London: Duckworth, 1988), p. 279.
28 Even Augustine sometimes thinks of himself in this way. Augustine, *Confessions*, p. 166.
29 Schelling, *Ideen zu einer Philosophie der Natur, Sämtliche Werke*, Pt I, II, pp. 13–14. Quoted and translated in Abrams, *Natural Supernaturalism*, pp. 181 and 182.
30 Preface to the 1795 version of *Hyperion, Sämtliche Werke*, Beissner (ed.), Vol. III, p. 236. Quoted and translated in Abrams, *Natural Supernaturalism*, p. 361.
31 Abrams, *Natural Supernaturalism*, p. 231.
32 Abrams, *Natural Supernaturalism*, pp. 230–31. The quotation at the end of the passage comes from, Hegel, *Phänomenologie*, p. 227.
33 Augustine, *Confessions*, pp. 214–26.
34 Hegel, *Phenomenology of Spirit* (Oxford: Oxford University Press, 1977), Translated by A.V. Miller, p. 492.
35 Hegel, Preface to *The Phenomenology of Spirit*, trans. Walter Kaufmann, in *Hegel: Reinterpretation, Texts, and Commentary* (New York, 1965), pp. 400–402; and *Phänomenologie des Geistes*, ed. Johannes Hoffmeister (6th edn: Hamburg, 1952), p. 559. Both quoted and the latter translated in Abrams, *Natural Supernaturalism*, pp. 192 and 235.
36 Fichte, *Die Grundzuge des Gegenwartigen Zeitalters* (1804–5); *Sämtliche Werke*, Vol. VII, pp. 5–11. Quoted and translated in Abrams, *Natural Supernaturalism*, p. 21. For a full investigation of the circular journey metaphor in Romantic philosophy and literature see Abrams, *Natural Supernaturalism*, pp. 140–324.
37 Hegel, *Phänomenologie des Geistes*, pp. 563–4. Quoted in Abrams, *Natural Supernaturalism*, p. 235.
38 I take this information from J. Bouveresse, 'Wittgenstein and the Modern World', in A. Phillips Griffiths (ed.), *Wittgenstein Centenary Essays* (Cambridge University Press, 1991), p. 37.
39 The lines are from the final verse paragraph of part V of Eliot's 'Little Gidding'. They are quoted as an epigraph to D. Pears, *The False Prison: A Study of the Development of Wittgenstein's Philosophy*, Vol. 1 (Oxford: Clarendon Press, 1987).

40 Wittgenstein makes a few remarks which indicate at least *some* knowledge of the Romantic philosophers' work, e.g.: 'Hegel seems to me to be always wanting to say things which look different are really the same. Whereas my interest is in showing that things which look the same are really different.' Quoted in Monk, *Ludwig Wittgenstein: The Duty of Genius*, pp. 536–7. This chapter, I'm afraid, falls on the Hegelian side of the divide.

41 Abrams, *Natural Supernaturalism*, p. 192.

42 *Wilhelm Meister* is referred to, for example, at OC:8.

43 'WM' indicates, *Wilhelm Meister's Apprenticeship*, ed. and trans. Eric A. Blackall in cooperation with Victor Lange (New York: Suhrkamp Publishers, 1989).

44 Hegel, *Phenomenology*, trans. Miller, p. 492.

45 Hamburg Edition, Vol. 9, p. 283. Quoted in T.J. Reed, *Goethe* (Oxford: Oxford University Press, 1984), p. 4.

46 Franco Moretti, *The Way of the World: The Bildungsroman in European Culture* (London: Verso, 1987), p. 4.

47 Moretti, *The Way of the World*, p. 24.

48 TS 220, pp. 89–90, quoted in S. Stephen Hilmy, 'Tormenting Questions in *Philosophical Investigations* section 133', in *Wittgenstein's Philosophical Investigations: Text and Context*, ed. Robert J. Arlington and Hans-Johann Glock (London: Routledge, 1991), p. 94.

49 Hamburg Edition, Vol. 13, p. 28. Quoted in Reed, *Goethe*, p. 99.

50 In this connection it is interesting to observe that Goethe and Wittgenstein's disapproval of anything vague, inner, idealistic and ineffectual, resulted in a common admiration for the world of *business*. Goethe is evidently not being ironic when he has Werner remark that the system of double-entry book-keeping is one of the great discoveries of the human mind, and Wittgenstein once remarked to Drury: 'My father was a businessman and I am a businessman too: I want my philosophy to be businesslike, to get something done, to get something settled.' M.O'C. Drury, 'A Symposium II', in K.T. Fann (ed.), *Ludwig Wittgenstein*, p. 69.

51 Moretti, *The Way of the World*, pp. 35 and 234.

52 *The Phenomenology of Spirit* is full of references to Goethe's work, particularly *Faust* and *Wilhelm Meister*. The most obvious similarity of outlook is that for Hegel the individual is only wholly himself in a society where he finds his needs and aspirations acknowledged and realized. Any kind of inward retreat or withdrawal – as in the case of a Stoic or Beautiful Soul – leads to the creation of an unhappy consciousness who cannot come to terms with 'the way of the world'. Such an individual striving after and identifying with an inward ideal in essentially alien circumstances, cannot flourish and is inwardly riven and debilitated. For discussion of these issues see Charles Taylor, *Hegel* (Cambridge: Cambridge University Press, 1975), pp. 148–96.

53 The page references for this and the next two quotations are to the Suhrkamp edition mentioned above, but I have used the translations found in Moretti, *The Way of the World*, p. 18. These capture more clearly the features to which I want to draw attention.

54 For a fuller examination of Goethe's conception of science and its relation to Wittgenstein's conception of philosophy see my article 'Goethe and Wittgenstein', this volume, pp. 1–21.

55 *Theory of Colours (Zur Farbenlehre)*, trans. C.L. Eastlake (Cambridge, MA: MIT Press, 1970).

56 Quoted in Monk, *Ludwig Wittgenstein: The Duty of Genius*, p. 180.

57 For more on the idea that philosophy, aims to produce a certain kind of vision that can be prompted but not simply handed on, see this volume, 'Goethe and Wittgenstein', pp. 1–21.

58 The final chapter of A.C. Grayling's book, *Wittgenstein* (Oxford: Oxford University Press, 1988), pp. 112–19, sets out an understanding and evaluation of Wittgenstein's work which requires, I would argue, a denaturing severance between his philosophy and personality.

59 I would like to thank Marie McGinn and Beth Savickey for helpful comments on earlier versions of this chapter.

Chapter 4

Arnold and the Socratic Personality

I

Arnold's notebooks and reading lists tell us that between 1845 and the end of his life he read – in Greek – the *Republic*, *Phaedrus*, *Menexenus*, *Lysis*, *Lesser Hypias*, *Ion*, *Phaedo*, *Symposium*, *Protagoras*, *Gorgias*, *Meno*, *Parmenides*, *Philebus* and *Statesman*, together with a number of other works now regarded as of more doubtful authenticity, the *Greater Hippias*, *Eryxias*, *Theages* and *Erastae*.[1] Several of these works – the *Republic*, *Phaedrus* and *Ion* – he read at least twice; many passages were copied into his notebooks for future reflection and contemplation; and, in all, there are about 60 significant references and discussions of Plato and Socrates in his collected published works.

Arnold thought Plato 'at once a great literary man and a great philosopher' [S:X:174],[2] but if we look for significant doctrinal parallels between the thought of the two men we shall be disappointed by their sparseness. The influence of the *Republic* is clear enough on *Culture and Anarchy*'s theory of the state, its account of the three classes, and its criticisms of Victorian democracy,[3] but generally the comparative dearth of shared beliefs has prompted the leading authority in this area, Warren Anderson, to write: 'Plato is useful as a source of quotation and illustration [for Arnold]. No deeper dimension appears, nor was any intended.'[4] In addition, Walter Hipple's[5] ingenious attempt to show that Arnold was a Platonist has been greeted with general scepticism.[6]

These negative conclusions, however, are largely due to restricting our conception of philosophical influence to something akin to the transmission of arguments and beliefs. If we do this, then we should not be surprised that Arnold's intense study of Plato produced so little, since Arnold's opinion of philosophy and philosophical argument – even though he acknowledged them to be 'noble and immortal aspiration[s] in man' [S:IX:63] – was low. When he considers particular metaphysical arguments from Plato they are usually dismissed out of hand. The arguments for the immortality of the soul in the *Phaedo* are 'sterile' [S:V:171]; most of the *Theaetetus* consists of 'barren logomachies' [S:IX:315]; and he had little time for logic generally: 'I have never been able to hit it off happily with the logicians … They imagine truth something to be proved, I something to be seen; they something to be manufactured, I something to be found' [S:III:535]. Similarly, philosophies conceived of as abstract and consistent sets of propositions, have little to offer the man of culture: 'So necessary, indeed, and so often shown by experience, is the want of solidity in constructions of this kind, that it argues, one may say, a dash of the pedant in a man to approach them, except perhaps in the ardour of extreme youth, with any confidence' [S:IX:63]. Only a few of the myths and theories of Plato escape this general dismissal on the quixotic ground that 'although he produces his abstractions like the rest, [he] produces them more than half in play and with a smile' [S:IX:63].

If we wish to locate the real source of philosophy's influence, Arnold believed, we must look to character: 'A philosopher's real power over mankind', he wrote in one of his essays on Spinoza, 'resides not in his metaphysical formulas, but in the spirit and tendencies which have led him to adopt those formulas. Spinoza's critic, therefore, has rather to bring to light that spirit and those tendencies of his author, than to exhibit his metaphysical formulas' [S:III:175]. It is, Arnold thinks, a mark of the very greatest thinkers that they have the power to transmit this spirit, thereby permanently influencing and forming their readers. In a letter of gratitude written to Newman in the early 1870s, for example, Arnold says: '[Nothing] can ever do away with the effect you have produced on me, for it consists in a general disposition of mind rather than a particular set of ideas.'[7]

For Arnold, character and spirit are revealed through *style*. 'Grand moral effects are produced by style', he wrote to Clough, 'for the style is the expression of the poet's character, as the matter is the expression of the richness of his mind.'[8] The idea is not restricted to poetry alone; in several later passages Arnold makes clear that this conception of style and personality also applies to philosophy and literature generally: 'The ethical influence of style in language – its close relations, so often pointed out with character' [S: III:234]: '[Addison's] style cannot equal in varied cadence and subtle ease the style of a man like Plato, because without range and force of thought all the resources of style, whether in cadence or subtlety, are not and cannot be brought out' [S:VIII:249 (see also S:X:171)].

If the most important aspects of a philosopher are his spirit and personality, and spirit and personality are revealed through style, then this would imply that a properly Arnoldian account of philosophical influence involves tracing the stylistic influence of a figure rather than documenting the origin of shared beliefs. Accordingly, the purpose of this essay will be to show that, during the period when Arnold thought of himself as primarily a social critic (roughly

1864–71), he modelled his literary persona upon the figure of Socrates, and that many of his most striking stylistic devices are modifications of the character traits by which Socrates achieved such an intimate and permanent effect on his followers. In addition, in the last section, I shall show how the literary form of Arnold's social criticism has a natural propensity to gravitate towards the genre through which Arnold came to know Socrates – the dialogue.[9]

In what follows I shall concentrate on four works: the essays, 'The Function of Criticism at the Present Time' (1864), and 'My Countrymen' (1866); the series of fictional conversations in letter form which were eventually collected in *Friendship's Garland* in 1871; and, *Culture and Anarchy*, published as a book in 1869. In all these writings, Arnold's central aim is to make the bluff, provincial, smug, practical-minded Englishman of the day aware of his condition, and to open him up to the ideals of reason, intelligence, impartiality and historical perspective to be found in contemporary Europe. Of course, Arnold's Socratic identification during this period was, to a certain extent, a pose adopted for particular polemical purposes; in part, it required him to assume a special manner, but it does not so much false-colour his real virtues as enhance them, and by doing so allows us to see the nature of his whole intellectual temper more clearly.

II

For Arnold, the human personality is made up of four basic elements: manners, conduct, intellect, and the sense of beauty [S:X:67]. Philosophical systems, he thinks, cannot engage the imagination or appeal to the emotions; they speak only to the intellect and neglect the three other equally important aspects of the psyche. If we wish to avoid a distorting onesidedness, therefore, and cultivate a harmonious expansion of human nature, we must give up our 'addiction to … abstract system' [S:V:109] and acquire a certain type of character: 'The Greek word [which means] a finely tempered nature, gives exactly the notion of perfection as culture conceives it: a harmonious perfection, a perfection in which the characters of beauty and intelligence are both present, which unites 'the two noblest of things sweetness and light' [S:V:99].

Clearly, the figure who embodied this character most perfectly for Arnold was Socrates, and throughout the late 1860s his identification with Socrates becomes increasingly evident: 'Even suppose I could get some followers', he wrote in 'My Countrymen', 'and assemble them, brimming with affectionate enthusiasm, in a committee room at some inn; what on earth should I say to them? what revolutions could I propose? I could only propose the old Socratic commonplace, Know Thyself; and how blank they would all look at that!' [S:V:28]. By 1869, the idea that Arnold was an English Socrates had achieved wide currency: the *Saturday Review* even asserted that he was 'played-out' in the role,[10] while Arnold ended *Culture and Anarchy* by endorsing it explicitly and at length:

> Pericles was perhaps the most perfect speaker who ever lived, for he was the man who most perfectly combined thought and wisdom with feeling and eloquence. Yet Plato brings in Alcibiades declaring that men went away from the oratory of Pericles, saying it was very fine, it was very good, and afterwards thinking no more about it; but they went away from hearing Socrates talk, he says, with the point of what he had said sticking fast in their minds, and they could not get rid of it. Socrates has drunk his hemlock and is dead; but in his own breast does not every man carry about with him a possible Socrates, in that power of disinterested play of consciousness upon his stock notions and habits, of which this wise and admirable man gave all through his lifetime the great example, and which is the secret of his incomparable influence? And he who leads men to call it forth and exercises it in himself, is at the present moment, perhaps, as Socrates was in his time, more in concert with the vital workings of men's minds, and more effectually significant, than any House of Commons' orator, or practical operator in politics. [S:V:228–9]

The reason why this passage actually claims identity with Socrates (Arnold, of course, is 'he who leads men to call it forth') is that Arnold was profoundly aware of how much more power to influence was possessed by a live human being than by a set of propositional beliefs. Socrates' 'incomparable influence' was largely due, Arnold felt, to his presenting 'the great example' to his followers; and in another place, he remarks: 'Your men of genius visible to you in the flesh, speaking to your ears bodily, a present object for your heart and imagination. That surely is the most potent of all influences! nothing can come up to it' [S:X:167]. Being obliged to communicate through print, Arnold could not of course be 'visible … in the flesh' but what he could do was construct a significantly heightened literary persona and have that exemplify the virtues he wished to advocate.

Culture and Anarchy is not therefore centrally concerned with proposing a list of political improvements, or with suggesting a method which would allow such a list to be arrived at; rather, its whole tone and manner give each reader an example of an ideally supple amenity on which he can model himself. Just as Arnold formed his literary persona by meditating on the character of

Socrates, so now each reader can find himself formed and moulded on the character of Arnold; and it is only by *experiencing* the Socratic personality – seeing how it approaches problems, infuses humour into dispute, responds to objections, refines its claims – that the reader can have his dormant Socratic virtues awakened. The profound effect that Socrates' character had on Arnold cannot therefore be demonstrated by considering the number of times his name or his beliefs occur in Arnold's works, but only by showing how Arnold's writings exemplify the Socratic virtues he claimed to embody.

As the passage from *Culture and Anarchy* makes clear, the virtue which Arnold most admired in Socrates was his disinterestedness. Socrates' only ambition was to establish the truth, and he set no value on the normal rewards of self-interested action: 'I do not care about the things that most people care about: making money, having a comfortable home, high military or civil rank, and all the other activities, political appointments, secret societies, party organizations, which go on in our city' [*Apology*: 36b].[11] On the other hand, those who sit in judgement on him, give their attention only to 'acquiring as much money as possible, and similarly with reputation and honour, and give no attention or thought to truth and understanding and the perfection of [the] soul' [*Apology*: 29e].

Socrates' complaints about his contemporaries hint at corruption as well as Philistinism; Arnold's are not so alarming, but they are still aimed at the baleful effects which self-interest, party, and political life have on clear-sighted thought. When, in 'The Function of Criticism', Arnold asks. 'What is at present the bane of criticism in this country?' the reply comes: 'It is that practical considerations cling to it and stifle it; it subserves interests not its own. Our organs of criticism are organs of men and parties having practical ends to serve, and with them those practical aims are the first thing and the play of the mind the second; so much play of the mind as is compatible with the prosecution of those practical ends is all that is wanted' [S:III:270]. Criticism, he asserts, must be, '*disinterested* ... Its business is ... simply to know the best that is known and thought in the world' [S:III:270], and to relish the truth for its own sake is the first step towards a Socratic perfection of self. In *Culture and Anarchy*, Xenophon's Socrates is recorded as saying: 'The best man is he who most tries to perfect himself' [S:V:171], and Socrates' words are echoed in the book's motto, '*Estote ergo vos perfecti*!' which makes manifest the intent of the entire work.

To delight in the correction of long-cherished beliefs was, for Arnold, one of the most important elements of disinterestedness. It is a virtue which Socrates frequently exemplifies. Just before his death, having given his reasons for endorsing faith in immortality, he can ask his friends, '[Do] you feel my account is inadequate? … [If] you feel any difficulty about our discussion, don't hesitate to put forward your own views, and point out any way in which you feel my account could be improved' [*Phaedo*: 84c]. While Arnold, commenting on Burke's acknowledged change of mind about the French Revolution, remarks, 'That return of Burke upon himself has always seemed to me one of the finest things in English literature, or indeed in any literature' [S:III:267]. In consequence, Arnold himself frequently – and lightheartedly – signals his own capacity for this kind of revision. In 'My Countrymen' he remarks: 'Being really quite the most teachable man alive, I could not help making, … a serious return, as the French say, upon myself: and I resolved never to call my countrymen Philistines again till I had thought more about it, and could be quite sure I was not committing an indecency' [S:V:4].

Thought, for Arnold, is not an end in itself, but he believed it would be all the more effective in the long run if it were treated as if it were an end in itself: 'Our ideas will, in the end, shape the world all the better for maturing a little' [S:III:282]. Because of this, he felt that his own ideas would ultimately be more influential than those of contemporary politicians who were, in the short term, more obviously successful. Unsurprisingly, therefore, one of his favourite quotations in later years (it occurs, for example, at S:VIII:130) was the passage in the *Gorgias* where Socrates claims that he is the only politician of his time. This is because he is the only person who tells the populace what is true rather than what it wants to hear: 'I think I am one of the very few Athenians, not to say the only one, engaged in the true political art, and that of the men of today I alone practise statesmanship. Since therefore when I speak on any occasion it is not with a view to winning favour, but I aim at what is best, not at what is most pleasant' [*Gorgias*: 52ld].

What the Victorian populace wanted to hear was that theirs was the most vigorous, powerful, practical, liberal, individualistic, and advanced country in the world; and there were plenty of contemporary orators (Adderley, Lowe, Bright, Roebuck) who were happy to tell them this. Arnold, on the other hand, regretted the lack of a properly supervised state education system; the extraordinary obsession with the most dismal kind of religion ('narrow, unintelligent, repulsive' [S:V:191]); the fascination with money and machinery; the insularity and self-satisfaction that seemed to be entering the national life; and, because of these, the fact that England's role in the modern world was actually in decline – it was in danger of becoming a 'second Holland' [S:V:27].

If Arnold, like Socrates, had harsh and unpalatable truths to tell, then he also learned from Socrates how they should be told. In the *Phaedo*, Socrates impressed his hearers with, 'the pleasant, kindly, appreciative way in which he received the two boys' objections' [*Phaedo*: 89], and he acknowledges in the *Apology* that the puncturing of pretensions 'has its amusing side' [33c]. In October 1863, Arnold wrote to his mother: '[Everything] turns upon one's exercising the power of persuasion, of charm; that without this all fury, energy, reasoning power, acquirement, are thrown away and only render their owner more miserable. Even in one's ridicule one must preserve a sweetness and good humour.'[12] His attempt to put this insight into practice had some success, and Henry James was entirely just to single out Arnold's 'degree of good feeling', the fact that 'he [had] never lost his good humour, never shown a touch of the odium theologicum, nor ceased to play fair'[13] as one of his major contributions to the literature of the age.

It is, of course, characteristic of the Socratic method to advance the discussion by means of questions, prompts, hints and examples rather than by bald exposition of a favoured view. The teacher does not stand above the pupil, he is not a pedagogue or instructor in any straightforward sense; on the contrary, he should try to be a window through which the pupil comes to see the world, and the less he explicitly imposes his own personality the more successful he is likely to be. This was certainly the ideal at which Arnold aimed: in the mid-1860s he wrote: 'In the long-run … one can only get oneself really accepted by men by making oneself forgotten in the people and doctrines one recommends';[14] and his constantly reiterated critical exhortations were to 'see the object as it really is' [S:III:258], and to 'get oneself out of the way and let humanity decide' [S:III:227]. Accordingly, the critic's judgement must be 'a sort of companion and clue, not … an abstract law-giver' [S:III:283], and he goes to great lengths to avoid any suggestion that he is imposing his views on the reader: 'Surely culture is useful in reminding us that …'; 'Keeping this in view, I have in my own mind often indulged myself with the fancy of …'; 'The prophets and philosophers whom I at any rate am disposed to believe …'.[15] He never seems to assert a view directly, but always draws our attention, reminds us and appeals to our better nature.

Arnold, like Socrates, makes every effort to turn potential opponents into fellow inquirers and to avoid an adversarial model of dispute. In works like 'My Countrymen' and *Friendship's Garland* he gives his unacceptable views of England to various fictional foreigners, and presents himself as vainly trying to defend the views of his real opponents. Often, he will pretend to erase himself altogether and let Culture do the exhorting and reminding for him ('Culture looks beyond machinery, culture hates hatred' [S:V:112]) as if Culture were some active and benign Platonic entity. At other times, he claims to share the fault he has identified in those who do not hold his views. In 'The Function of Criticism', for instance, he writes: 'The mania for giving an immediate political and practical application to all these fine ideas of the reason was fatal. Here an Englishman is in his element: on this theme *we can all go on for hours*' [S:III:265] (my italics). It is actually most unlikely that Arnold could 'go on for hours' on this point as he was directly opposed to it, but by taking his opponents' self-satisfaction on himself, he turns what could have been a polemic into some reflective self-criticism, and thereby gives an example of good practice to his critics.

Socrates does have a number of positive doctrines ('nobody errs willingly', and 'the good man cannot be harmed', for example), but they are secondary to his method and manner. Consequently, we quite understand him when he claims that his superiority to his interlocutors lies solely in the fact that he knows he is ignorant whereas they do not [*Apology*: 21d]; that he has nothing to teach; and that his vain search for knowledge and wisdom has resulted only in showing up the false beliefs of politicians, artists, and professional educators [*Apology*: 21c–22e]. Arnold also has a number of positive views about political issues, but we can also see why he thinks the Socratic 'know thyself' is all he would have to say to his followers, and why James hit on an important truth when he said that Arnold 'never pretended to have a body of doctrine'.[16] Like Socrates, Arnold sets himself up in opposition to professional politicians, sophists, and educators by disclaiming all pretensions to knowledge or expertise: 'Everyone is now boasting of what he has done to educated men's minds and to give things the course they are taking. Mr Disraeli educates, Mr Bright educates, Mr Beales educates. We, indeed, pretend to educate no one, for we are still engaged in trying to clear and educate ourselves' [S:V:229]. Arnold's principal service therefore, like Socrates', is not to tell us what to believe, but to prick the pretensions of others' claims to certainty, and give an example of the disinterested spirit in which beliefs should be held, discarded, and revised.

In this anti-doctrinal stance, he was clearly influenced by the elaborations of the sceptical Socratic temper found in the Cambridge Platonists and their associates. From one of the latter's books, Joseph Glanvill's *The Vanity of Dogmatising*, he took the story of 'The Scholar-Gipsy', and a glance at Glanvill's book shows how close it is to Arnold's outlook. 'The knowledge I teach is ignorance',[17] wrote Glanvill, and he then sets about dogma with Arnoldian zest: '(1) 'Tis the effect of ignorance. (2) It argues untamed passions. (3) It disturbs the world. (4) It is ill-manners, and immodesty. (5) It holds men captive in errour. (6) It betrays narrowness of spirit.'[18] Later, when Arnold reviewed a book by Tulloch which contained a history of Cambridge Platonism, he commended Burnet's description of them as 'those who, at Cambridge, studied to propagate better thoughts, to take men off from being in parties, or from narrow notions, from superstitious beliefs and fierceness about opinions'. Finally, he reasserts his main complaint about Plato and philosophy generally: Tulloch's book, he says, gives 'somewhat too much space to their Platonic philosophy, to their disquisitions on spirit and incorporeal essence. It is not by these that they merited to live, or that, having passed away from men's minds, that they will be brought back to them. It was by their extraordinary simple, profound, and just conception of religion. Christianity was [to them] … a *temper*, a behaviour' [S:VIII:122].

III

For Socrates, philosophy was an oral activity conducted among a small group of people – ideally of friends and companions. In this section I want to show that some of the most distinctive features of Arnold's style seek to recreate the tone of Socratic inquiry in another medium and in a wholly different set of circumstances.

The most important aspect of a man's physical presence, for Arnold, was the actual sound of his voice. Forty years after their first encounter, the inflexions of Newman's voice, 'the most entrancing of voices' [S:X:165] still haunted Arnold's imagination: 'When I was an undergraduate at Oxford, voices were there in the air which haunt my memory still. Happy the man who in that susceptible season of youth hears such voices! they are his possession for ever … The name of Cardinal Newman is a great name to the imagination still' [S: X:165]. Again, an author who has to communicate through print cannot hope to reproduce such an effect, but when we look in detail at Arnold's prose style we realize that he is attempting to transcend the limitations of the written, and that many of his stylistic habits are those of a man trying to persuade through speech rather than written prose.

The most important of these characteristics are his long sinuous sentences with their frequent interpolations; his repetitions, particularly a tendency to reintroduce the grammatical subject of a sentence rather than use a pronoun; the emphatic use of 'I say'; his penchant for beginning a new section with a striking, often monosyllabic, call to attention, 'But', 'Still', 'Nay', 'Now, really'; and the insouciant, conversational casualness with which so many of his main ideas are introduced. These, together with the way stress is manipulated by the use of hyperbation and inversion, and the deliberately awkward, homely and slang expressions which pepper even his most rarefied discussions, give a very powerful impression of an individual speaking.[19]

But not all speech has the same persuasive power. Arnold says that men soon forgot even the masterful oratory of Pericles, but when they heard Socrates talk, 'they went away with the point of what he said sticking fast in their minds and they could not get rid of it'. In part, this would suggest the radical superiority of personal talk to public oratory as an instrument of persuasion. Arnold knew full well that if someone felt he was being talked at by a speaker who was personally indifferent to him, then the words would create a disagreeable impression and have little effect. Many of Arnold's essays originated as lectures, but the tone is frequently playful, informal and conversational. Indeed, Arnold's is a style which seeks to make the reader his intimate and collaborator: when we respond to him, it is as friends and intimates aspiring to something higher, rather than as dutiful pupils or well-briefed followers. Somehow or other we feel we come to know *him* rather than merely what he says; we know his voice rather than his style, and this brings into play questions of manners, gratitude, loyalty, and other attitudes which the printed word normally leaves untouched.

Arnold's preference for conversation and intimacy made him share both Socrates' distrust of the sophists' ambition to sway large assemblies and the style they had perfected for achieving it [for example, *Phaedrus*: 267a6]. It is notable how frequently, when Arnold quotes an opponent, he is keen to emphasize that the remarks were made in the course of a speech, an anonymous leading article, a statement to the House, or some other grand impersonal form of discourse directed at a mass audience: 'Mr Gladstone well pointed out, in a speech at Paris …' [S:V:105]; '[This] doctrine is preached in the *Times* with great clearness and force of style …' [S:V:156]; 'Mr Bright … said forcibly in one of his great speeches …' [S:V:117]. These forms of delivery ensure that the reader cannot respond personally to the writer or speaker either because he does not know whose words he reads, or because he feels he is simply one of a crowd which is being hectored or addressed – a situation where a proper, reciprocal, personal response is impossible. This gives Arnold the opportunity to become the friend at our elbow whose raised eyebrow turns the speaker's thunderings into bombast and his appeals into bathos.

The excesses of Palgrave's style Arnold ascribes to the fact that he 'feels himself to be speaking before a promiscuous multitude therefore he has no calm confidence and no self-control; he relies on the strength of his lungs; he knows that big words impose on the mob, and that, even if he is outrageous, most of his audience are apt to be a great deal more so' [S:III:254–5]. The style of the popular historian Kinglake has all the sophistical virtues of the 'good editorial': 'Its characteristic is, that it has no soul; all it exists for, is to get its ends, to make its points, to damage its opponents, to be admired, to triumph' [S:III:255]. Finally, Arnold contrasts himself, 'a mere seeker for truth with nothing trenchant or authoritative about me' [S:V:12], with 'the newspapers, who have so many more means than I of knowing the truth, and who have that trenchant and authoritative style for communicating it' [S:V:6].

One of the most striking affinities between Arnold and Socrates is their persistently ironic manner. In a letter to his mother, Arnold makes clear that he, like Socrates, uses irony primarily to disturb complacency:

> For my part, I see more and more what an effective weapon … is irony, or according to the rather strict meaning of the original Greek word, the saying rather less than one means. The main effect I have had on the mass of noisy claptrap and inert prejudice which chokes us has been, I can see, by the use of this weapon; and now, when people's minds are getting widely disturbed and they are beginning to ask themselves whether they have not a great deal to learn which is new to learn, to increase this feeling in them is more useful than ever.[20]

However, irony is also an excellent way to further a sense of intimacy with the well-disposed section of one's audience, because, as Fowler nicely phrases it: '[Irony is] the use of words intended to convey one meaning to the uninitiated part of the audience and another to the initiated, the delight of it lying in the secret intimacy set up between the latter and the speaker.'[21] The impression that an ironist is writing for friends and confederates is furthered by the fact that from reading a few remarks in isolation it may not be at all clear whether they are intended ironically or not. To determine this, we may have to be familiar with the rest of a man's oeuvre, and this reinforces the sense that he is writing for those who are already familiar with his position and beliefs.[22]

It is for a related reason that irony makes a point 'stick fast in the [people's] minds so they can not get rid of it'. We are conscious of thinking through an ironic remark for ourselves, and we do not have the sense that we are merely recording or registering it. Thus irony, like the Arnoldian/Socratic manner of prompting, hinting, questioning, has the effect not merely of presenting us with another piece of forgettable information but of teasing us into thought and making us see the limitations of our own positions. The effects of this interaction are clearly much deeper-lying and more permanent than simply being told something, or having one's own position refuted by somebody else.

For neither Arnold nor Socrates is irony simply a verbal trope to he used for polemical purposes; it follows directly from their whole mode of inquiry. Indeed, irony is the final element needed to see the unity of the Socratic personality. Its overall ambition is to obtain what Nagel calls the 'objective view'.[23] This can only be achieved by overcoming the distorting influences of one's position in the world – self, action, and party – and setting one's sights on the truth.[24] Abstracting oneself from one's normal viewpoint has the effect of lessening one's self-interested prejudice and giving one far more sympathy with other people's positions; and the lowered profile of the self and the raised awareness of others helps neutralize the polemical urge. However, the subjective view can never be abolished, otherwise knowledge would be subjectless, and the best we can hope for is that the self be educated and enlightened. This entails that the two views have to consort uneasily together in one subject: moods, emotions and passions persistently recoiling from the chilliness of seeing myself as simply one person among others; objective thought continually undercutting the claims of self and party. The result of the latter, as Nagel[25] emphasizes, can frequently be a sense of absurdity, but also a pervasive sense of irony as the claims of self are viewed *sub specie aeternitatis*. Of course, this irony can be bitter, but just as often it results in the wry, amused detachment that Arnold and Socrates both exemplify; indeed, the sense of conceptual tension which is the origin of irony is also, as Schopenhauer[26] argued, the basis of humour.

IV

If one's main philosophical purpose is to show that others do not know what they claim to know, or that they do not hold their ideas in the right way, then one requires opponents, antagonists, those who stand in need of cure. Without Euthyphro, Gorgias, Callicles, and Thrasymachus, Socrates would have been paralysed; and without Fitzjames Stephens, Roebuck, Lowe and Bright, Arnold would have been left with nothing to say – in spite of his studiously unpolemical pose. Fittingly, therefore, *Essays in Criticism: First Series*, the work which collected some of Arnold's first and most important social criticism, is furnished with an epigraph from Burke: 'Our antagonist is our helper.' And Henry James later observed that Arnold was first and foremost a controversialist: 'Rejoinder and refutation have always furnished him with texts and examples and offered a spring-board, as it were, to his polemical agility … [He] has been only a skirmisher and a suggester.'[27] The natural medium for the elenchical thinker is therefore dialogue, and the natural literary mode for the representation of these conversations is the dialogue form. Below, I shall show how Arnold's social criticism is essentially dialogic: it is itself part of a dialogue, and his own works have an irresistible tendency to transmute themselves into a representation of dialogue. In other words, because of their shared conception of intellectual inquiry, Arnold finds it natural to represent himself or his spokesman in the same way that Plato represents Socrates.

By the mid-nineteenth century philosophers no longer met for discussions outside the law courts or in the market-places, and the functions of colloquia had been largely taken over by printed exchanges in periodicals. This was the origin of all Arnold's social criticism: 'The Function of Criticism at the Present Time' replies to criticism of his lectures on translating Homer; the preface to *Essays in Criticism: First Series* and 'My Countrymen' reply to Fitzjames Stephen's article, 'Mr Matthew Arnold and His Countrymen'; *Friendship's Garland* responds to criticism of these, and so on. The controversial origin of Arnold's social writings are at their most marked in *Culture and Anarchy*. Here it is absolutely essential to realize that the work was written and published piecemeal over a period of 13 months, because later chapters, very confusingly, reply to published criticism of earlier chapters. To understand the book properly, therefore, we have to have read at least the responses of Sidgwick and Harrison, preferably at the appropriate textual moments, and there is at least one edition of the work which inserts these responses in the spaces between Arnold's chapters.[28] Arnold has sometimes been criticized for writing monologues,[29] but this is true only insofar as his works are frequently one half of a dialogue, and he could reasonably expect his audience to know the other. In his book, *Two Classes of Men*, David Newsome remarks that much of Plato's appeal for Arnold had to do with the dialogue form in which the philosopher wrote.[30] There are at least four clusters of reasons why this should be so.

i) The dialogue form gives the appearance of being studiously fair and unegoistic: the author gives the impression of asserting nothing directly and he need not be committed to any of the positions articulated. Even if the author's point of view is represented, the mode of representation still treats it as one position among others. This makes it a very attractive form for those who want to overcome the snares of self and the distortions endemic in adversarial dispute.
ii) Dialogue is also closely related to irony, and the two most famous philosophical writers of irony – Plato and Hume – were also the two philosophers who handled the dialogue form most successfully. Just as

the ironist is not committed to what his statements literally say, so the author of a fiction is not committed to assertions made by his characters; both irony and the creation of speaking characters are therefore ways an author can distance himself from the utterances he pens. If a fictional or factitious character makes a speech and we are simultaneously aware of the author's opposing view, then we have an ironized monologue. If the author's opposing view is articulated by another character then we have the kind of ironic dialogue found in *Gulliver's Travels* and *Friendship's Garland*. An interest in dialogue thus grows naturally out of an ironic cast of mind.

iii) Just as – at least in theory – the speakers within a dialogue are equal to one another, so the author and reader of a dialogue are on far more of a parity than in conventional didactic writing. The roles of teacher and pupil, speaker and listener, disappear, to be replaced by circumstances in which both the author and reader appear to overhear what is said, and the plurality of voices suggests a place for the reader's own. As in irony, the author pays the reader the compliment of assuming he is competent to decide which, if any, of the statements or speakers are to be relied upon. This means that the sentences in a dialogue are not meant to be immediately believed and pressed into action, but first have to be entertained and weighed by the reader; if, having considered the proffered views, the reader then wishes to affirm them, then that is his privilege. Dialogue, like irony, has a closer association with the disinterested spectator than the engaged agent; it prompts, it does not insist, and no one would dream of trying to exhort, brow-beat or hector an audience by reading them a dialogue.

iv) Dialogue is far more suited to the demonstration of a method or a spirit of inquiry than it is to the exposition of a system, and dialogue's antipathy to fixities and definites, the monologic assertion of truth, consorts well with Arnold's wholly dynamic conception of culture: 'not a having and a resting, but a growing and a becoming, is the character of perfection as culture conceives it' [S:V:94]. Dialogue is also the most literary form of philosophical writing. It is traditionally the most amusing philosophical genre;[31] it is a narrative form which, unlike the treatise or critique, represents a passage of time; it is the style of writing which brings us closest to the human voice (dialogue, we have the impression, is transcribed rather than described); it is the form in which we are least likely to abstract someone's ideas from their personality or cultural background, and is therefore particularly appealing for a writer like Arnold who insists on the importance of those things [for example, S:V:97].

One of the most important virtues of the Socratic personality, for Arnold, is the way he conducts himself in dispute: his manners, his conduct, his tone, his disinterestedness. Arnold wishes not merely to describe but to *show* this conduct, and therefore the controversial and dialogic origins of *Culture and Anarchy* come to be represented in the book's pages. In this work we see Arnold in dialogue with, and being superiorly Socratic to, his contemporaries; indeed the book is so full of quoted speeches from minor contemporaries that extensive footnotes are now required for its full comprehension.

Arnold develops a number of characteristic devices for making these opponents look unappealing, just as Plato biases our opinion against Thrasymachus and Callicles by representing in full their contemptuous rudeness. The figures Arnold quotes are often given a tone of voice, a tone which, in marked contrast to Arnold's reminders and suggestions, is invariably sour, or monotonous, or pompous: 'Mr Roebuck is never weary of reiterating ...' [S:V:96], 'Mr Bright complains with a sorrowful indignation ... [S:V:108], 'That Alcibiades, the editor of the *Morning Star* taunts me ...' [S:V:115]. He also manages to make them look boorish, insensitive and ill-mannered by means of the peculiarly Arnoldian torture of inelegant non-variation. He selects an opponent's weakest, most self-satisfied or combative phrase, and then has him blurt it out endlessly in contexts where it is horribly dissonant. Thus, into the elegant and tolerant discussion of sweetness and light in the opening chapter of *Culture and Anarchy* come the nonconformists with their slogan, 'The Dissidence of Dissent and the Protestantism of the Protestant Religion!' [S:V: 101]; into a particularly harrowing account of a child's murder barges Roebuck with his 'I pray that our unrivalled happiness may last!' [S:III:273].

In several of his essays, we can actually see this kind of ironic, discursive prose transmuting itself into genuine dialogue. 'The Function of Criticism' is full of Arnold's replies to quoted opponents, and his own ironic assertions of opponents' positions, but during at least one moment of high excitement he creates a speechifying fictional figure to reply to: '"We are all *terra filii*" cries their eloquent advocate; "all Philistines together. Away with the notion of proceeding in any other way than the way dear to the Philistines; let us have a social movement, let us organize and combine a party to pursue truth and new thought, let us call it *the liberal party*"' [S:V:276]. In the next important work of social criticism, the essay 'My Countrymen', which established the fully developed tone of Arnold's social criticism, Arnold greatly extends this technique. He begins with an extensive review of contemporary newspaper reports about the state of England, often quoting verbatim. He then counters these with opinions from foreign newspapers and from remarks people made to him while abroad. Finally, he ends up inserting several very long speeches into the mouths of some fictional 'envious foreigners'. These are soon engaged in controversy with the author:

> 'Why, the capital, pressing danger of England, is the barbarism of her middle class; the civilisation of her middle class is England's capital, pressing want.'
>
> 'Well, but', said I, still catching at Mr Lowe's powerful help, 'the parliament of this class has performed exploits unrivalled … in the whole history of representative assemblies …'.
>
> 'Let us distinguish', replied the envious foreigners, 'let us distinguish. We named three powers, – did we not? – which go to spread that rational humane life which is the aim of modern society'. [S:V:20]

The conversation lasts for at least a third of the article, and the foreigners soon develop concrete, individual characters: 'an Italian, who was one of our party, [fumbled] with his notebook, from which he presently produced a number of grey newspaper slips'; and acquire names, 'Little Pompco Pococurante. [All the rest of the criticism comes from] Arminius' [S:V:23]. We have now arrived at the full-fledged dialogue form in which *Friendship's Garland* is presented. The conversations take place between Arnold's spokesman Arminius, a brusque Prussian savant, and a fictionalized 'Matthew Arnold'. This character, while patriotic, is no match for his interlocutor because he is altogether too impressed by Prussian intellectualism and French wit. All the resources of fiction are drawn upon – descriptions of place and persons, for example – as the pair travel around England visiting nonconformist households, watching a bench of magistrates in action, and conversing with a number of emblematic Englishmen – the Reverend Esau Hittall, Viscount Lumpington, Bottles Esquire, Zephaniah Diggs.

Arnold's social criticism has its moments of Dickensian sprightliness, but its true intellectual origin and aspirations – particularly in *Culture and Anarchy* – were not lost on two of his best-informed contemporaries. 'I wish to give Mr Arnold the full benefit of his resemblance to Plato',[32] wrote Henry Sidgwick before embarking on a comparison of the two which is very much in Plato's favour. And perhaps the most affectionate and insightful acknowledgment of this affinity came in Fredrick Harrison's, 'Culture: A Dialogue'. Here, in a gesture Arnold much appreciated,[33] Harrison decided to send up Arnold's work in the form of a mock-Socratic dialogue between himself and Arnold's Arminius; a dialogue in which the former remarks not only that '[The first chapter of *Culture and Anarchy*] recalls many a fine bit from Plato', but that the style suggests 'It might have come … straight from some lost dialogue'.[34]

Friendship's Garland plays a series of virtuoso variations on the whole idea of dialogue. It consists of a set of letters, and in the public world of print the published letter is as close as one can get to a conversation: a letter has a particular addressee – even if only 'Sir' or 'The Editor' – and it anticipates, makes a space for, a reply. One of these letters is real. This is where Arnold replies to a French correspondent calling himself 'Horace' who wishes to contest some remarks Arnold made in 'My Countrymen'. The rest of the letters are purely fictional and purport to be an exchange between the editor of *The Daily Telegraph*, Arminius, and the fictionalized 'Matthew Arnold'. The work is thus a dialogue which represents a dialogue; or rather, a dialogue which represents its own earlier self. The whole is then edited and annotated by the fictional Matthew Arnold and published under the name of the real one. Compared with these layers of irony, this hubbub of unreliable voice, this thoroughgoing send-up of literary scholarship, Nabokov's *Pale Fire* fades into simplicity.

Friendship's Garland is second only to *Culture and Anarchy*, among Arnold's works of social criticism and yet for many years it was ignored and remained out of print. Now, however, there has been a revival of scholarly interest, and we can well understand why one specialist – Brian Nellist – claims it is the work which 'allows us to hear, through its magnification of them, the variations and shifts of voice throughout Arnold's work' and that it is the book in which 'Arnold's style is seen most completely'.[35] However, the style of *Friendship's Garland* would not suit all occasions. By the mid-nineteenth century, the serious use of the dialogue form was as antique as the colloquium it represents, and the form could only be used for comic and satirical purposes (Mallock's *The New Republic* comes to mind). Serious issues required something weightier and less anachronistic, and the style Arnold develops in 'My Countrymen' and *Culture and Anarchy*, which, we might say, aspires to the condition of dialogue, is an excellent solution to the problem. It manages to retain many of what are, for Arnold, the dialogue's most congenial features – the direct presentation of personality and manner, the impression of an open-ended debate where different voices each give their account of the truth, the impression that the author is not asserting anything – while preserving the seriousness and integrity of discursive prose.

Certainly, therefore, Anderson is right to think that Arnold shares very few beliefs or doctrines with Plato and Socrates, but quite wrong to think that Plato or Socrates are merely sources of quotation and illustration. In fact, the influence of Plato's dialogues, and the character of Socrates they reveal, penetrates below the level of belief and into the very texture of Arnold's personality, thought and prose style; and this, as Arnold himself emphasizes, is altogether more important.

Notes

1 Howard Foster Lowry, Karl Young and Waldo Hilary Dunn (eds), *The Note-Books of Matthew Arnold* (London: Oxford University Press, 1952) and Kenneth Allot, 'Matthew Arnold's Reading Lists in Three Early Diaries', *Victorian Studies*, 11 (1959), pp. 254–66.

2 'S' followed by volume and page numbers indicates, R.H. Super (ed.), *The Complete Prose Works of Matthew Arnold*, 11 vols (University of Michigan Press: Ann Arbor, 1960–77).

3 These criticisms are examined in my 'Arnold, Plato, Socrates', in Anna Baldwin and Sarah Hutton (eds), *Platonism and the English Imagination* (Cambridge: Cambridge University Press, 1994), pp. 242–56.

4 Warren D. Anderson, *Matthew Arnold and the Classical Tradition* (Ann Arbor: University of Michigan Press, 1965), p. 125.

5 Walter J. Hipple Jr, 'Matthew Arnold, Dialectitian', *The University of Toronto Quarterly*, 32 (1963), pp. 1–26.

6 See, for example, David Newsome, *Two Classes of Men: Platonism in English Romantic Thought* (London: Murry, 1974), pp. 126–31. An exception to this scepticism is R.H. Super, see S:V, pp. 416–17.

7 *Unpublished Letters of Matthew Arnold*, ed. Arnold Whitridge (New Haven: Yale University Press, 1923), p. 56.

8 *The Letters of Matthew Arnold to Arthur Hugh Clough*, ed. Howard Foster Lowry (London Oxford University Press, 1932), p. 101.

9 When this chapter was originally published in *Prose Studies*, 18, 2, August 1995, I included a lengthy section on the accuracy of Arnold's view of Socrates, and the idea of responding to the personalities of thinkers we admire. I omit this section in the current reprint.

10 *Saturday Review*, 6 March 1869, 17, p. 318.

11 All quotations from Plato are from *Plato: The Collected Dialogues*, ed. Edith Hamilton and Huntington Cairns (Princeton, NJ: Princeton University Press, 1973).

12 29 October 1863. Russell, *Letters*, 1, p. 201.

13 Henry James, 'Henry James on Arnold's Importance', *English Illustrated Magazine*, 1 (January 1884), 241–6. Reprinted in Carl Dawson, ed., *Matthew Arnold: The Poetry: The Critical Heritage* (London: Routledge and Kegan Paul, 1973), p. 284.

14 Letter to his mother, January 1864. Russell, *Letters*, 1, p. 219.

15 I take these three examples from John Holloway's brilliant discussion of Arnold's style in 'Matthew Arnold', in *Matthew Arnold: A Collection of Critical Essays*, ed. D.J. DeLaura (New Jersey: Prentice-Hall, 1973), p. 121.

16 Henry James, 'Arnold's Importance', p. 284.

17 The preface to *The Vanity of Dogmatizing*, quoted in Ruth apRoberts, *Arnold and God* (Berkeley: University of California Press, 1983), p. 11.

18 Joseph Glanvill, *The Vanity of Dogmatizing* (New York: Columbia University Press, 1931), p. 224.
19 I owe a great deal to – without suggesting the riches of – the discussions of Arnold's style in Stephan Collini, *Arnold* (Oxford: Oxford University Press, 1988), pp. 1–17; Holloway, 'Arnold', pp. 119–40; Geoffrey Tillotson, 'Matthew Arnold's Prose: Theory and Practice', in DeLaura, *Critical Essays*, pp. 141–9.
20 5 December 1867. S:V:414.
21 *Modern English Usage* (Oxford: Oxford University Press, 1954), p. 306.
22 See Denis Dutton, 'Why Intentionalism Will Not Go Away', in Anthony J.Cascardi (ed.), *Literature and the Question of Philosophy* (Baltimore: Johns Hopkins University Press, 1989), p. 202.
23 Thomas Nagel, 'Subjective and Objective' in *Mortal Questions* (Cambridge: Cambridge University Press, 1979), pp. 196–213, and *The View from Nowhere* (Oxford: Oxford University Press, 1986), esp. pp. 3–12.
24 It seems paradoxical to say that Arnold, like Socrates, is interested in the overcoming of personality, when I have spent the first two sections arguing that he is interested, above all, in Socrates' character and in establishing a similar character for himself. However, as David Newsome once remarked, the only way to capture Arnold's personality is through paradox. He is the fanatic of moderation, the unpolemical polemicist, the elegantly inelegant stylist, the self-depreciating egotist, the teacher with nothing to teach.
25 Nagel, *Mortal Questions*, p. 23.
26 Arthur Schopenhauer, 'On the Theory of the Ludicrous', in *The World as Will and Representation*, trans. E.F.J. Payne (New York: Dover Books, 1958), pp. 91–101.
27 Dawson, *The Poetry*, p. 284.
28 Ian Gregor (PhD dissertation, University of Durham [Kings College, Newcastle-upon-Tyne]). Mentioned in S:V:viii.
29 Collini, *Arnold*, p. 77.
30 Newsome, *Two Classes*, p. 87.
31 Hume's character Pamphilus remarks: '[Dialogue] afford[s] an agreeable amusement ... and unites the two greatest and purest pleasures of human life, study and society.' *Dialogues on Natural Religion*, ed. J.M. Bell (Harmondsworth: Penguin Books, 1990), p 38.
32 Henry Sidgwick, 'The Prophet of Culture', *MacMillan's Magazine*, 16 August 1867, pp. 271–80. Reprinted in Carl Dawson and John Pfordresher, (eds) *Matthew Arnold. Prose Writings: The Critical Heritage* (London: Routledge, 1979), pp. 209–24.
33 '[It is] in parts so amusing that I laughed till I cried.' Letter to Lady Rothschild, 30 October 1867. Russell, *Letters*, 1, p. 372.
34 Frederic Harrison, 'Culture: A Dialogue', *Fortnightly Review*, 11 (November 1867), pp. 603–14 Reprinted in Dawson and Pfordresher, *Prose Writings*, p. 227. Of course. Arnold's dialogic style could have been the result of reading other dialogue writers apart from Plato, but I can find no evidence of Arnold having read any of them extensively. He read three dialogues by Berkeley in 1845, but there is only one mention of Hume and that is to his *History of England*. See K. Allott, 'Reading Lists', pp. 254–66, and Arnold, *Notebooks*, p. 383.
35 Brian Nellist, 'Disconcerting the Reader: *Friendship's Garland* and the True Voices of Mr Arnold', in *Matthew Arnold: A Centenial Review, Essays and Studies*, ed M. Allott (London: Murry, 1988), p. 31.

Chapter 5

The Dissolution of Goodness: *Measure for Measure* and Classical Ethics

Measure for Measure: A Plot Synopsis

The Duke of Vienna feels that the laws against immorality are being flouted, and he therefore places the city in the charge of his puritanical deputy, Angelo. The Duke explains this hand-over by announcing that he is going on a pilgrimage, but in actual fact he returns, disguised as a friar, to watch Angelo enforcing the regulations. The latter goes about his work with a will. His first acts are to demolish the brothels, and arrest the young nobleman Claudio for making his fiancée Juliet pregnant.

Claudio is sentenced to death, and he begs his sister – the novice nun, Isabella – to intercede with Angelo on his behalf. When she does so, Angelo finds himself overcome by lust for her. He says that he will release Claudio if she will have sex with him, an offer which she indignantly refuses. In prison, a miserable Claudio, now despairing for his life, is comforted by a friar (the Duke in disguise) who suggests a plan. He explains that Angelo was once engaged to a woman called Mariana, but cruelly abandoned her. If Isabella pretends to agree to sex, then, in the right circumstances, she and Mariana can change places without Angelo being aware. It will then seem that Isabella has performed her part of the bargain, and Angelo will set Claudio free.

Angelo is taken in, but he treacherously orders Claudio's execution anyway, and demands to see his severed head. The Friar suggests dressing Barnadine, a convicted murderer, in Claudio's clothes, but Barnadine, most inconveniently, will not allow himself to be executed. Fortunately, a pirate has just died in the prison, and his head, suitably disguised, is then sent to Angelo.

At this point the Duke throws off his disguise, and Isabella and Mariana confront Angelo. At first he denies all wrongdoing, and it is only when the Duke explains how he himself witnessed Angelo's crimes that Angelo finally admits to them. The Duke orders Angelo to marry Mariana and then be executed. Isabella and Mariana plead for Angelo's life, and when Claudio is brought in alive, the Duke pardons Angelo. Claudio is now free to marry Juliet, Angelo is made to marry Mariana, and the Duke himself decides that he should marry Isabella.

I

'There is very little for [classicists] in *Measure for Measure*', wrote J.A.K. Thompson in 1952, and certainly the points of classical influence he identifies – one reminiscent of Plutarch and one of Ovid – are few and unimportant.[1] Of course, the classical influence is now acknowledged to be greater than this. It is agreed, for example, that the Duke's speech on death contains echoes of Cicero's *Tusculan Disputations*,[2] and some interpreters have heard classical resonances in the title,[3] but it cannot be said that the search for classical sources has inspired a single interpretation of the play, or thrown any light on its most pressing problems. In what follows, I shall argue that the play's debt to classical sources is much greater than has been hitherto supposed, and that understanding this inheritance allows us to give an interpretation of the work which dissolves difficulties that have long disturbed commentators.

II

The Duke gives two reasons for leaving Vienna. Initially, he says it is to allow Angelo to enforce the long-neglected laws against sexual vice. It soon becomes clear, however, that this is merely cover for, or perhaps part of, a more ambitious moral project:

> More reasons for this action
> At our more leisure shall I render you;
> Only this one: Lord Angelo is precise;
> Stands at guard with Envy; scarce confesses
> That his blood flows; or that his appetite
> Is more to bread than stone. Hence shall we see
> If power change purpose, what our seemers be.[4] [I, iii, 48–54]

The testing of people like Angelo (the experimental subject is 'our seemers', not 'our seemer') is itself soon seen to be part of a larger ethical interest. When Escalus asks the disguised Duke what news there is abroad in the world, the Duke characteristically replies, not with specifics, but with a brief and despairing lecture on ethics:

> None, but that there is so great a fever on goodness that the dissolution of it must cure it. Novelty is only in request; and it is as dangerous to be aged in any kind of course as it is virtuous to be constant in any undertaking. There is

> scarce truth enough alive to make societies secure; but security enough to make fellowships accurst. Much upon this riddle runs the wisdom of the world. This news is old enough, yet it is every day's news. [III, ii, 216–24]

As befits a lover of mystification, these lines are gnomic and obscure, but I see no reason to quarrel with Wilson Knight's gloss-cum-paraphrase:

> No news, but that goodness is suffering such a disease that a complete dissolution of it (goodness) is needed to cure it. That is, our whole system of conventional ethics should be destroyed and rebuilt. A change (novelty) never gets beyond request, that is, is never actually put into practice. And it is as dangerous to continue indefinitely a worn-out system or order of government, as it is praiseworthy to be constant in any individual undertaking. There is scarcely enough knowledge of human nature current in the world to make societies safe; but ignorant self-confidence (i.e., in matters of justice) enough to make human intercourse within a society a miserable thing. This riddle holds the key to the wisdom of the world (probably, both the false wisdom of the unenlightened, and the true wisdom of the great teachers). This news is old enough, and yet the need for its understanding sees daily proof.[5]

The usual interpretation of the Duke's project is Christian. He wishes to root out deceit and hypocrisy, and replace it by a true understanding of Christian morality based on the texts 'what measure ye mete, it shall be measured to you again' and 'forgive us our debts as we forgive our debtors'.[6] However, such an understanding of the Duke's project could hardly be more conventional, and it scarcely accords with the radicalism of his desire for a complete 'dissolution of [goodness]' where 'our whole system of conventional ethics should be destroyed and rebuilt'. In this essay, I shall take the Duke at his word, and argue that he really does want to rethink our whole concept of what goodness – and hence morality – is. In what follows, I shall show that under the Christian surface we can see the deep and pervasive influence of classical – particularly Aristotelian – ethics, and that this influence, properly understood, really does prompt us to re-evaluate our whole way of thinking about morality.

III

The extremes of conventional morality are extensively peopled in this play. On the one hand there are those who are very moral (Angelo, Isabella); and on the other, there are those who are very immoral (Pompey, Mistress

Overdone, Lucio, Barnardine). Barnardine is the most primitive of this latter group because he is only interested in sleeping, drinking, and swearing; the others are all involved – either for pleasure or profit – in the world of sexual vice. We are unlikely to follow Schlegel[7] in thinking these people 'wretches'. We genuinely admire Lucio's wit and poetical moments, Barnadine's churlish refusal to be beheaded, and Pompey's ability to bore and baffle his judges. We also sympathize with the difficulties of their existence. Living on the fringes of legality they are always at the mercy of rulers, fashion, and the agents of the law; and, above all, we are constantly aware of the easy-going, gossipy creatureliness of their humanity. However, this does not disguise the fact that they are not, we feel, people who could ever amount to anything; lacking any notion of judgement, responsibility, discipline or rational planning, they are constantly at the mercy of desires for drink, sex or small profit.

At the other extreme stand Angelo and Isabella. Isabella is a novice in the convent of Saint Clare, the strictest of the Italian convents. Even so, she feels its rules are not strict enough:

> I speak not as desiring more,
> But rather wishing a more strict restraint
> Upon … the votarists of Saint Clare. [I, iv, 3–5]

Angelo too, 'a man of stricture and firm abstinence' [I, iii, 12], wishes to place the citizens of Vienna under stricter restraint, and two of his first actions on gaining power are to arrest Claudio on the now capital charge of fornication, and to give orders for the brothels in the suburbs to be demolished.

The result of this repression, however, is less superhuman virtue than inhumanity. Repeatedly, Angelo's denatured coldness is remarked upon: he is

> … a man whose blood
> Is very snow-broth; one who never feels
> The wanton stings and motions of the sense. [I, iv, 57–9]
> […]
>
> Some report, a sea-maid spawned him. Some that he was begot between two stockfishes. But it is certain that when he makes water, his urine is congealed ice. And he is a motion ungenerative; that's infallible. [III, ii, 304–5]

The difficulty with such absolute restraint is that, inevitably, it cracks, and the agent is overwhelmed by desires that have grown huge and distorted through long repression. When Angelo succumbs to Isabella's charms, he unleashes forces so powerful that they almost destroy his sense of self-identity:

> What's this? What's this? Is this her fault, or mine?
> The tempter, or the tempted, who sins most, ha? O fie, fie, fie!
> What dost thou, or what art thou, Angelo?
> [...] What, do I love her, That I desire to hear her speak again?
> And feast upon her eyes? What is't I dream on?
> [. ..] Ever till now
> When men were fond, I smil'd and wonder'd how. [II, ii, 163–87]

The result of this onslaught is that all restraint is swept aside and Angelo completely loses control of himself. He says to Isabella that he will spare Claudio if she will agree to sleep with him, and, when she refuses, threatens to have Claudio tortured to death. When he thinks she has relented, he reneges on his bargain and sends a message to the prison saying that Claudio's execution must be brought forward. His moral collapse is swift, spectacular and complete.

Although not so extreme, Isabella's psychology exemplifies the same rule-governed repression. When she comes before Angelo for the first time she tries to distance herself both emotionally and intellectually from Claudio's misdemeanour by arguing that Angelo should condemn Claudio's fault and not Claudio himself, an extraordinarily feeble argument that Angelo has no difficulty in brushing aside. With that, she feels she has done all she can: 'O just but severe law! / I had a brother, then: heaven keep your honour. [Going]' [II ,ii, 40–41]. Lucio is appalled at her cold detachment and urges her to more emotional entreaty:

> Kneel down before him, hang upon his gown;
> You are too cold. If you should need a pin,
> You could not with more tame tongue desire it.
> To him, I say. [II, ii, 44–7]

In spite of this appeal, her halfheartedness continues to exasperate Lucio ('You are too cold' [II, ii, 56]). Eventually, however, Angelo's unresponsiveness begins to rile her; her tongue finds the concepts of pity, forgiveness and mercy, and she begins to develop her case. When she arrives at the 'man, proud man, / Dress'd in a little brief authority' speech, her emotions are at last fully engaged and success looks in prospect. Lucio is delighted and cries: 'O, to him, to him, wench! He will relent; / He's coming: I perceive't' [II, ii, 125–6].

In this scene, opposition and the heat of the moment overcome her emotional inhibition, but when she visits Claudio in prison she is once again implacable. Even allowing for her religious ambitions, the seventeenth-century belief in the afterlife, and the sanctity of virginity, her response to Claudio's request to save him is astonishingly cold and vehement:

> [...] O, you beast!
> O faithless coward! O dishonest wretch!
> Die, perish! Might but my bending down
> Reprieve thee from thy fate, it should proceed.
> I'll pray a thousand prayers for thy death;
> Not word to save thee.
> [...] O fie, fie, fie!
> Thy sin's not accidental, but a trade;
> Mercy to thee would prove itself a bawd;
> 'Tis best that thou diest quickly. [III, i, 135–49]

People who try to renounce a central human desire often end up being tyrannized by one of its uglier forms. Angelo's repressed sexuality does not go away but manifests itself in the sadistic and unfeeling application of rules. When it finally emerges into daylight it is found to be repulsive: it is likened to a cesspit [III, i, 92–3], and instead of blooming like a flower it rots like carrion in the sun [II, ii, 165–8]. Similarly, Isabella's sexuality does not disappear, but re-emerges in a number of perverse and unappealing guises. When she refuses to sleep with Angelo, she sketches what she imagines to be a preferable alternative to sex, unaware that it is masochistic sex she imagines:

> Th' impression of keen whips I'd wear as rubies,
> And strip myself to death as to a bed
> That longing have been sick for, ere, I'd yield
> My body up to shame. [II, iv, 101–4]

And her heated imagination transmutes saving Claudio into a form of incest: 'Is't not a kind of incest, to take life / From thine own sister's shame?' [III, i, 138–9]. By the end of the play, her religious calling and horror of sexuality are quietly pushed to one side as she willingly accepts the Duke's proposal of marriage.[8] Her strict principles have evaporated as completely as Angelo's.

The image of morality this play presents us with is self-deceived and hypocritical. It would be a mistake, however, to feel that this is the morality's only fault. I think we can feel grateful that Angelo and Isabella have not succeeded in denaturing themselves entirely, and that their attempt to deny and repress their true feelings has not met with complete success; indeed, Isabella's anger and Angelo's vanity can seem like genuinely human moments amongst much that is stony and frigid. Even now, if we are told a man is moral, our pulse hardly quickens at the prospect of meeting him; it is difficult to imagine anything other than someone who is stiff, self-conscious and slightly inhuman. *Measure for Measure* faces squarely the problem that our concept of virtue has become deeply unattractive and life-denying; and the Duke's desire to attempt a dissolution of goodness is an attempt to replace the rule-governed puritan conception of virtue with a better one.

IV

What is the conception of ethics with which the Duke wishes to replace the puritan model? Some commentators detect an important clue in the title *Measure for Measure* itself. Stauffer suggests that 'the title [should be] taken as a praising of the Aristotelian mean … the hope for man is that measured or temperate action may meet with a like response',[9] and Lever, endorsing this remark, suggests that the title has 'connotations of weight set against weight and of mutual tempering of extremes'.[10] However, these remain little more than fugitive observations, and something far more deeply interfused is needed if the Duke's ethical ideal is to reveal itself. The passage immediately following his speech on the dissolution of goodness is significant:

> *Duke*: I pray you, sir, of what disposition was the Duke?
> *Esc*: One that, above all other strifes, contended especially to know himself.
> *Duke*: What pleasure was he given to?
> *Esc*: Rather rejoicing to see another merry, than merry at anything which professed to make him rejoice. A gentleman of all temperance.
> [III, ii, 224–31]

The word 'temperance' is evidently carefully chosen. It is not a word which Shakespeare uses frequently. Sometimes, its use has no ethical significance [*The Tempest*, II, i, 41–2]; usually it is a slightly colourless opposite to some disequilibrating – frequently temporary – emotional state: lust [*Antony and Cleopatra*, IV, xiii, 121; *The Rape of Lucrece*, 884]; passion and anger [*Coriolanus*, III, iii, 27; *Antony and Cleopatra*, V, ii, 49]; madness [*King Lear*, IV, vii, 24]. The use of 'temperance' in the conversation quoted above is the only occasion in Shakespeare's plays when it receives its full ethical weight, and is used to characterize the emotional tenor of an entire life.[11]

Unlike charity, humility, and mercy we do not immediately think of temperance (except in the Salvation Army sense) as a Christian virtue. It is, however, the central virtue of Aristotle's *Nicomachean Ethics.* He explicates the concept as follows:

> The temperate man holds a mean position with regard to pleasures. He enjoys neither the things that the licentious man enjoys most (he positively objects to them) nor wrong pleasures in general, nor does he enjoy any pleasure violently; he is not distressed by the absence of pleasures, nor does he desire them – or if he does, he desires them moderately, and not more than is right, or at the wrong time, or in general with any other qualification. But such pleasures as conduce health and bodily fitness he will try to secure in moderation and in the right way … [Bk 3, 1119a][12]

In the earlier part of their conversation, Escalus tells us that the Duke 'above all other strifes, contended especially to know himself'. Although we now regard the search for self-knowledge as a central theme of Shakespearean drama, it is, again, not a project which characters allude to frequently; and, when it is mentioned, is more often noted in the breach than in the observance [e.g., *King Lear*, I, i, 293]. Escalus's description of the Duke is the only place in Shakespeare where self-knowledge is held out as one character's acknowledged, life-long, and defining task.

What is the origin of 'Know thyself'? It was one of the maxims of the Oracle at Delphi, but since classical times it has been associated with the life and inquiries of Socrates. In the *Phaedrus*, Socrates makes clear that he regards the search for self-knowledge as the most fundamental of all intellectual inquiries:

> I can't as yet 'know myself', … and as long as that ignorance remains it seems to me ridiculous to inquire into extraneous matters. Consequently … [I] direct my inquiries, as I have just said, rather to myself to discover whether I really am a … complex creature. [230][13]

So far, I have referred to temperance and self-knowledge as if they were separate virtues; but this is not the case. They are two aspects of *sophrosyne*, the most important concept of ancient Greek ethics. Although this word is usually translated as 'temperance', *sophrosyne* is in fact an idea of considerable complexity and no direct translation exists in our language. Its precise nature was a matter of considerable debate even amongst the Greeks, and Plato devotes his early dialogue, the *Charmides*, to its exploration. Here we find the young nobleman Charmides asserting the essential unity of self-knowledge and temperance in *sophrosyne*:

> I would almost say that self-knowledge is the very essence of temperance, and in this I agree with him who dedicated the inscription 'Know thyself' at Delphi .... 'Know thyself' and 'Be temperate!' are the same, as I maintain, and as the words imply, yet they may be thought to be different. [*Charmides*, 164d–165a]

For our purposes, it is also worth noting that the English pairing of 'temperance' and 'measure' is also shadowed in Greek. In civic and jurisprudential contexts (the context of *Measure for Measure*) a traditional synonym for *sophrosyne* is *metriotes*.[14]

Nietzsche once remarked that nothing which has a history can be defined,[15] and the history of *sophrosyne* is particularly rich and complicated. Originally, in the time of Homer, *sophrosyne* simply meant being sane, rational, and of sound mind. These qualities naturally show themselves in action, and *sophrosyne* soon came to mean being shrewd, wise in practical matters, and knowing what was in your own self-interest. The concept had begun to acquire greater ethical significance by Hesiod's era, and its central connotations include self-restraint, moderation, and not overstepping boundaries – particularly those laid down by the gods. Socrates emphasized the place of self-knowledge in *sophrosyne*; and from his middle period onwards, Plato talks about the inner harmony necessary to achieve the *sophron* character.

Sophrosyne was frequently associated with self-sufficiency, responsiveness and mercy; and opposed to mania, drunkenness, gluttony, sexual excess, overweening ambition, criminal activity, and all other forms of heedless or profligate behaviour.[16] (In Aristophanes' *The Clouds*, it is even attacked on the grounds that it is opposed to the delights of love, gaming, drinking and feasting – in short, to everything that makes life worth living.[17]) Thus, if one had to give a brief definition of the word as used in fourth-century philosophy, it would be: 'Inner harmony and integration attained through self-knowledge and experience, which gives rise to moral excellence; in particular, wise, prudent and temperate desires that never over-step natural and appropriate boundaries.'

Sophrosyne is obviously opposed to the strict restraint and potential fanaticism of the puritan conception of morals, and many early Protestants denounced Aristotle's *Ethics* wholeheartedly. Luther, for example, fulminated, 'I can only believe the Devil has introduced this study [sc., of Aristotle's books]. For the same reasons his book on ethics is the worst of all books. It flatly opposes divine grace and all Christian virtues';[18] and the idea of such an opposition is endorsed when, at the end of the play, Escalus points to 'lack of temper'd judgement' [V, i, 471] as one of Angelo's central faults. As the Duke aspires to, and approaches the condition of *sophrosyne*, it seems reasonable to suppose that the dissolution of goodness he wishes to bring about is to replace the rule-governed view of morality with an enlightened classical ethic of moderation and psychical harmony; the action of the play, which the Duke instigates, therefore represents his inquiry into this possibility.

The Duke's desire to inquire into the nature of goodness helps to confirm his exemplification of *sophrosyne*, since, as Socrates makes clear in the *Charmides*, only the man who approaches *sophrosyne* is capable of making such an investigation into ethical knowledge; indeed, undertaking such a project is almost a necessary condition for possessing the virtue:

> Then the wise or temperate man, and he only, will know himself, and be able to examine what he knows or does not know, and to see what others know and think they … know … No other person will be able to do this. And this is wisdom and temperance and self-knowledge ….[*Charmides*, 167a; see also *Apology*, 37e–38a]

If we turn to the Duke's celebrated speech on death [III, i, 4–41], we find that here too the influences are classical rather than Christian.[19] There is no mention of God or divine love; sin is omitted; Christ is wholly absent; immortality is not even considered as a possibility. The self or soul is held to be a mere fiction, and a materialism reminiscent of Democritus or Epicurus is hinted at:

> Thou art not thyself;
> For thou exists on many a thousand grains
> That issue out of dust. [19–21]

Man is not master of his own mind:

> Thou art not certain;
> For thy complexion shifts to strange effects after the moon. [23–5]

There is no divine providence, the events which occur are a matter of chance or astrological influence:

> A breath thou are,
> Servile to all the skyey influences

> That dost this habitation where thou keep'st
> Hourly afflict. [8–11]

Finally, was there ever a more cynical portrait of human nature, completely bereft of kindness, love and charity, than this?

> Friend hast thou none;
> For thine own bowels which do call thee sire,
> The mere effusion of thy proper loins,
> Do curse the gout, serpigo, and the rheum
> For ending thee no sooner. [III, i, 28–32]

The idea that life is worthless, and death a kind of desirable sleep, is common enough in Christian literature, but the arguments for these propositions could not be more different from the Duke's. In orthodox literature, life is found worthless in comparison with the joys and splendours of heaven; and the sleep of death is only a blessing because we shall awake to know a larger love (e.g., Donne: 'One short sleep past we wake eternally'[20]). One can only think that the fact the Duke is disguised as a friar while he delivers this speech is designed to emphasize by contrast its profoundly unChristian content.

V

Neoplatonism

The Duke, we know, is 'a scholar' [III, ii, 148], but how much did Shakespeare know about classical ethics at this date?

There are signs of Platonic influence on *Venus and Adonis*, *The Phoenix and the Turtle*, Sonnet 53,[21] *Henry V*,[22] and *Julius Caesar*.[23] Although Shakespeare rarely mentions authorities, Aristotle is explicitly mentioned at the beginning of *The Taming of the Shrew* [I, i, 32] in a context that suggests some knowledge of his ethical views.[24] Authorities are agreed, however, that the influence of Plato and Aristotle reaches its height in *Troilus and Cressida*, probably written in 1602, two years before *Measure for Measure*.[25] This is not surprising. The play is deeply philosophical in tone and centres around a number of ethical debates: the nature of honour and justice, the need to give public demonstration of one's virtues, moral responsibility, and voluntary action. I.A. Richards in '*Troilus and Cressida* and Plato'[26] demonstrates the influence of the *Republic* on these debates, and, more recently, Stephen Medcalf has shown how the concepts of what is probably Ficino's translation of the *Euthyphro* permeate the language of the play.[27] It seems reasonable to suppose that before writing a major philosophical play about ancient Greece, Shakespeare refreshed his knowledge of Greek philosophy, possibly using Jonson's learning and library.[28]

In *Troilus and Cressida*, however, it is the influence of Aristotle which is most pervasive. In an appendix to the Arden edition, Kenneth Palmer[29] demonstrates that many of the major debates are structured on explicitly Aristotelian lines. The most obvious case is the section where Troilus, Hector and Paris debate whether Helen should be returned to Menelaus. Here we find Shakespeare's second explicit reference to Aristotle: 'Aristotle thought [young men] / Unfit to hear moral philosophy' [II, ii, 167–8; Bk 1, 1095ab]. We also find the following shared ideas: pleasure and passion are incompatible with free and rational decision-making (a point which Aristotle illustrates by citing the superior wisdom of the Trojan elders who wished to see Helen returned – the very case Shakespeare is dramatizing) [169–74; Bk 3, 1111b and Bk 2, 1109b]; the distinction between natural and conventional justice [174–5 and 177–83; Bk 5, 1134b]; natural justice is best illustrated by the justice between husband and wife [174–7; Bk 5, 1134b]; the law has to act when natural justice does not prevail [177–83; Bk 3, 1113b].

Aristotle's central concepts reverberate throughout the text. At I, i, 347–8, Shakespeare uses 'choice' to mean an action taken after rational deliberation, a sense that sounds slightly portentous in English but which is entirely natural as a translation of the Greek '*proairesis*' – discussed by Aristotle in Bk 3, 1111b. We also find discussions of whether honour is more important than life [V, iii, 25–8; Bk 4, 1124b], the relation of voluntary action to coercion [II, i, 96–9; Bk 3, 1109b–1111b], and the idea that appropriate action is not necessarily moderate – extreme circumstances require extreme emotions [IV, iv, 1–10; Bk 2, 1106a]. There is even – a most extraordinary fact if it were merely accidental – a joint mention of Milo, the prodigiously strong wrestler from Croton in southern Italy [II, iii, 247; Bk 2, 1106b].

The sheer detail of these reminiscences suggests that when Shakespeare came to write *Measure for Measure* some two years later, his knowledge of Aristotle's *Ethics* was recent, first-hand and extensive. He would not have had trouble in finding the book. Shakespeare's command of Latin and Greek is, of course, a deeply disputed matter, but Greek texts were commonplace, and reliable and idiomatic translations into Latin (those for example of Bruni[30] [1416–19] and Lambin[31] [1558]) enjoyed wide currency. In 1547, Richard Grafton published an abridged English version of an Italian translation – *The Ethiques of Aristotle ... now newly translated into English*,[32] and Italian and

French editions circulated widely: a catalogue compiled about 1575 shows James VI of Scotland's library to have included *Les Ethiques d'Aristote en francoys*, fol.,[33] and if we can judge by *Henry V* [III, iv], Shakespeare had a good command of French.

The *Ethics* acquired an important place on English grammar school curricula,[34] and there were many study aids to facilitate learning: John Case's *Mirror of Moral Question* and his elementary *ABCedarium moralis philosophiae* of 1596 were two of the most popular.[35] The widespread study of the *Ethics* caused considerable alarm amongst the godly. In 1578, a puritan called John Stockwood preached a sermon attacking the amount of time allotted to classical authors in grammar schools:

> I would haue you, that setting aside all care of religion in your schollers, to make it your only profession to read them profane Authors, shewe me the example but of one person, whome, eyther *Tullie* his Offices or *Aristotle* his Ethickes, or *Plato* his Preceptes of maners, euer yet made a godly and a vertuous man. I am not against the teaching of profane writers: I know they haue their vse. But I vtterlye mislike your preposterous, backewarde, and euerthwarte care in labouring, chiefly about these, onmitting that whiche should be formoste, namelye instruction out of the worde.[36]

Attacks of this kind are the strongest possible evidence for the widespread study of the *Ethics.* They indicate that written curricula requiring the study of Aristotle were not merely expressions of good intention but were actually put into effect, and that study of the *Ethics* was not just restricted to the individual institutions whose written curricula happen to have come down to us.

There are also two important indirect sources for Shakespeare's knowledge of classical ethics. The first is John Florio's translation of Montaigne's *Essays*. This was printed in 1603, although the book had been circulating in manuscript for at least a decade earlier. It was well known to Shakespeare and his circle: Florio was a friend of Ben Jonson, and language tutor to Shakespeare's patron, the Earl of Southampton; one of the British Library's copies of the first edition contains a signature of Shakespeare which may well be genuine, and another contains the signature of Ben Jonson. The most well known instance of Shakespeare utilizing Montaigne is when he versifies five lines of Montaigne's essay 'On Cannibals' and puts them into the mouth of Gonzalo in *The Tempest* [II, i, 138–47]. But Robertson, in his study of Montaigne and Shakespeare, adduces over ninety parallel passages, arguing that the period from 1600 to 1604 is the most heavily influenced period, and that *Hamlet* and *Measure for Measure* are the most heavily influenced plays.[37]

Montaigne's essays are soaked in classical literature, sometimes including page-long quotations from Plato; but he was himself in many ways a rebirth and exemplification of the classical temper. Montaigne's attitude to Christianity is, at best, cool: R.W. Church remarked, 'His views, both of life and death, are absolutely and entirely unaffected by the fact of his professing to believe the Gospel';[38] and John Stirling goes further: 'All that we find in him of Christianity, would be suitable to apes and dogs rather than to rational and moral beings.'[39] He was the first modern European to learn Latin as his first language; he is generally credited with the modern rediscovery of Pyrrhonean scepticism;[40] he describes himself as 'a worshipper of [Aristotle's] golden mean';[41] Socrates is, for him, the 'master of masters';[42] indeed, as Emerson points out, Socrates is the one topic on which Montaigne's prose glows with ardour;[43] the most distinguished recent historian of scepticism describes him with good reason as 'the French Socrates'.[44]

Cicero's *Tusculan Disputations*[45] are usually cited as a main source for the Duke's speech on death, and the argument as a whole is reminiscent of the writings of Lucretius and Epicurus. It seems likely, however, that the Duke's argument draws directly on a work which influenced all three writers and which Cicero mentions as one of his sources – Socrates' *Apology*. The whole of the relevant passage is quoted in Montaigne's essay, 'Of Physiognomy', and the most pertinent section runs as follows: 'if it (death) be a consummation of one's being, it is also an amendment and entrance into a long and quiet night. Wee finde nothing so sweete in life as a quiet and gentle sleepe, and without dreames.'[46] No one can read this passage, I take it, without being immensely struck by its resemblance (particularly in its use of the word 'consummation') to Hamlet's 'To be, or not to be' soliloquy.[47] Although the Duke's speech lacks the precise verbal echo, his contention that death is something benign and not to be feared is much closer in spirit to Socrates' position.

The Duke's argument that we should be contemptuous of death because it only takes something away that is not worth having is stated at least ten times in Montaigne's corpus, but the following is fairly typical:

> Our religion hath no surer humane foundation, than the contempt of life. Discourse of reason [*Hamlet* again] cloth not only call and summon us unto it. For why should we feare to lose a thing, which being lost, cannot be moaned?[48]

> It is not without reason we are taught to take notice of our sleepe, for the resemblance it hath with death. How easily we passe from waking to sleeping; with how little interest we lose the knowledge of the light, and of our selves.[49]

Similarly, Claudio's heterodox opinion that in Hell we are punished by extreme cold rather than extreme heat, appears to have its origin in this passage:

> Amongst them [barbarous nations] was also found the beliefe of Purgatory, but after a new forme, for what we ascribe unto fire they impute unto cold, and imagine that soules are both purged and punished by the rigor of an extreame coldness.[50]

The second important indirect source for Shakespeare's knowledge of classical ethics is James VI of Scotland's *Basilicon Doron* [1599],[51] at once 'a text-book of political ethics and a statement of personal aims'.[52] As James had been proclaimed James I of England on 24 March 1603, it was one of the most extensively discussed books of the year. Because of Shakespeare's close connection with James, the affinities between the king, Shakespeare, and *Measure for Measure* are rich and complicated,[53] but the following are worthy of brief notice in the present context. James, like the Duke in *Measure for Measure*, had dislike of crowds; was a very considerable scholar ('a Living Library and a Walking Study', according to one contemporary[54]); and profoundly interested in the relationship between justice and mercy at a practical as well as theoretical level.[55] He also had a low opinion of puritans (they are a frequent foil throughout *Basilican Doron*), and was much struck by the idea of using dissimulation to find out what his people and courtiers were doing. He writes:

> And therefore delite to haunt your Session, and spie carefully their proceedings; … Remit everything to the ordinary indicature, for eschewing of confusion: but let it be your owne craft, to take a sharpe account of every man in his office.[56]

Following his own precepts, he made a would-be secret expedition to the Exchange in March 1604 to watch unobserved his merchants at work.[57]

Only ten days after his arrival in the capital, James instructed Lord Cecil to prepare the letters patent which were to make Shakespeare's company 'The King's Men',[58] and on 26 December 1604, *Measure for Measure* was acted in front of the Court in the Banqueting House at Whitehall – although it was probably written between May and August of the same year.[59] What could be more appropriate on this occasion than a play whose main protagonist exemplifies many of James's traits, and whose plot demonstrates the wisdom of his ethical and political views? *Basilican Doron* shows these views to be founded on Aristotle's *Ethics*, and one important section is worth quoting at length:

I need not trouble you with the particular discourse of the foure Cardinall vertues, it is so trodden a path, but I will shortly say vnto you; make one of them, which is Temperance, Queene of all the rest within you. I meane not by the vulgar interpretation of Temperance, which onley consists in *gustu & tactu,* by the moderating of these two senses: but, I meane of that wise Moderation, that first commanding of your selfe, shall as a Queene, command all the affections and passions of your minde, and as a Phisician, wisely mix all your actions according thereto .... The like say I now of Justice, which is the greatest vertue that properly belongeth to a Kings office.

Use Iustice, but with such Moderation, as it turne not in Tyrannies otherwaies *summum Ius, is summa iniuria* ... for lawes are ordained as rules of vertuous and social living, and not to be snares to trap (!) your good subjects: and therefore the lawe must be interpreted according to the meaning, and not to the literal sense thereof: *Nam ratio est anima legis.*

And as I say of Justice, so I say of Clemencie, Magnanimitie, Liberalitie, Constancie, Humilitie, and all the other Princely vertues; *Nam in medio stat virtus.* And it is but the craft of the Diuell that falsely coloureth the two vices that are on either side thereof with the borrowed titles of it, albeit in very deede they have no affinitie therewith and the two extremities themselves, although they seem contrarie, yet growing to the height, runne ever both in one: For *in infinitis omnia concurrunt*; and what difference is betwixt extreame tryrannie ...; and extreame slacknesse of punishment ...?[60]

This passage contains an explicit discussion of the doctrine of the mean in the context of a ruler's virtues, and is concerned above all to show that temperance (*sophrosyne*) is 'the Queene of all the rest within you'. The marginal notes refer us directly to James's Platonic and Aristotelian sources: at the first mention of 'Temperance' we find '*Arist. 5. pal.*'; at the first mention of 'Tyrannie' we find '*Pla. 4. de Leg. Arist.* nag. *mor.*'; at 'sociall living' the reference is to '*Arist. 5. aeth. & 1. rhet.*' ('*aeth.*' is the *Nicomachean Ethics*; '*mag. mar.*' is the *Magna Moralia*, a text not now regarded as genuinely Aristotelian but as first- or second-generation Peripatetic). I shall show the importance of James's distinction between interpreting the law 'according to the meaning' and not to 'the literal sense thereof' in the context of *Measure for Measure* when I come to discuss law and morality in section VII.

VI

The concept of *sophrosyne* only makes sense in the context of the entire Greek ethical outlook, just as the concept of sin only makes sense in the context of

Christian metaphysics. The ethical outlook of the Greeks was very different from that of Christianity. If, therefore, the Duke wishes to restore the concept of *sophrosyne* to full and active life, he will indeed have to bring about an entire dissolution of goodness.

Let me call the kind of moral world-view held by Angelo and Isabella 'puritan morality'.[61] It has the following characteristics: (i) morality is not primarily a matter of this world or of the human point of view; it is transcendental and concerned with the point of view of God and the world to come; (ii) morality is about rules, constraints and prohibitions; (iii) one's emotions, desires and inclinations frequently come into conflict with these rules, and the agent commits a sin if he yields to temptation.

None of these presuppositions is present in Aristotle's *Ethics*; in fact, it is not at all clear that the Greeks possessed a concept akin to our notion of morality.[62] The human, psychological, naturalistic perspective of Greek ethical thought becomes clear when we learn that the word which we translate as 'ethics' is from the Greek word '*êthos*' which literally means 'character', and that this in turn is etymologically related to '*êthos*' which literally means 'habit'. The moral or transcendental overtones of the word 'ethics' in *Nicomachean Ethics* are entirely our own projection; 'Aristotle on Character' would be much less misleading. In addition, our modern concept of moral behaviour is often made to stand in opposition to mere prudential reasoning, and we all understand what is meant when a man is described as good but not wise in practical matters. Aristotle would have understood no such distinction. For him, a man is good if he acts in accordance with practical wisdom; indeed, 'prudence' is one common translation for this faculty of mind (*phronesis*).

One of the most cogent arguments for adopting a transcendental, and therefore potentially fanatical, point of view is the positing of an afterlife: if a short period of immoral behaviour is to be followed by an eternity of torture, or a finite period of moral behaviour is to be followed by an infinity of bliss, then this is a good reason for behaving morally. Thus the Duke, in his speech on death, neutralizes the main motivation for transcendental ethics by ignoring God and downplaying the existence of the world to come. In the *Nicomachean Ethics* too, immortality is not even considered as a possibility; we are concerned with this world alone. The gods also have only a very subordinate role to play: two typical references are when we are told that contemplation is the most god-like activity [Bk 10, 1178b] and that the stars are more divine than we are [Bk 6, 1141b].

In Aristotle, there is no thought that I should take up an objective perspective and consider myself only as one amongst others. The *Ethics* attempts to show what kind of life will most increase *my* chance of happiness (*eudaimonia*), not how or why the happiness of an entire society should be maximized; although, of course, Aristotle is happy to emphasize that the happiness of my family and friends are *part* of my happiness. Because there is no potential conflict between the ethical and the prudent, or between the human and the transcendental, the idea of a moral fanatic does not seem to have occurred to Aristotle; when he searches for the opposite of the licentious man, he merely comes up with the possibility of someone who is numb or insensible [Bk 2, 1104a].

Aristotle also rejects the possibility of hard and fast moral rules.[63] He distinguishes between practical and theoretical reason. Theoretical reason results in something being known, whereas practical reason results in something being done; and while the former is based on theories, abstractions, algorithms, and true beliefs, the latter is based on the response of an experienced man to the particularities of a concrete state of affairs. Morality is a matter of practical reasoning because 'things of this sort are among the concrete particulars, and the discernment rests with the perception' [Bk 2, 1109b]. Such knowledge cannot be entirely written down, and can only be acquired through repetitious training and practice. To consider some contemporary examples: the knowledge of a moral agent is less like knowledge of a theory or calculus than it is like the knowledge of a connoisseur who is adept at spotting forgeries, a coastguard who senses when a rescue is too dangerous to attempt, a son who knows how tactfully to defuse his father's anger.

Clearly there is some role for rules here, but the rules act merely as guiding principles, rules of thumb, useful summations of past experience; they are general descriptions of how to do something *well*, they do not legislate or stipulate a practice. As Aristotle puts it: 'Among statements about conduct, those that are universal are more general, but the particular are more true – for action is concerned with particulars, and statements must harmonize with these' [Bk 2, 1107a]. Such guiding principles or rules of thumb are useful for the beginner or for people acting under conditions of uncertainty, but one thing that distinguishes the expert from the tyro is that the expert knows when principles should be ignored. If you have only just begun to play chess, then it is useful to know that the queen should not be brought out early, or that rooks should be saved for the endgame, but no grandmaster would dream of adhering rigidly to these principles if he saw there was enormous advantage to be gained by flouting them.

Puritan morality, like most modern moral theories, is act-centred: it lays down rules which define what the good act is, and then defines the good agent as someone who (generally) performs good acts.[64] However, Aristotle does not believe in binding moral rules and therefore this kind of theory is not available to him. Thus, the theory put forward in the *Ethics*, like most ancient theories of ethics, is agent-centred: we are given a description of the good agent, and then the good act is defined as whatever it is that such agents (usually) do. The theory Plato presents in the *Republic*, which had an immense influence on Aristotle and the ancient world generally, is a good example. Plato divides the psyche into three: reason, spirit and desire. He then defines justice, not in terms of certain kinds of public rules or norms as we might expect, but in terms of how the three parts of the soul must interrelate in the psychology of the virtuous agent:

> Justice, therefore, we may say, is a principle of this kind; its real concern is not with external actions, but with a man's inward self, his true concern and interest. The just man will not allow the three elements which make up his inward self to trespass on each other's functions or interfere with each other, but, by keeping all three in tune, like the notes of a scale . ... will in the truest sense set his house to rights, attain self-mastery and order, and live on good terms with himself. When he has bound these elements into a disciplined and harmonious whole, and so become fully one instead of many, he will be ready for action of any kind ... whether it is political or private. [443d–e][65]

Thus goodness is equated not with following rules but with psychical harmony. This condition is to be maintained not by acquiring true beliefs or theories but by training and educating the whole of the psyche (moods, emotions, desires, habits, dispositions to act, etc.) from early childhood. As Aristotle remarks: 'Pleasure induces us to behave badly, and pain to shrink from fine actions. Hence the importance (as Plato says) of having been trained in some way from infancy to feel joy and grief at the right things; true education is precisely this' [Bk 2, 1104b].

In Aristotle's moral theory, our emotional responses to particulars are an essential part of our sensibility. There is, therefore, no thought of ignoring or defeating the emotions; rather, they should be included and educated. For some Christians (Kant,[66] for example) an action is only moral if it ignores or overrules inclination, but for Aristotle this already represents a falling away from virtue, since the virtuous man will *want* to do what is right. Self-control in the ancient world was often seen as a psychological state below that of complete virtue. Plutarch's view is representative:

> People do not consider self-control a complete virtue. For it has not yet become a mean state as a result of harmony of the worse part in relation to the better, nor has the excess of feeling been removed, nor is the desiring part of the soul

> obedient to and in agreement with the intelligent part; rather it pains and is pained and is repressed by necessity, and lives alongside [the intelligent part] like a hostile enemy element in a civil war.[67]

Aristotle correctly sees that only a man in whom duty and inclination are one can be expected to perform virtuously in all circumstances. This ideal of Aristotelian virtue, a condition where there is no disparity between inclination and just action, is exemplified in Montaigne's description of Socrates and Cato:

> We see in these two men … so perfect a habit of virtue that it has become their common complexion. It is no longer a painful virtue, nor one dictated by reason, for the maintenance of which the soul needs to brace itself; it is the very essence of the soul, it is its natural and habitual way.[68]

Judged by these standards, the two sets of characters discussed in the first section of this essay fare badly. The low-life characters – Pompey, Mistress Overdone, Lucio, Barnardine – are at the mercy of their basic drives. In Aristotelian terms they are licentious and the victims of uneducated desire; in Platonic terms they have allowed reason and spirit (the part of the mind devoted to ambition and civic honour) to be over-run by appetite. They are thus condemned to a life of vice or triviality or both. Angelo and Isabella fare little better. They have not genuinely educated their desires, they have merely subjected them to rules and external restraint. The result is that they are both internally riven: Angelo 'stands at guard with Envy' [I, iii, 51], Isabella is 'at war 'twixt will and will not' [II, ii, 33]. This repression means that they have little knowledge of their own feelings, and that the feelings themselves, because never examined or cultivated, are alien and unruly. *Measure for Measure* criticizes lack of temperance in both the senses distinguished by James I: 'gustu & tactu', and the ability to command 'all the affections and passions of your minde'.[69]

Both the conventional conception of the moral life and the conventional conception of the immoral life are therefore shown to be thoroughly unsatisfactory. The only way to progress beyond them is to isolate and neutralize the presupposition that both sets of characters share, and this turns out to be the idea that morality is a matter of following external rules. This shared conception of morality is made clear at the start of the play. At the beginning of the first act, Angelo introduces the new restrictions on the populace of Vienna; at the end, we hear of Isabella's desire for stricter restraint. Between the two, we find three low-life characters discussing which of the Ten Commandments should be dropped if one wishes to be a soldier or a pirate;

and see the trial of Pompey and the arrest of Claudio for violating the laws against vice. The theme of rules – new rules introduced and old rules ignored – is already firmly in place by the end of the first act.

If one has this conception of morality, then it is very natural to think of it as a fetter or a strait-jacket. Matthew Arnold, discussing the later stages of the problem which Shakespeare examines in this play, introduces a significant image:

> A few years [after the flowering of Tudor and Jacobean literature] the great English middle class, the kernel of the nation, the class whose intelligent sympathy had upheld a Shakespeare, entered the prison of Puritanism, and had the key turned on its spirit there for two hundred years.[70]

It is not merely coincidental that so much of Shakespeare's only play about puritan rule should take place in a prison; indeed, all the prison scenes take place during the period of Angelo's deputyship. Nor is it accidental that the final judgement scene, when all wrongs are righted, should – most unusually – take place in the open air.

Shakespeare's reading of Aristotle allowed him to see that there is a conception of ethics which is a form of self-realization rather than constraint, depends on psychical harmony rather than rules, involves the feelings as much as the intellect, depends on responses to particulars rather than abstractions, can withstand the reality of power and temptation, allows for exceptions and modifications according to circumstance, and is human rather than transcendental. This is the outlook in which the Duke's search for *sophrosyne* has its home, and it is this enlightened ethical culture that implicitly criticizes both the triviality of the low-life characters and the cramping narrowness of puritan moral life.[71]

VII

The account of ethics I sketched in the last section is all very well for personal life, but how can it be applied to the questions of law and government which play such a central role in *Measure for Measure*?

For Aristotle, there is certainly a place for laws, but they are never treated as sacrosanct. They must be tempered by equity [Bk 5, 1138a] and they must be adjusted so as to fit the intentions of the lawgiver and the particularities of the circumstances being considered:

> When the law states a general rule, and a case arises under it that is exceptional, then it is right, where the legislator owing to the generality of his language has erred in not covering that case, to correct the omission by ruling such as the legislator himself would have given if he had been present there, and as he would have enacted if he had been aware of the circumstances ... This in fact is ... the reason why everything is not regulated by law; it is because there are some cases that no law can be framed to cover, so that they require a special ordinance. An irregular object [like human behaviour] has a rule of irregular shape, like the leaden rule of Lesbian architecture: just as this rule is not rigid but is adapted to the shape of the stone, so the ordinance is framed to fit the circumstances.[72] [Bk 5, 1137b]

Again, measured by these standards, Angelo performs extremely badly. First of all, admittedly at the Duke's instigation, he eagerly revives a prurient, intrusive law that the Duke was happy to let lapse. Secondly, the original purpose of the law against fornication was obviously to control the brothels in the suburbs of Vienna; it was not intended to be used against people like Claudio and Juliet, who, in the eyes of the common law, were already married; the couple had merely delayed the public announcement of their marriage because of difficulties with the dowry. Thirdly, Angelo is repeatedly urged to see this case as an exception: Claudio is of good family, it was the kind of offence which anybody might have committed, nobody died because of it. But these arguments fall on deaf ears. Fourthly, he is asked on several occasions [e.g., II, i, 8–16 and II, ii, 137–9] to use his powers of sympathy, imagination and empathy in judging the case, but this, once more, he resolutely refuses to do.

His perpetual defence is that he is the mere agent or administrator of the law: 'Your brother is forfeit of the law' [II, ii, 71]; 'It is the law, not I, condemn your brother' [II, ii, 80]; '... the most just law / Now took your brother's life' [II, iv, 52–3]; 'I – now the voice of the recorded law' [II, iv, 61]. Angelo attempts to throw all the responsibility for Claudio's condemnation onto the law itself, ignoring the fact that the law is made and administered by men who must use their own judgement. (Isabella shows a similar inclination to hypostatize abstractions when she first of all suggests that Angelo condemn Claudio's fault and not Claudio.) When Escalus is forced to tell Angelo that he is 'so severe ... he is indeed justice' [III, ii, 247–8] this is not intended as a compliment; it implies that Angelo is simply being a legal cipher who is not bringing the full resources of a human being to bear on the case in hand.

This runs contrary to the Duke's explicit instructions. When the Duke left Vienna, he commanded Angelo to be 'at full ourself. / Morality and mercy in Vienna / Live in the tongue and heart' [I, i, 43–5].[73] Clearly, part of his meaning is that Angelo, in his capacity as temporary ruler, should use his heart, imagination and emotion in responding to the particularities of cases in exactly the same way as the Duke would do if he were present; but, by simply treating the law as a kind of calculus which already contains all the answers, Angelo is utterly failing in his task. Just as a navigator who can only reckon courses by using textbook rules is a poor navigator, so a judge who can only apply written laws – with no thought for justice, equity, or fairness – is an incompetent judge.

From the ethical point of view, Escalus acts as a dramatic foil to Angelo. He is, of course, the first to try and make Angelo moderate his judgement of Claudio, but there are several other points of contrast which are more important. Escalus' views on authority and government are the result of both theory and practice [I, i, 11–12] whereas Angelo's views are the product of theory alone. From the Aristotelian point of view this places Escalus in much the stronger position since the ability to rule justly can only be acquired by ruling justly:

> [The] virtues we do acquire by first exercising them, just as happens in the arts. Anything that we have to learn how to do we learn by the actual doing of it: people become builders by building and instrumentalists by playing instruments. [Bk 2, 1103a]
>
> That is why some people who do not possess <theoretical> knowledge are more effective in action (especially if they are experienced) than those who do not possess it. [Bk 6, 1141b]

Pompey's interrogation can seem like an over-long comic interlude, but it is clearly intended to bring out the differences between Escalus' and Angelo's approach to justice. Angelo says little and is testy and impatient; eventually, exasperation drives him to stalk out, but not before saying that he hopes Escalus will find cause to have everybody whipped. Escalus, on the other hand, treats the defendants with considerable courtesy, and is evidently intrigued and amused by the motley crowd before him. Exercising his judgement on the particularities of the case, he sees that the punishments the law decrees for the crimes being tried are inappropriate. Far from having them all whipped, therefore, he lets Pompey off with a warning, and makes a few tactful enquiries about the men in Elbow's district who might be interested in replacing him.

Both Escalus and Angelo grow angry and threaten torture, but their motives could not be more different. Angelo's anger is mere pettish vexation at people who are of no interest to him; and he threatens to torture Claudio when Isabella

are a number of reasons for not believing this. Firstly, if stamping out vice were his intention then he would have appointed a reliable deputy. Escalus is the obvious choice since the Duke says that he is 'pregnant in / … art and practice' [I, i, 11–12] and knows more about government than the Duke can tell him [I, i, 6–7]. However, although Escalus is 'first in question' (i.e., the first to be considered) he is passed over in favour of Angelo and only made the 'secondary' [I, i, 46–7]. We are given no reason for this, and neither Escalus nor any other courtier questions the decision. The Duke also knows that Angelo is completely untested in positions of authority and has, as I pointed out above, already let down Mariana.

Secondly, if the Duke wanted to enforce the statutes against fornication there is no reason why he could not have done it himself. This is the first thing that crosses Friar Thomas's mind on hearing the explanation about the statutes: 'It rested in your Grace / To unloose this tied-up justice when you pleased …' [I, iii, 31–2]. The Duke tries to explain that such an action coming from him would seem too dreadful since he winked at the populace's permissive behaviour from the first. He then asks to borrow a friar's habit so he can watch how Angelo's rule develops. Immediately after making this request he returns to his motives for leaving Vienna, for no reason I can see apart from thinking that the explanation he has already offered is unconvincing. It is here that he says he wants to test people like Angelo.

Thirdly, after the Duke's 'return' to Vienna, we hear nothing whatever about the general success or failure of Angelo's policy or any indication that the Duke intends to continue with it. The whole focus of the final scene is on tidying up the consequences of Angelo's moral collapse, and the statutes about vice are forgotten. Fourthly, if the Duke made Angelo his deputy in order to stamp out vice there is no particular reason why the Duke should have stayed in Vienna to watch how things proceeded; indeed, it would have been better to have gone away, and returned to enjoy the fruits of the policy once all the harshness and unpleasantness were over. If, on the other hand, his intention was to see how Angelo's character withstood the test of power, then there was every reason for him to stay; there is no point in setting up an experiment if the only person who understands it is not on hand to observe. The best way to understand the explanation about vice is to see it not only as a cover to disguise the Duke's real reason for leaving, but as way of making Angelo reveal the extremity of his hand from the beginning – a catalyst shall we say.

There are still three aspects of the Duke's character and behaviour which need explaining: his love of mystification; his cruelty to Isabella; and his proposal of marriage to her at the end of the play [V, i, 489–90] which contradicts his prediction to Friar Thomas that he will never fall in love: 'Believe not that the dribbling dart of love / Can pierce a complete bosom' [I, iii, 1–3]. Of course, we can always claim that he, like most of the other characters in the play, just happens to learn something about himself, or that mystification and the odd moment of cruelty just happen to be aspects of his personality. But I think it is possible to see that these three aspects of his behaviour are more than random character traits, and are related to the central theme of the play.

In his essay on Iago, 'The Joker in the Pack',[84] W.H. Auden points out that those who are addicted to practical jokes and confidence tricks always think that they are much cleverer than their apparently gullible victims. In fact, Auden continues, they are much more likely to be emotionally inadequate because they cannot bear the risks involved in normal relationships. These relationships are typically reciprocal: if I know you then you also know me (otherwise you simply know about me); if you are my friend then I am also your friend, and so on. Thus to enter into a normal relation with other people not only requires an ability to like and love other people, but also the self-confidence to feel that you are capable of being liked and loved. Typically, therefore, normal reciprocal relationships contain a potentiality for pain and hurt caused by loss of self-esteem. The practical joker, the confidence trickster, the man who likes to observe people through one-way mirrors, avoids this risk, but at the cost of not knowing other human beings at all; and we are all aware there is something sadistic and manipulative in the practice of spying on, tricking, or reducing people to experimental subjects. Full, non-theoretical knowledge of human beings is intersubjective; it can only be gained by interacting with them, and that means they must interact with you.

The devotee of the one-way gaze is a common enough character type in Shakespeare: Polonius makes himself slightly ridiculous through his addiction to spying, eavesdropping, underhanded schemes and secret knowledge; and Cavell bases his whole interpretation of *King Lear* on Lear's horror of being known, loved or recognized.[85] There is something of this character in the Duke. He wants to know his people but he ardently dislikes the public gaze; he likes to skulk in dark corners (places from which you can see but not be seen); he loves disguises (the perfect way to know about others without them knowing about you); he eavesdrops on the conversation in the cell between Isabella and Claudio; he delights to spread false rumours of his motives and whereabouts (while knowing all the time of the motives and whereabouts of others); he evidently relishes sending letters of 'strange tenour' to Angelo and imagining Angelo's confusion and discomfort on receiving them. Above all, there is something just a little chilly and manipulative in performing an ethical experiment on his court and people, especially on those he knows intimately. We would not take it well if we discovered that what we took to be a series of appalling and agonizing crises that nearly destroyed us was actually a set of emotional hoops designed to test our mettle and extend our self-knowledge.

He knows that Isabella has over-intellectualized and denatured herself, and has denied her desires and emotions. He realizes that the beginning of a remedy must be to make her feel, and acknowledge her long-repressed emotional life. This, I take it, is the reason why he does not reveal himself earlier, and, having revealed himself, does not tell her of Claudio's survival. However, his delight in manipulation, his profound interest in her as a case, which were always slightly suspect motives, here spill over into cruelty; her interest as an experimental subject, a patient, has occluded her dignity as a human being. It is almost as if her suffering and fortitude at last engages his sympathy as well as his curiosity, and makes him aware of the emotional poverty of detachment. He proposes marriage, and it is at this point that he finally gives up the certainty of the objective gaze, gives up the role of controlling intelligence and spectator, and enters the human world of reciprocal relationships as a participant, with all the risks that entails.

Oddly, we see that the Duke and Angelo share the same fault. Both try to transcend the human world by taking up an objective, impersonal stance: Angelo by adopting a series of abstract rules; the Duke by adopting the perspective of the quasi-scientific onlooker. It is not insignificant that these are the only two characters in the play who are described as bookish: the Duke is a scholar, Angelo blunts his natural edge with 'profits of the mind, study and fast' [I, iv, 61]. The Duke's experiment, of course, succeeds admirably; but its greatest and most unlooked for achievement is to show the limits of the experimental attitude itself.[86]

Notes

1 J.A.K. Thompson, *Shakespeare and the Classics* (London: George Allen and Unwin, 1952), p. 129. Now see also J.W. Velz, 'The Ovidian Soliloquy in Shakespeare', *Shakespeare Studies*, 18 (1986), pp. 1–24 and cf. Ch. and M. Martindale, *Shakespeare and the Uses of Antiquity* (London and New York: Routledge, 1990), p. 83; J. Bate, *Shakespeare and Ovid* (Oxford: Clarendon Press, 1993), pp. 70–71, 116 and 154.

2 See, for example, *Measure for Measure*, The Arden Edition, ed. J.W. Lever (London: Routledge, 1988), p. 67.

3 Donald A. Stauffer, *Shakespeare's World of Images. The Development of his Moral Ideas* (New York: Norton, 1949; repr. Bloomington, IN: Indiana University Press, 1966), p. 156. Quoted in Lever, Arden Edition, p. xci. Also Lever's own remarks.

4 All quotations from *Measure for Measure* are from Lever's Arden Edition.

5 G. Wilson Knight, '*Measure for Measure* and the Gospels', in: *Measure for Measure: A Casebook*, ed. G.K. Stead (London: Macmillan, 1971), pp. 91–121.

6 '*Measure for Measure* and the Gospels', pp. 91 and 94.

7 Schlegel's word is '*Gesindel*'. August Wilhelm Schlegel, *Vorlesungen über dramatische Kunst and Literatur* [1808, publ. 1809–11, vol. 2 = Id.], *Kritische Schriften und Briefe*, ed. Edgar Lohner, vol. 6, *Sprache und Literatur, 38* (Stuttgart: Kolhhammer Verlag, 1967), p. 152. The passage is translated in *The Romantics on Shakespeare*, ed. Jonathan Bate (Harmondsworth: Penguin Books, 1992), p. 451 (John Block's translation [1815], revised by A.J.W. Morrison [1848]).

8 Isabella, of course, makes no verbal response to the Duke's proposal, and exactly how she behaves is a matter for directorial decision. I have tried to steer a middle course between the ecstasy with which she responds in some productions and the stony silence or look of horror with which she responds in others. Generally, the negative reaction – which has only been considered a possibility in the last 15 years or so – strikes me as ingenious and topical rather than in accordance with the spirit of the play; I therefore prefer to stay with the traditional reading at this point.

9 Stauffer, *Shakespeare's World of Images*, p. 156. Quoted in Lever, Arden Edition, p. xci.

10 Lever, Arden Edition, p. xci.

11 Perhaps Sonnet 18, l.2, 'Thou art more lovely and more temperate', comes closest to Escalus's concept of temperance. although the primary focus here, as in the *Tempest*, is on the climate.

12 All quotations from Aristotle are from *The Ethics of Aristotle. The Nicomachean Ethics*, trans. J.A.K. Thompson, with an Introduction and notes by Jonathan Barnes, revised with notes and appendices by Hugh Tredennick (Harmondsworth: Penguin Books, 1976).

13 All quotations from Plato, except for the *Republic*, are from *Plato: The Collected Dialogues*, ed. Edith Hamilton and Huntington Cairns (Princeton: Princeton University Press, 1973).

14 Helen North, *Sophrosyne: Self-knowledge and Self-restraint in Greek Literature*, Cornell Studies in Classical Philology 35 (Ithaca, NY: Cornell University Press, 1966), p. 102 on the relationship of *sophron* and *metrios.*

15 *[Alle] Begriffe, in denen sich ein ganzer Prozess semiotisch zusammenfasst, entziehen sich der Definition; definirbar ist nur Das, was keine Geschichte hat*', F. Nietzsche, *Zur Genealogie der Moral*, ed. C. Colli and M. Montinari, *Nietzsche Werke*, Kritische Gesamtausgabe, Vol. 6.2 (Berlin: Walter de Gruyter, 1968), p. 333. I use the translation found in Nietzsche, *The Genealogy of Morals: An Attack*, Second Essay: '"Guilt," "Bad Conscience," and Related Matters', section XIII, trans. Francis Golffing (New York: Doubleday, 1956), p. 210.

16 North, *Sophrosyne*, pp. 16–21, 124, 140, 178–9.

17 Lines 1071–4. See North, *Sophrosyne*, pp. 97–8.

18 Martin Luther, 'To the Christian nobility of the German nation concerning the reform of the Christian estate', trans. H.E. Jacobs and J. Atkinson, in *Luther's Works*, ed. J. Pelikan and H.T. Lehmann, vol. 44 (St. Louis, MO: Concordia, 1958), 201 = Luther, 'An den christlichen Adel deutscher Nation von des christlichen Standes Besserung', in *Werke*, Kritische Gesamtausgabe, vol. 6 (Weimar/Graz: H. Böhlau, 1888), p. 458. Cf. Brian

P. Copenhaver and Charles B. Schmitt, *Renaissance Philosophy*, A History of Western Philosophy, vol. 3 (Oxford: Oxford University Press, 1992), p. 39.

19 Here I rely heavily on Clifford Leech, 'The Meaning of *Measure for Measure*', in Stead (ed.), *Measure for Measure: A Casebook*, pp. 152–65.

20 *Divine Meditations* 10, in John Donne, *The Complete English Poems*, ed. A.J. Smith (Harmondsworth: Penguin, 1980), p. 313.

21 See John Roe, 'The Poetry of Sidney, Shakespeare, Chapman and Donne', and Stephen Medcalf, 'Shakespeare on Beauty, Truth and Transcendence', in *Platonism and the English Imagination*, ed. A. Baldwin and S. Hutton (Cambridge: Cambridge University Press, 1994), pp. 107–10 and 117–25. John Vyvyan, *Shakespeare and Platonic Beauty* (London: Chatto and Windus, 1961), is also relevant in this context.

22 Emrys Jones, *The Origins of Shakespeare* (Oxford: Clarendon Press, 1977), p. 20.

23 I.A. Richards, '*Troilus and Cressida* and Plato', in his *Speculative Instruments* (Routledge and Kegan Paul: London, 1955), pp. 205–6. These pages contain a brief discussion of *Julius Caesar*. It must be pointed out that this article has been criticised for tendentious overstatement. See John Paul Russo, *I.A. Richards: His Life and Work* (London: Routledge, 1989), pp. 290–93.

24 The relevant lines of Tranio's speech [I, ii, 25–45] are as follows: 'I am … / Glad that you thus continue your resolve / To suck the sweets of sweet philosophy. / Only, good master, while we do admire / This virtue and this moral discipline, / Let's not be no Stoics nor no stocks, I pray, / Or so devote to Aristotle's checks / As Ovid is an outcast quite abjur'd' [I, ii, 26–33]. *The Taming of the Shrew* is one of Shakespeare's earlier plays, being written in 1593–94, and this passage betrays a less sophisticated understanding of Aristotle than his later explorations in *Troilus and Cressida* and *Measure for Measure*. In Tranio's speech, morality is pictured as a matter of restraints ('checks') or eradicated feelings ('stocks'), and Aristotle is portrayed as siding with the Stoics against the passion and sensuality of Ovid. It is part of the argument of this paper to show that, after (re)reading Aristotle for *Troilus and Cressida*, Shakespeare came to see that Aristotle and the Stoics do not share the same conception of morality, and that a proper understanding of Aristotle's *sophrosyne* shows it to be quite compatible with intense feeling. Helen North states the correct view, and surely Shakespeare's later view, succinctly: *sophrosyne*, she observes, is 'the harmonious product of intense passion under perfect control' *(Sophrosyne*, p. x), and that '[whereas] Aristotle required only that the appetites be moderated, the Stoics demanded that passion be extirpated' (*Soprosyne*, p. 215).

25 Richards, '*Troilus*', pp. 98–113, and Medcalf, 'Shakespeare on Beauty', pp. 122–5.

26 Richards, *'Troilus*', pp. 122–5.

27 Medcalf, 'Shakespeare on Beauty' (above, n. 21), pp. 122–5.

28 On the relationship with Jonson, see Medcalf, 'Shakespeare on Beauty', pp. 118–19.

29 *Troilus and Cressida*, Arden Edition, ed. Kenneth Palmer (London Methuen, 1982), Appendix III, pp. 311–20. The relationship between the *Ethics* and this play has recently been re-explored by W.R. Elton in 'Aristotle's *Nicomachean Ethics* and Shakespeare's *Troilus and Cressida*', *Journal of the History of Ideas*, 58 (1997), pp. 331–7.

30 R. Pfeiffer, *History of Classical Scholarship from 1300 to 1850* (Oxford: Clarendon Press, 1976), p. 29. For an account of Bruni's translating activities, see Copenhaver and Schmitt, *Renaissance Philosophy* (above, n. 18), pp. 76–84.

31 Charles B. Schmitt, *Aristotle and the Renaissance* (Cambridge, Mass.: Harvard University Press, 1983), p. 77.

32 Schmitt, *Aristotle and the Renaissance*, p. 125.

33 T.W. Baldwin, *William Shakespere's Small Latine & Lesse Greeke* (Urbana: University of Illinois Press, 1944), vol. 1, p. 547.

34 The development of grammar school curricula is discussed in Baldwin, *William Shakespere's Small Latine*, pp. 75–185, and 285–436.

35 Copenhaver and Schmitt, *Renaissance Philosophy* (above, n. 18), p. 124, and Schmitt, *Aristotle and the Renaissance* (above, n. 31), p. 53.

36 John Stockwood, *A Sermon Preached at Paules Crosse on Barthelmew day, being the 24. of August. 1578*, quoted in Baldwin, *Shakespere's Small Latine*, vol. 1, p. 111.

37 J.M. Robertson, *Montaigne and Shakespeare* (London: Adam and Charles Black, 1909), p. 42. Robertson uses an edition of Florio's translation by Henry Morley (*The Essays of Michael Lord of Montaigne*, trans. John Florio (1603), ed. Henry Morley [London: Routledge, 1886]; hereafter = Morley); a more recent and accessible edition can be found in the 'Everyman's Library' series (*Montaigne's Essays in Three Volumes*, trans. John Florio, Everyman's Library 440–42 [London: Dent 1910; repr. 1965]; hereafter = Everyman).

38 R.W. Church, 'The Essays of Montaigne', in *Oxford Essays*, contributed by Members of the University [vol. 3] (London: John W. Parker and Son, 1857), p. 279. Cf. Robertson, *Montaigne and Shakespeare*, p. 194.

39 John Stirling, *London and Westminster Review*, July 1838, p. 346. Quoted in Robertson. *Montaigne and Shakespeare*, p. 194.

40 Richard H. Popkin, *The History of Scepticism from Erasmus to Spinoza* (Berkeley: University of California Press, 1979), p. 42.

41 Michel de Montaigne, 'On Experience' (Bk 3, ch. 13) in *Essays*, ed. and trans. J.M. Cohen (Harmondsworth: Penguin, 1981), p. 389 = 'De l'experience', in id., *Essais*, ed. M. Rat, vol. 2 (Paris: Editions Garnier, 1962), p. 560. I have used Cohen's translation, rather than the most recent one by Screech, because in these particular instances I think Cohen's renderings are more idiomatic. The relevant page reference in Screech is *The Essays of Michel De Montaigne*, ed. and trans. M.A. Screech (Harmondsworth: Penguin, 1987), p. 1251.

42 *Montaigne*, 'On Experience' (Bk 3, ch. 13), in Cohen (trans.), p. 357 = id., 'De l'experience', in Rat (ed.), vol. 2, p. 529 (Screech, p. 1221).

43 Ralph Waldo Emerson, 'Montaigne; Or, the Skeptic', in Ralph Waldo Emerson, *Selected Essays*, ed. Larzer Ziff (Harmondsworth: Penguin, 1982), p. 325.

44 Popkin, *The History of Scepticism*, p. 56.

45 See Lever, Arden Edition, p. 67.

46 Robertson. *Montaigne and Shakespeare*, p. 48, quoting Montaigne, 'Of Physiognomy', trans. Florio, i: Morley, Bk 3, ch. 42, p. 540.

47 Hamlet's fifth soliloquy ('To be or not to be …' [III, i, 56–89]) also lacks any mention of sin. This is noted by William Kerrigan, *Hamlet's Perfection* (Baltimore: Johns Hopkins University Press, 1994), p. 97.

48 Robertson, *Montaigne and Shakespeare*, p. 87, quoting Montaigne, 'That to Philosophic, is to learne how to die', trans. Florio, in Morley, Bk 1, ch. 19, p. 33 (= Everyman, vol. 1, p. 86).

49 Robertson, *Montaigne and Shakespeare*, p. 91, quoting Montaigne, 'Of Exercise or Practice', trans Florio, in: Morley, Bk 2, ch. 6, p. 185 (= Everyman, vol. 2, p. 51).

50 Robertson, *Montaigne and Shakespeare*, p. 95, quoting Montaigne, 'An Apologie of Raimond Sebonde', trans. Florio, in Morley, Bk 2, ch. 12, p. 294 (= Everyman, vol. 2, p. 291).

51 I would like to thank Professor Wolfgang Haase for drawing my attention to the relevance of this work. Part of this passage is quoted and discussed in Lever, Arden Edition, p. xlix,

and also in Elizabeth Pope, 'The Renaissance Background of *Measure for Measure*', *Shakespeare Survey*, 2 (1970), pp. 66–82, especially 73 ff.

52 Lever, Arden Edition, p. xlvii.

53 See, for example, Donald Lloyd Stevenson, 'The Historical Dimension in *Measure for Measure*: The Role of James I in the Play', an appendix to, *The Achievement of Shakespeare's Measure for Measure* (Ithaca: Cornell University Press, 1966), pp. 134–66, and Richard Levin, 'The King James Version of *Measure for Measure*', *Clio*, 3 (1974), pp. 129–63.

54 William Barlow, *The Summe and Substance of the Conference ... at Hampton Court (1604)*, p. 84. Cited by David Lloyd Stevenson, *ELH. A Journal of English Literary History*, 26 (1959), p. 200 and quoted in Lever, Arden Edition, p. xlvii.

55 See the account in Lever, Arden Edition, p. 1, of James's late pardoning of several men condemned to hang in Winchester for their part in Raleigh's conspiracy in the winter of 1603–4.

56 James VI and I, *Political Writings*, (ed) Johann P. Sommerville, ser. Cambridge Texts in the History of Political Thought (Cambridge, New York, Oakleigh, and Melbourne: Cambridge University Press, 1994), pp. 45–6. Elizabeth Pope, 'The Renaissance Background of *Measure for Measure*' (above, n. 51), also discusses this parallel.

57 Lever, Arden Edition, pp. xlix–1.

58 S. Schoenbaum, *William Shakespeare: A Compact Documentary Life* (Oxford: Oxford University Press, 1987), p. 250.

59 Lever, Arden edition, p. xxxv.

60 James VI and I, *Political Writings*, pp. 43–4.

61 I am using the phrases 'puritan morality' and 'Christian morality' as semi-technical terms to denote the kind of views held by Angelo and Isabella. I do not intend to imply that the presuppositions I isolate are either necessary or sufficient for a Christian conception of morality. Many Christians would, of course, regard what I call 'puritan morality' as a complete travesty of Christianity; they would wish to emphasize purity of heart, empathy, human responsiveness, etc.

62 In this I follow Bernard A.O. Williams, *Ethics and the Limits of Philosophy* (London: Collins, 1985), p. 6, and Jonathan Barnes, 'Introduction' to Aristotle, *Ethics*, p. 31. My understanding of Greek ethics has been heavily influenced by both of these works. For the view that Greek – especially Homeric – notions of morality, action, responsibility etc. are utterly remote from ours, see the interpretations of Bruno Snell and others criticized in Williams, *Shame and Necessity*, Sather Classical Lectures 57 (Berkeley: University of California Press, 1993), esp. pp. 21–49. For an opinion which is more conservative than Williams's, and argues that Greek notions of morality and virtue are more like our own, see Julia Annas, *The Morality of Happiness* (New York: Oxford University Press, 1993).

63 My reading of Aristotle has been particularly influenced by Martha Nussbaum, 'The Discernment of Perception: An Aristotelian Conception of Private and Public Rationality', in her *Love's Knowledge. Essays on Philosophy and Literature* (Oxford: Oxford University Press, 1990), pp. 54–105.

64 I take this distinction from Julia Annas, *An Introduction to Plato's Republic* (Oxford: Oxford University Press, 1991), pp. 153–69.

65 *The Republic*, ed. and trans. Desmond Lee (Harmondsworth: Penguin, 1987).

66 Immanuel Kant, *The Moral Law (Groundwork of the Metaphysic of Morals)*, ed. H.J. Paton (London: Hutchinson, 1976), pp. 63–5.

67 Plutarch, *De Virtute Morali*, 445c–d. Quoted in Annas, *The Morality of Happiness*, p. 53.
68 Montaigne, 'On Cruelty' (Bk 2, ch. 11), in Cohen (ed.), p. 178 = id., 'De La Cruaute', in Rat (ed.), vol. 1, p. 467 (Screech, p. 476).
69 James VI and I, *Basilicon Doron*, pp. 43–4.
70 Matthew Arnold, 'Heinrich Heine', in, *Essays Literary and Critical*, ed. G.K. Chesterton (London: Dent, 1919), p. 115.
71 A great deal of English literature can be seen as mounting a campaign against abstract rule-governed conceptions of morals on behalf of the good heart and educated emotions. *Tom Jones* is an obvious example, but the following sentence from George Eliot puts the matter succinctly: 'There is no general doctrine which is not capable of eating out our morality if unchecked by the deep-seated habit of direct fellow-feeling with individual fellow-men'. *Middlemarch*, ch. 61 (Harmondsworth: Penguin, 1994), p. 619.
72 Moulding on the island of Lesbos was ogival, i.e., took the form of a double curve. This could not be measured with a rigid ruler, and consequently builders used a leaden ruler which could be bent to the shape of the object being measured.
73 On mercy, see the collection of passages in Theodor Meron, *Henry's Wars and Shakespeare's Laws: Perspectives on the Law of War in the Later Middle Ages* (Oxford: Clarendon Press, 1993), p. 30.
74 See Nussbaum, 'The Discernment of Perception' (above, n. 63), pp. 97–101.
75 Samuel Taylor Coleridge, *Literary Remains* (1836), quoted in Bate, *The Romantics on Shakespeare* (above, n. 7), p. 453.
76 Algernon Charles Swinburne, *A Study of Shakespeare* (1880), quoted in R.W. Chambers, 'Measure for Measure', in *Measure for Measure*, The Signet Classic Shakespeare, ed. S. Nagarajan (New York: New American Library, 1963), pp. 207–8.
77 W.W. Lawrence, *Shakepeare's Problem Comedies* (New York: Macmillan, 1931), p. 112, quoted in Chambers, 'Measure for Measure', p. 192.
78 *The Times Literary Supplement*, 16 July 1931, p. 554, quoted in Chambers, 'Measure for Measure', p. 192.
79 Wilson Knight, '*Measure for Measure* and the Gospels', p. 92.
80 Roy W. Battenhouse, '*Measure for Measure* and the Christian Doctrine of Atonement', *Publications of the Modern Language Association*, 61 (1946), pp. 1029–59. Quoted in Leech, 'The Meaning', p. 157.
81 'The Renaissance Background of *Measure for Measure*' (above, n. 51), p. 71.
82 It might be objected that, in my eagerness to demonstrate the non-Christian origins of the Duke's morality, I overlook the occasion when Angelo says that the Duke '... like power divine, / Hath looked upon my passes ...' (V, i, 367). But this is *Angelo*'s interpretation of the Duke's behaviour and he still views the Duke's actions through the categories of the puritan worldview. He is the character whose conception of morality is most remote from temperance and self-knowledge, and, unlike Isabella (a less extreme case), he is only just beginning to arrive at a position where self-knowledge is possible. For an article which argues that Angelo's fault is lack of self-knowledge rather than hypocrisy, see W.H. Durham, 'What art thou, Angelo?', *University of California Publications in English*, VIII (2) (1951), p. 169.
83 For the evidence that Shakespeare's father had Catholic sympathies see S. Schoenbaum, *William Shakespeare*, pp. 45–54
84 W.H. Auden, 'The Joker in the Pack', in *Othello: A Casebook*, ed. J. Wain (London: Macmillan, 1985), pp. 119–223.

85 S. Cavell, 'The Avoidance of Love: A Reading of *King Lear*', in *Must We Mean What We Say? A Book of Essays* (Cambridge: Cambridge University Press, 1976 [originally New York: Scribner, 1969]), pp. 267–353.

86 I would very much like to thank Marie McGinn, Stephen Wall, Ann Pasternak-Slater, Hermione Lee, A.W. Price, Alan Heaven and, above all, the editor of the *International Journal of the Classical Tradition*, Wolfgang Haase, for suggestions which led to significant improvements in this paper. I would also like to record a general debt to Ruth Nevo's '*Measure for Measure:* Mirror for Mirror', *Shakespeare Survey*, 40 (1988), pp. 107–22. Although she has nothing to say about classical ethics, her views of Angelo, Isabella and Escalus are similar to my own.

Chapter 6

Lamarque and Olsen on Literature and Truth

Who sayes that fictions onely and false hair
Become a verse? Is there in truth no beautie?
George Herbert

In *Truth, Fiction and Literature*, Peter Lamarque and Stein Haugom Olsen defend a no-truth theory of literature [1],[1] and argue that the concepts of truth, knowledge and insight play no ineliminable role in accounting for literature's value. This does not mean that they favour a form of aestheticism which sees no connection between art and life; indeed, they urge that great literature is centrally concerned with moral dilemmas, individuals and their relation to society, love, the passing of time, death, and other themes of perennial concern to human beings. But rather than state *theses* about such themes or seek to imply *truths*, it is the purpose of literature to explore, enact, develop and imaginatively realize them.

Lamarque and Olsen acknowledge that authors sometimes appear to assert general propositions about human nature, as in, for example, the first sentence of *Anna Karenina*, 'All happy families are alike but an unhappy family is unhappy after its own fashion'. They also acknowledge that some works of literature *imply* general propositions about human nature: the Lydgate story in *Middlemarch*, they suggest, implies that 'The best human hopes and aspirations are always thwarted by forces beyond human control' [338]. However, they urge that the truth-value of such propositions is not relevant to the literary assessment of the works which contain them, and that attempting to assess their truth-value should play no part in either literary appreciation or criticism.

They support this contention with the following argument. If these propositions occurred in a sociological or philosophical text, then they would be (or at least ought to be) backed up with evidence and argument designed to impart belief and persuade the reader. The authors, however, claim to notice a distinct absence of such argument in literary critical contexts:

> Perhaps the first feature to notice concerning the discourse about literature which one finds in criticism and conversation is that it does not contain much *debate* about the truth-value of these propositions. There is an absence of argument about whether or not a particular proposition or set of propositions … is true or false … Debate about the truth or falsity of the propositions implied by a literary work is absent from literary criticism since it does not enter into *the appreciation of the work as a literary work.* [332–4]

From this they conclude that these general propositions, whether stated or implied, play a different logical role in literary contexts from that which they perform in philosophy or sociology. First, the literary function of general propositions is '[to characterize] a theme which gives focus and interest to the fictional content' [66] and 'to organize the events, characters and situations … into a significant and meaningful pattern' [331]. Second, it is sufficient in literary contexts to understand the meaning or content of a proposition; there is no pressure to push on to determine its truth-value. 'The question of truth', they write, 'is separate from the question of intelligibility … It is the *content* of the proposition, what it is about, not its truth as such, that confers interest on the … story' [329–30].

If a critic tries to show how a work develops, elaborates, fleshes out, realizes a theme, then this *is* relevant to aesthetic evaluation. If, on the other hand, he tries to show how such a propositional truth does or does not conform to the world, then 'there is no reason for maintaining that the criticism constitutes a step in aesthetic appreciation' [338]. When a critic moves from showing how the theme of free will manifests itself in *Middlemarch* to considering the truth of the free-will hypothesis, then he has left criticism behind and moved on to philosophy:

> [Appreciation] does not involve the reader asking further questions about the truth of the proposition 'The best human hopes and aspirations are always thwarted by forces beyond human control' … A debate about the substance of this thematic statement will be a debate about the possibility of free will and this is central in philosophy. The critic is free to join this debate, of course, but when he does he has moved on from literary appreciation of *Middlemarch.* [336]

The authors are happy to accept that readers can pick up numerous facts about people, places, points of etiquette and so forth from literature, but these truths, they insist, are merely incidental to a work's value *as* literature. 'Our principal debate', they write, 'is with those who want … [to] see the aim of literature as conveying or teaching or embodying universal truths about human nature, the human condition, and so on, in a sense at least *analogous* to that in which scientific, or psychological, or historical hypotheses can express general truths' [6].

In what follows, I shall argue that this account of literature and truth is seriously at variance with the way writers, critics and readers behave in the real world. It is of course possible that these people are mistaken, and that they ought to behave in the manner the authors describe, but it is surely more likely that common practice has not been corrupted by ignorance or false theory, and that it has a good deal to tell us about literature and truth. My primary method of argument is counter-example, and this means that I shall use more quotation than is normal in this kind of article. It seems important, however, to show that writers and critics actually say what I claim they say. I shall not discuss the authors' account of fiction, but if what I have to say about their theory of literature and truth is correct then it will have consequences for their analysis of fiction as well.

I

Lamarque and Olsen claim that general propositions asserted by authors are only very rarely discussed by literary critics and that this shows that the truth-value of such propositions is not relevant to the aesthetic assessment of literary works. Is this true? The literature discussing the penultimate line of Keats' 'Ode on a Grecian Urn', 'Beauty is truth, truth beauty', is colossal (hundreds of pages according to Paul de Man's modest estimate[2]), largely because everybody's first response is incredulity. Some lies and untruths, we want to say, are beautiful (Renaissance cosmology); some truths are horrific and ugly (Auschwitz). Similarly, one's doubts are not allayed when Keats goes on to make the extravagant claim that 'that is all / Ye know on earth and all ye need to know'. Most people, we reflect, seem to have got by pretty well without knowing this truth (and where they did badly it was not for lack of it), and there are plenty of other things which one definitely *does* need to know: what foods to eat, who your friends are, and so on.

Some confusion over the correct text offers two ways of distancing the importance of truth in this context besides that mentioned by the authors above. No manuscript of the poem exists in Keats' hand, but he oversaw the publication of two editions in his lifetime. An anonymous version in the *Annals of Fine Arts* reads 'Beauty is Truth, Truth Beauty. – That is all …'.

The other, in Keats' 1820 volume, *Lamia, Isabella and Other Poems*, reads '"Beauty is truth, truth beauty," – that is all …'.[3] If the first of these is correct, then the whole of the last two lines would seem to be said *by the urn*, in which case they may no more express Keats' opinion than Iago's remarks express Shakespeare's. If the second is correct, so that 'that is all … ye need to know' is endorsement and elaboration from the narrator, then it is still possible to argue that Keats and the implied narrator of this poem are not one and the same. However, neither strategy works. The main reason is that towards the end of his life Keats began to work out a complex philosophy of truth and its relation to beauty. Reflections on this topic can be found in several other poems (the sonnet 'On Sitting Down to Read *King Lear* Once Again' is clearly important here) and, more significantly, in his letters. On 22 December 1818 he writes to his brothers George and Tom that he has been to see Benjamin West's picture *Death on the Pale Horse*:

> It is a wonderful picture, when West's age is considered [nearly eighty]. But there is nothing to be intense upon; no woman one feels mad to kiss: no face swelling into reality. The excellence of every Art is its intensity, capable of making all disagreeables evaporate, from their being in close relationship with Beauty & Truth – Examine King Lear & you will find this exemplified throughout: but in this picture we have unpleasantness without any momentous depth of speculation excited, in which to bury its repulsiveness …. [With] a great poet the sense of Beauty overcomes every other consideration, or rather obliterates all consideration.[4]

To say that beauty overcomes or obliterates all other considerations, or that art causes disagreeables to evaporate by bringing them into a close relationship with beauty and truth, is not quite to say that beauty and truth are one and the same, but one can well understand why a critic like Lionel Trilling feels these remarks can illuminate the last two lines of the ode in a way that allows them to express a profound truth:

> What [Keats] is saying in his letter is that a great poet (e.g., Shakespeare) looks at human life, sees the terrible truth of its evil, but sees it so intensely that it becomes an element of the beauty which is created by his act of perception – in the phrase by which Keats describes his own experience as merely a reader of *King Lear*, he 'burn[s] through the evil'. To say, as many do, that 'truth is beauty' is a false statement is to ignore our experience of tragic art. Keats' statement is an accurate description of the response to evil or ugliness which tragedy makes: the matter of tragedy is ugly or painful truth seen as beauty. To see life in this way, Keats believes, is to see life truly.[5]

The last two lines of the ode 'On a Grecian Urn' are an instance of a general proposition in literature that has been widely discussed, and a great deal of this discussion centres on whether the lines are true. Trilling, for example, endorses them for being 'accurate': they say how we can see life truly; those who think they are false ignore our experience of tragic art. We are left in no doubt that someone who simply dismisses them as false has responded inadequately to the poem. If these lines can receive such discussion then it is hard to see why analogous lines in other works should not be treated in the same way.

The discussion of Keats is useful for a further reason. Lamarque and Olsen remark that as far as literary criticism is concerned we do not have to know whether a general proposition is true, we merely have to know its meaning. The discussion of Keats shows it is frequently impossible to separate questions of meaning from questions of truth. If a line appears to express a large and resounding falsehood, then this may be a good reason for thinking one has not understood it. Applying the principle of charity and adjusting one's interpretation of Keats' meaning until it expresses something plausible is one way to rectify this. Sometimes one can only get started on this process by looking at other works (the sonnet on *King Lear*), other documents by or about the author (Keats' letters), by considering other artists and the author's reactions to them (Shakespeare), and everyone's general experience of life (our response to tragic art). It is also worth remarking that obvious falsehood is at least one way in which we are alerted to the presence of fictional narrators, and authorial irony and sarcasm. These kinds of rhetorical strategies do not undermine or neutralize the role of truth in fiction, they are inconceivable without it.

It is not difficult to find other debates about the meaning and truth of propositional claims in literature. In 1964, Auden gave an account of returning to his poem 'September 1, 1939'. On reacquainting himself with the famous line 'We must love one another or die', he recalled:

> I said to myself 'That's a damned lie! We must die anyway.' So, in the next edition, I altered it to 'We must love one another and die.' This didn't do either, so I cut the stanza. Still no good! The whole poem, I realized, was infected with an incurable dishonesty and must be scrapped.[6]

Naturally enough a debate then ensued as to whether the line really was a lie (or at least false). As in the 'Grecian Urn' case, this debate about the line's truth-value was inseparable from the debate about the line's meaning. Some critics objected that the later Auden was misled by the earlier Auden's erroneous punctuation; others that Auden, as a Christian, should have found nothing objectionable in the line read in the normal way: it is simply an echo of John 3.14, 'He that loveth not his brother abideth in death.' There is nothing strange or illegitimate about the interpretative strategy these critics are pursuing. Like Auden and Trilling, they assume that if an important line is false then it damages the poem that contains it; if it expresses a profound truth then the value of the poem is enhanced. They are therefore attempting to show that Auden's line falls into the latter category.

II

What of Lamarque and Olsen's positive analysis of the function of general propositions in literature? The idea, that is, that they guide our response to a work, alert us to certain themes, point up particular parallels, allow us to see the ideas which are being enacted, embodied and dramatized in the text? This idea seems plausible if you only consider general sentences in novels, particularly opening sentences, but it works much less well for propositions in other kinds of literature.

To take poetry first, here is the whole of 'XXVII' from A.E. Housman's *More Poems*:

> To stand up straight and tread the turning mill.
> To lie flat and know nothing and be still,
> Are the two trades of man: and which is worse
> I know not, but I know that both are ill.[7]

This poem, I suppose, contains three propositional claims: the lot of man is either weary life or death; both are bad; it is not clear which is worse. Clearly these generalities cannot guide our perception through dramatic particulars and so forth, because there are no dramatic particulars of any kind to guide our perceptions through. This means that it is impossible for these propositions to function in the way the authors say general propositions ought to function in literary contexts. Of course, it would always be possible to claim that the poem is a failure, even to the extent that it is not a work of literature at all, but Housman is obviously well loved by the general public, and respected by a number of outstanding critics – John Bayley and Christopher Ricks, for example. Philip Larkin[8] quotes this very poem in support of his contention that 'no one else has reiterated his single message so plangently', and Julian Barnes even selects it as his favourite poem. He justifies his response as follows:

> Housman sets orderly form against disorderly despair: his pessimism is epic, astringent, untrammelled, unmatchable. You get pretty glum at the notion that life's light is snapped off, that an eternity of non-existence gapes? Yield, then, to someone who can't even decide which is worse, being alive or being dead. Four-line poems are usually squibs, products of some brief, bright idea; 'More Poems XXVII' is the opposite, a sauce reduction of the broth of despair. Housman pointedly rhymes three of his four lines, thus throwing extra weight on the unrhymed word *worse*.[9]

To me it seems clear that an adequate response to the poem *demands* a thoughtful reflection on the truth of its *Weltbild.* Surely Housman wants us to reflect on his view of life, wants us to compare it with our own, wants us to notice how it contrasts with Christianity and blithe hedonism, wants us to feel the superior force and truth of his own vision? If some people say they love the poem because of its Heracleitian weight and finality, or others say that they find it insignificant, merely the self-pitying whine of an elderly adolescent striking the *lacrimae rerum* note, am I obliged to answer that these have no bearing on the poem's quality *as a poem*? Does this mean aesthetic discussion will have to be restricted to matters of rhyme, rhythm, diction and imagery? Housman's romanticized pessimism has been the object of much explicit critical disparagement, but it is worth observing that disagreement can be expressed in forms other than critical prose. Parody can be one way of expressing dissent, and Housman has attracted a good deal: Hugh Kingsmill's 'What, still alive at twenty-two, / A clean, upstanding chap like you?' is probably the best known example.[10] If poems make no claims to present general truths, then it is hard to see why poets as well as critics should feel the urge to express their disagreement.

I think Lamarque and Olsen would be less inclined to play down the role of truth and argument if they also considered what goes under the inadequate name of *belles lettres*. By this I mean such non-fiction as the essays by Montaigne, Bacon, Steele, Addison, Johnson, Lamb, Hazlitt, Leigh Hunt, Emerson, Carlyle, Stevenson, Arnold, Huxley and Orwell, and various longer works by de Quincy, Borrow and Thoreau. These works are not just useful adjuncts to literature (like Mayhew's *London Labour and the London Poor*); nor are they works which are usually read as literature, but were actually written as contributions to some other subject (like Gibbon's *Decline and Fall*). They were frequently written as literature, and they are now virtually never classified in any other way. For the most part, they do not present themselves as fictions, and are full of general observations about human nature, God, the universe, politics, and all the other things novelists and poets are inclined to generalize about.

(Interestingly, some of these prose writings begin to develop a fictional element: Steele and Addison's Sir Roger de Coverley and Mr Spectator are cases in point, and Arnold's Arminius grew out of his essay 'My Countrymen'.[11]) If one started to think about literature by considering these works, then moved on to poems of exposition and argument (like Sir John Davies' 'Nosce Teipsum' or Kipling's 'If'), and only then on to lyrics, plays and novels, there would be much less temptation to cut literature adrift from truth, and what Wordsworth called the knowledge which all men carry about with them.[12]

Lamarque and Olsen largely concern themselves with general propositions in novels, but even here their arguments do not seem wholly convincing. I do not see why a novelist should not just throw off an aphorism which, at the beginning of a work, may simply be a striking call to attention, or which, in the middle, may be prompted simply by what has gone before. Not every general statement functions like an epigraph, as the following passages from Edith Wharton's *The House of Mirth* show:

> [Grace Stepney] had in truth no abstract propensity to malice: she did not dislike [Lily Bart] because the latter was brilliant and predominant, but because she thought that Lily disliked her. *It is less mortifying to believe oneself unpopular than insignificant, and vanity prefers to assume that indifference is a latent form of unfriendliness.* Even such scant civilities as Lily accorded to Mr Rosedale would have made Miss Stepney her friend for life: but how could she see that such a friend was worth cultivating?

> Lily's visit to the Dorsets had resulted, for both, in the discovery that they could be of use to one another: and *the civilized instinct finds a subtler pleasure in making use* of *its antagonist than in confounding him.*[13]

Neither of the italicized general propositions prompts us to see, or summarizes, a theme of the novel. They are occasioned, of course, by incidents that have just occurred, but their ramifications do not extend beyond these. I would not, however, regard these remarks as *worthless* from the literary point of view simply because they do not embody central themes in the text. It also seems odd that if some of these remarks were collected in a book of aphorisms, then on Lamarque and Olsen's analysis they *do* become asserted. It seems counter-intuitive that Edith Wharton should not assert her remarks when she pens them in her own person, but that she *should* come to assert them years after her death when they are put into another book edited by somebody else.

It would be dangerous critical practice to assume that the only literary function of a general proposition, especially one in a prominent position, is to point up the central themes of a work. Is it so clear that the contrast between happy, and unhappy families is the most important theme of *Anna Karenina*? Is this novel notably richer in examples of many, similar happy families and many dissimilar unhappy families than other novels of the period? Is that how we remember it? When Tolstoy wrote the novel he said his intention was 'to represent the woman as not guilty, but merely, pitiable'.[14] Of course, this remark need not be authoritative. It is possible that Tolstoy incorrectly summarized his own novel, modified his intention, or simply failed to carry it out. It is striking, however, that most of the critical debate about the novel centres on the issue Tolstoy identifies. One of the first essays on the novel in English, Matthew Arnold's, spent most of its time arguing that Anna was at fault for breaking her marriage vows, and it is Anna's agony and suicide we all remember. It should be odd, on Lamarque and Olsen's view, that this theme receives no comparable general proposition in such a high-profile position.

If the function of general propositions in a novel is to alert us to themes and dramatic particulars then there is no need for them to take the universal form. 'All nineteenth-century Russian families are alike …', or 'All aristocratic nineteenth-century Russian families in this novel are alike …' would serve as equally good openings to *Anna Karenina.* 'It is a truth acknowledged by all English people of late Georgian times, that a single man in possession of a good fortune …' would introduce the reader to *Pride and Prejudice* just as efficiently. However, it seems essential, and is clearly part of the author's intention in using the universal form, that these propositions should refer beyond the pages of the novel and embrace the general experience of humanity. This is important because novelists will often want to show what aspects of their characters' behaviour are unique to the individual, and which are typical of human nature generally.

If a general proposition is just straightforwardly false – 'Failure always improves the moral character', 'Short men fear heights; fat men don't' – and it is not ironic, asserted by an unreliable narrator, etc., then this can only point to the writer's lack of psychological penetration. This in its turn can only damage a novel's literary standing. Of course, some general propositions are pretty vague and metaphorical ('The past is a foreign country, they do things differently there'), and one cannot imagine what kind of proof or evidence could possibly tell for or against them. On the other hand, 'All happy families …' *does* look the kind of remark which could be refuted by reflection, further experience of life, watching documentaries, reading sociological reports and other novels.

In fact, I am not at all sure that Tolstoy's observation is true. It is surely possible to imagine a large number of different ways in which a family can be happy. There are those which are always laughing and joking; those which live a life of quiet, harmonious contentment; those whose members seem to bicker a lot but hold one another in deep affection; those which consist of separate, tolerant individuals who give one another plenty of space, and so on. The second half of Tolstoy's proposition has more going for it, but I should have thought that the varieties of unhappiness are permutations of four basic archetypes (taciturn, rowing, unaffectionate and backstabbing) and, just to be intolerably flat-footed for a moment, that there are certainly not as many varieties of unhappiness as there are unhappy families although of course the *causes* of the unhappiness may be more various. To a very limited extent these considerations make me think less well of the novel. I shall therefore be pleased if I come across evidence to show that unhappiness is more diverse than I can imagine at the moment, and that the forms of happiness I have listed share common factors I cannot currently see.

A general proposition in literature is like a general proposition anywhere: if there are no special reasons for thinking otherwise, it is asserted, and it means what it says. It should be evaluated for its interest, and part of that evaluation will involve consideration of its truth-value. If it also organizes our perception of a text, then that is even better, but it does not *have* to.

III

The main difficulty I experience with Lamarque and Olsen's discussion of propositions *implied* by works of literature is that there is something seriously askew about their main example. The truth-value of 'The best human hopes and aspirations are always thwarted by forces beyond human control', which they use on at least half a dozen occasions, *does* seem inessential to an understanding of the Lydgate story in *Middlemarch.* This, however, is not because of its status as a general proposition implied by a work of literature, but because it does not emerge naturally, from either the story or the authors' more detailed analyses of it.

Lydgate's tragedy is rooted in his character, and, as Aristotle argued,[15] we are at least partly responsible for our characters. Lydgate is therefore at least partially responsible for his own eventual destruction. He is an intelligent man of high principle, but he is conceited ('Lydgate's conceit was of the arrogant sort, never simpering, never impertinent, but massive in its claims' [M:149][16]); his intelligence is not of the kind that can operate easily in some of the more important areas of everyday life ('that distinction of mind did not penetrate his feeling and judgement about furniture, or women, or the desirability of its being known (without his telling) that he was better born than other country surgeons' [M:150]); he thinks very little about money although he assumes he will always live well ('it had never occurred to him that he should live in any other than what he would have called an ordinary way, with green glasses for hock, and excellent waiting at table' [M:348]); and he is tactless and high-handed in his treatment of the ordinary townsfolk (for example, his comments on Plymdale's literary annual [M:270]).

Above all, Lydgate has a notion that women are light and charming creatures whose central function is to ease and soothe the lives of serious men ('[he thought he had found perfect womanhood] who would create order in the home and accounts with still magic, yet keep her fingers ready, to touch the lute and transform life into romance at any moment; who was instructed to the true womanly limit and not a hair's-breadth beyond – docile, therefore, and ready to carry out behests which came from beyond that limit' [M:352]). He has already had one disastrous *amour* when he fell in love with, and passionately defended the innocence of, Mme Laure, a French actress who later admits to murdering her husband because she was bored with him. Consequently, when Lydgate ill-advisedly marries Rosamond Vincy and slides into serious debt, we can hardly think that these developments are unexpected. The forces that destroy him are not beyond human control; they are not even beyond his control. I shall therefore substitute the old tragic insight 'Admirable but arrogant men can sometimes be brought down by fundamental faults in their character' for the proposition which Lamarque and Olsen derive from the story.

Once we see how an implied proposition connects with the detail of a story, we can see that the truth of implied propositions is even more important than the truth of stated propositions. When an author wants to summarize the themes of his work – and this can be one reason for asserting a general proposition – there is no reason why his summary must be infallible. Sometimes, as I suggested in my discussion of Tolstoy, what the author says and what he shows are quite different. According to Blake, Milton in *Paradise Lost* was of the Devil's party without knowing it (i.e., Milton's general condemnations of Satan and his cronies are at variance with the overwhelming imaginative sympathy he shows when he describes the dramatic details of their anguish); and no one can read the moral which Coleridge added to *The Rime of the Ancient Mariner* ('He prayeth best, who loveth best / All things both great and small') without feeling that it is totally inadequate to the complexity of the story.[17] If a stated proposition is false or silly then this need have very little implication for a work's value, as the rest of it may be perfectly true and serious. If, however, the proposition actually *implied* by a work is false or silly, then this will infect large tracts of the work: in all likelihood the concrete incidents will be imperfectly imagined, the drama forced, the motives implausible. Accordingly, the discovery of such a proposition could only have serious implications for the way we value a work.

IV

A surprising feature of *Truth, Fiction and Literature* is that the authors do not test their no-truth theory against works of literature which contain or presuppose serious falsehoods. This is not just a matter of general propositions of the kind discussed above, but of particular concrete incidents which turn out to be inaccurately described or impossible. The authors offer only a few brief remarks:

> It is not part of the literary stance to test the work for a percentage of false statements. Indeed, the skill with which all author moulds and changes historical facts to suit artistic purpose is an object of praise not of censure. When Shakespeare in *Julius Caesar* moves Caesar's victory over Pompey's sons to 45 BC this is no ground for artistic criticism. [297]

It is quite possible that Shakespeare moved the date of Caesar's victory intentionally; but what of straightforward errors? Soon after the publication of *Middlemarch*, a London surgeon pointed out to George Eliot that she describes Lydgate's eyes as *dilated* with the effects of opium, whereas under the influence of opium the pupils *contract.* Even though the eyes can be wide while the pupils are contracted, Eliot felt sufficiently uncomfortable with the relevant passages to alter them in a later edition.[18] She clearly thought even such a minor error was a blemish, otherwise her desire to correct it is inexplicable.

There is a more serious error in Golding's *Lord of the Flies.* Jack's group of hunters on the tropical island steal the shortsighted Piggy's glasses so that they can light fires. Without his glasses Piggy can hardly see, so he fails, for example, to see and avoid the rock with which Jack and his gang finally murder him. This is a crucial incident in the plot, as it signals the moment when all the constraints of civilization are finally cast off. The difficulty, however, is that the correction of myopia requires concave lenses. These diffuse rather than concentrate the sun's rays and therefore cannot be used for lighting fires; indeed, you would have much more chance of setting fire to a branch by exposing it to direct sunlight without any lens at all. The error is almost impossible to put right. Golding could hardly make Piggy longsighted because it would be very difficult to see how this could be an important disadvantage – one which is worth facing serious danger to overcome – on an island where there is no reading matter and no work requiring delicate visual discriminations close to the body.[19]

Sometimes factual errors are nearly fatal, as at the beginning of Larkin's poem 'Absences':

> Rain patters on a sea that tilts and sighs.
> Fast running floors, collapsing into hollows,
> Tower suddenly, spray-haired. Contrariwise,
> A wave drops like a wall: another follows,
> Wilting and scrambling, tirelessly at play
> Where there are no ships and no shallows.[20]

In 1961, Larkin received a letter from an oceanographer, Frank Evans, pointing out an important mistake:

> When I first read the poem … I thought: he's got his images wrong. Like so many people who walk along the shore and watch the breakers rolling in he thinks that waves in the ocean do the same. But it is only waves coming in to the beach that roll over and drop like a wall; offshore, no matter how big the waves are, when they break the water just spills down the front. It is the size not the shape of the deep water waves that changes with the wind strength. Whether in storms or summer breezes makes no difference to the profile of the breaking waves.[21]

Larkin was understandably upset by this. He replied to Evans as follows: 'I was confusing two kinds of waves …. This makes nonsense of dropping like a wall, if they in fact never slope more than 1 in 7. I hope not many of my readers are oceanographers.'[22] Later, he added a note to an American edition of the poem: '[my confusion] seriously damaged the poem from a technical viewpoint. I am sorry about this, but I do not see how to amend it now.' Larkin could have replied that this error did not affect the poem from a literary point of view, but I think we can all sympathize with his initial hope that not too many of his readers were oceanographers, and his final, commendably honest, decision to admit to non-oceanographers that the error seriously mars his poem.

The errors of Golding and Larkin strike me as damaging because their work no longer harmonizes with the world as we know it. We are asked to visualize the *jeux de vagues* where there are no shallows, and yet the kind of wave described is *only* found where there are shallows; similarly, we are asked to imagine circumstances where concave lenses focus light when they can *only* cause light to diverge. Somehow, we can never be quite comfortable with these works again because, while we read, we have to make a conscious effort to suppress the knowledge that what they describe is impossible. With Larkin's poem, in particular, imagery becomes thin and intermittent, and then stops altogether.

It is worth noticing, however, that the damage these errors inflict is not as severe as it would be if the two works belonged to some non-literary *genre*. Suppose that 'Absences' and the plot of *Lord of the Flies* had been specially written for a school physics textbook, as concrete examples to make the laws governing lenses and waves accessible to an adolescent audience. If, after publication, the errors were then pointed out. the book would have to be withdrawn or emended; it would be too misleading to stay in the public domain. Truth, or at least the well founded belief that a statement is true, is a necessary but insufficient condition for reading non-fictional writings as non-fiction. In fiction, truth is neither necessary nor sufficient for literary merit, since our interest can always be sustained by a work's wit, energy, epic sweep, pathos or humour, etc., but truth is always a virtue and falsehood always a vice.[23]

V

At the moment, the academy is particularly sensitive to inaccurate portrayals of *classes of people*, and complaints about T.S. Eliot's anti-semitism, Dickens' portraits of women or Mark Twain's portrayal of negroes are too familiar to require documentation. The most commonly voiced complaint, however, and the charge which is most damaging to a writer's literary standing, is that his vision of reality and human nature in general is fundamentally flawed. This is unsurprising given that the hope of discovering profound truths about human nature, unlike discovering scientific truths about waves and lenses, has always been one of the traditional reasons for reading literature. Here, for example, is Leavis on late James:

> [The later James] came to … live the life of a spiritual recluse: a recluse in a sense in which not only no novelist but no good artist of any kind can

> afford to become one. His technique came to exhibit an unhealthy vitality of undernourishment and etiolation. His technical preoccupation, to put it another way, lost its balance, and instead of being the sharp register of his finest perceptions, as informed and related by his fullest sense of life, became something that took his intelligence out of its true focus and blunted his sensitiveness .... Correlated with this tendency is that manifested in the extraordinary specialized living of his characters.[24]

And here, making an interestingly, related point but from the opposite direction, is Lionel Trilling on Sherwood Anderson:

> The nature of the falsehood seems to lie in this – that Anderson's affirmation of life by love, passion, and freedom had, paradoxically enough, the effect of quite negating life, making it grey, empty and devoid of meaning. We are quite used to hearing that this is what excessive intellectation can do; we are not so often warned that emotion, if it is of a certain kind, can be similarly destructive. Yet when feeling is understood as an answer, a therapeutic, when it becomes a sort of critical tool and is conceived of as excluding other activities of life, it can make the world seem abstract and empty. Love and passion, when considered as they are by Anderson as a means of attack upon the order of the respectable world, can contrive a world which is actually without love and passion and is not worth being free in.[25]

At the beginning of this passage, Trilling chooses to express himself in the language of truth and falsehood, but at this level of concreteness metaphors may be more appropriate. Accordingly, he later speaks of therapeutics, critical tools, weapons, and a vision of the world which makes it seem empty and abstract. Perceptual metaphors dominate the passage from Leavis: James' technical preoccupations could not register his finest perceptions; they took his intelligence out of its true focus; they blunted his sensitiveness. Whatever the metaphor, the basic message is the same: these writers are not true to life and they are the worse for it. They either do not see the world as it is, or they see only part of the world as it is and mistake it for the whole.

These quotations from Trilling and Leavis are paradigmatic passages of criticism. They were intended to assess Anderson and James as novelists, and they strike me as thoughtful, tactful, true, and well supported (in the rest of the essays) by carefully analysed examples. Nothing, it seems to me, could be more relevant to the task for which they were intended. However, according to Lamarque and Olsen, these passages are not relevant to the literary evaluation of Anderson and James, and to suppose they are is to commit a kind of category mistake. This strikes me as far too extreme, and entails that most of the world's criticism, especially that written before the second half of the twentieth century, is going to be based on a category mistake as well.[26]

There are works that express philosophies which, according to many critics, are more harmful and erroneous than those in James and Anderson – the right-wing novels of Ayn Rand, for example. And it is easy to imagine works which assert or enact ideas which are more vicious and implausible still. If someone wrote a novel attempting to show that nudism makes you intelligent, or that cruelty to children makes them outgoing and well adjusted, then it is unlikely to be published, let alone read or remembered. How could the people in such novels possibly feel or be motivated by anything remotely human? How could their behaviour be coherent? How could we possibly be interested in seeing such ideas enacted, explored, developed and imaginatively entertained? We shall not find such controversies about literary works, not because truth is irrelevant to literary evaluation, but because truth is so important that obviously idiotic ideas automatically debar the books which express them from the category of literature.

This makes Lamarque and Olsen's attempt to detach interest from truth look as unpromising as their attempt to detach meaning from truth. They write:

> Judgements about interest are made with regard to content and are independent of judgements concerning truth. What gives the Lydgate story in *Middlemarch* depth is not so much that it implies a true proposition, but that it can be interpreted as about humanly interesting concerns – for example, the nature and consequences of noble human desires. The thematic statement that noble human desires and aspirations are thwarted by forces beyond an individual's control gives focus to the treatment in the novel. No doubt a different artistic treatment could present a theme of equal interest albeit formulated in a proposition which is the precise negation of this one. [329–30]

There are certain propositions that a work of literature could enact ('Hope triumphs over adversity') when an equally fine work could enact the opposite, but again this does not show that truth is *irrelevant* to literary evaluation; it merely shows how difficult it is to establish what the truth *is*. The point about negation, however, does not apply to Lamarque and Olsen's proposition about *Middlemarch*. If we take its complete negation to be 'The best human hopes and aspirations are never thwarted by forces beyond human control', then it seems most unlikely that any serious work of literature could ever embody it. It is best if a work of literature enacts a fresh and profound insight into human nature; we are happy enough if a work endorses an obvious truth, but no work which embodies an obvious, glaring falsehood could be placed on a par with

King Lear and *War and Peace*. A work which enacted 'The best human hopes and aspirations are never thwarted ...' could only be a puerile fantasy.[27]

If we move from the evaluation of particular works to the kind of general vices encapsulated in standard critical predicates, then the importance of truth becomes more evident still. Words like 'sentimental', 'unrealistic', 'improbable', 'priggish', 'immature', 'adolescent', and so forth all require some notion of truth or adequacy to the facts for their analysis. Anthony Savile, for example, argues persuasively that the sentimentalist either distorts the world in a way which gives him direct pleasure (by editing out faults or projecting false virtues), or distorts it in a way which allows him to have a more favourable view of himself.[28] Thus Dickens' portrayal of Paul Dombey is sentimental because no child was ever so selfless, precocious, religious and sweet; and no child's death was ever so bland, unmessy and ennobling. What would criticism without such predicates look like?

VI

Three important factors relevant to the significance of falsehood in evaluative criticism remain to be discussed: when the false assertion (or assertion presupposing a falsehood) was made; why it was made; the *genre* that contains it.

We have no difficulty with Homer believing in his gods, but when Yeats decides to make an earnest attempt to believe in fairies we think him seriously silly. Similarly, believing the earth was made in 4004 BC was quite a different thing in the seventeenth century from believing that piece of information now. We have access to all kinds of techniques and information to which the seventeenth century did not have access. Not to use them lays us, but not of course the seventeenth-century writer, open to charges of laziness and incompetence. We may not believe in the factual truth of a writer's *Weltbild,* but it must at least be the kind of view which a mature, intelligent person could have believed in, i.e., not *that* remote from what the best evidence available to the writer showed the truth to be. It is striking that proposed general truths about human nature seem to be the least subject to historical variation, and that there are few excuses to offer when writers, however ancient and benighted, get them wrong.

Literature is not always concerned with unvarnished truth. It will frequently distort a truth, exaggerate it, simplify it in order to bring out an underlying pattern, stimulate our critical faculties by presenting half-truths or shock us into furious disagreement by asserting outright lies. It is clear, however, that works of literature gain their interest and value from their *relation* to truth, and their ultimate purpose is to make the reader see the world more clearly.[29] Frequently, when we are reading a text, we have to bear in mind both the way the world is portrayed in the text, and the way it actually is.

In order to evaluate the significance of literal falsehoods, we also need to be clear about the author's intention, and this can sometimes be difficult to establish. Elizabeth Bishop, for example, appears to suppose that there is such a thing as an 80-watt lightbulb:[30]

> Meanwhile the eighty-watt bulb
> betrays us all,
>
> discovering the concern
> within our stupefaction.

Is she making a mistake or a point? She may know perfectly well that there is no such thing, in which case she may be implying that we are never likely to be betrayed; or she may have imagined that the poem's events occur in a dream or hallucination. Clearly the poem cannot be judged responsibly before one has taken a careful look at the relevant biographical evidence, although this, of course, need not provide a conclusive answer.

How damaging an error or distortion is will also depend on the literary *genre* that contains it, as we clearly have different standards for historical novels, satires, realistic novels, science-fiction adventures, farces, romances, works of magical realism, fairy stories, myths, surrealist jottings, and so forth.

In the case of historical novels and films, for instance, reading a historical novel because you want to find out what living in a certain era was like strikes me as a perfectly reasonable *literary* reason for reading it. We do not usually mind if an author intentionally telescopes events or writes minor characters in or out – although it has become conventional to signal such changes in a preface to stop readers being misled. We also tolerate a certain amount of historical error so long as it has no serious moral implications, although good novelists have high standards in these matters. In *Barnaby Rudge* a man is hanged for passing bad £1 notes. Someone wrote to Dickens that at the time his novel is set there were no £1 notes: notes under £5 were not issued until 1797. Dickens checked the fact, altered the text of his novel, and wrote to thank the correspondent for his information.[31] Clearly, historical accuracy counts for something.

However, we do mind if events or characters are changed in such a way as seriously to distort history and make unjustifiable moral points. Paul Bew, professor of history at Queen's University, Belfast, has recently criticized Neil Jordan's film about Michael Collins because of its historical inaccuracies. In one scene, for example, we see the Black and Tans firing machine-guns from armoured cars at a football crowd in Dublin's Croke Park, whereas in reality there were no machine-guns and no armoured cars. In another we see an IRA agent called Ned Broy beaten to death by the British, whereas in actual fact he lived for another 60 years. On the basis of such distortions, Bew accuses the film of having that cruel self-absorption spliced with sentimentality that is characteristic of fascist art.[32]

We can also object if we feel that the whole character and atmosphere of an era has been fundamentally misrepresented, even when there are no straightforward factual inaccuracies. Pat Barker's trilogy about the First World War (which became famous when the last volume, *The Ghost Road*, won the Booker Prize in 1995) has inspired an instructive controversy. Discussing the book in the *TLS*, Ben Sheppard writes:

> [Barker's] exploitation of the contemporary codes of gender, class and sexuality is rooted in post-feminist pieties and the chic abstractions of modern historians, not in solid historical originals. Its tone is, nearly always, false. It would help if Billy Prior [the central character] was a credible character, rather than an assemblage of attributes – working-class, officer, bisexual, embittered about war, yet determined to return to it. His class attitudes are those of a confidently stroppy grammar-school boy of the 1950s, worlds away from the likes of Wilfred Owen and R.C. Sherriff who emulated, rather than mocked, public-school officers. His promiscuity, the occasion for frequent passages of airport-novel sex – is grounded (needless to say) in childhood abuse …. The falseness of this strand goes far beyond asking us to believe that Prior has read Freud, and is familiar with terms like negative transference, in 1917 when only Bloomsbury intellectuals were aware of psycho-analysis. Prior … is a vehicle for modern baggage about shrinks and psychotherapy. In 1917 … the whole subject of nerves was treated with jocular dismissal or alcoholic denial, and discussing your state of mind was not the respectable activity it has since become least of all by anyone of working-class origin, for whom mental illness carried the horror and stigma of the madhouse. Things were still pre-Freudian.[33]

Now if these charges are accurate, they seem to me to damage Barker's trilogy as novels. I suppose one might say 'I am reading *The Ghost Road* as a novel, not a history book', but this would be like saying 'When I read *Hamlet*

I am not interested in psychological insights', or 'I am reading Keats for the sound, not the sense'. The genre of the historical novel is, amongst other things, supposed to render a certain kind of historical awareness. If it does not, it may still survive, but that will mean it will not sustain the full level of imaginative engagement. If you imagine trying to re-read Endo's novels about the Christianization of Japan after you had discovered that there never were any Christians in Japan before 1800, or that all the Japanese were happily converted in a fortnight, you might still manage the task, but they would be different novels.

The same applies to other novels based on real contemporary people or set in real geographical places. Consider the following: a novel set in contemporary Harlem which shows the life lived there to be one of cocoa and jumble sales; a play about the Krays, showing that they were motivated by entirely philanthropic concerns; a satire based on Tony Blair's vast nose and advanced age. These works would be too remote from the truth to be interesting in themselves (although the pathologies of their authors would be worth investigating), and they would have to be pushed quietly to one side.

* * *

Conveying the truth has always been viewed as one of the central values of literature, and while Lamarque and Olsen have made me seriously question this, they do not ultimately say anything which makes me think it false.[34]

Notes

1 All page references in this style are to Peter Lamarque and Stein Haugom Olsen, *Truth, Fiction and Literature* (Oxford: Clarendon Press, 1994).

2 Paul de Man (ed.), *The Selected Poetry of Keats* (New York: New American Library, 1966), p. 254. Here is a small sample of essays and books which contain discussions of the issue: J. Middleton Murry, *Studies in Keats, New and Old* (Oxford: Oxford University Press, 1939), pp. 60–61; M. Dickstein, *Keats and his Poetry: a Study in Development* (Chicago: Chicago University Press, 1971), p. 32n and pp. 227–8: K. Burke, 'Symbolic Motion in a Poem by Keats', in C.S. Fraser (ed.), *Keats: Odes* (London: Macmillan, 1971), pp. 113–21: M. Levinson, *Keats' Life of Allegory: the Origin of a Style* (Oxford: Blackwell, 1988), p. 178; H. Vendler, *The Odes of John Keats* (Harvard: Harvard University Press, 1983), pp. 131–6, 139, 147–51.

3 This information is taken from de Man, *Selected Poetry*, pp. 253–4.

4 Robert Gittings (ed.), *Letters of John Keats* (Oxford: Oxford University Press, 1970), p. 42.

5 L. Trilling, 'The Poet as Hero: Keats in his Letters', in *The Opposing Self* (Oxford: Oxford University Press, 1980), p. 32. This is, of course, only one way of trying to make sense of Keats' remark. Another promising line of enquiry is suggested by Einstein's claim that the general theory of relativity had to be true because it was so beautiful. For a full discussion of this criterion of scientific truth see J.W. McAllister, *Beauty and Revolution in Science* (Ithaca: Cornell University Press, 1996).

6 See E. Mendelson, *Early Auden* (New York: Viking Press, 1981), pp. 326–7.

7 J. Sparrow (ed.), *A.E. Housman. Collected Poems* (Harmondsworth: Penguin, 1956), p. 187.

8 P. Larkin, *Required Writing* (London: Faber & Faber, 1983), p. 264.

9 Julian Barnes, 'Favourite Lines', *Sunday Telegraph Review*, 25 February 1996, p. 14.

10 Quoted in Sparrow, *A.E.Housman*, p. 2.

11 See my 'Arnold and the Socratic Personality', this volume, pp. 73–91.

12 In 'Preface to the Lyrical Ballads' (1802) in Stephen Gill (ed.), *William Wordsworth* (Oxford: Oxford University Press, 1984), p. 606.

13 Edith Wharton, *The House of Mirth* (Harmondsworth: Penguin, 1986), pp. 122 and 128 (my italics).

14 *Diaries* of *Sofya Andreyevna Tolstoya 1860–91* (Leningrad, 1928), p. 32, quoted in Ernest J. Simmons, *Tolstoy* (London: Routledge & Kegan Paul, 1973), p. 94.

15 Aristotle, *Ethics*, ed. J. Barnes (Harmondsworth; Penguin, 1976), pp. 111–41.

16 'M' followed by a page number indicates George Eliot, *Middlemarch* (Harmondsworth: Penguin, 1986).

17 Blake, *The Marriage of Heaven and Hell*, Section II, 'The Voice of the Devil', in *Blake: Complete Writings*, ed. Geoffrey Keynes (Oxford: Oxford University Press, 1989), p. 150. The quotation from *The Rime of the Ancient Mariner* is from Part VII, stanza 23. It can be found in *Selected Poems of S.T. Coleridge*, ed. James Reeves (London: Heinemann, 1988), p. 44. This stanza was added to the poem after the first edition when Mrs Barbauld complained that besides being implausible the ballad 'had no moral'. See S.T. Coleridge, table talk of 31 May 1830, *The Table Talk and Omniana of Samuel Taylor Coleridge, with Additional Table Talk from Allsop's Recollections etc.*, ed. H.N. Coleridge (Oxford: Oxford University Press, 1917), quoted in Norman Fruman, *Coleridge and the Damaged Archangel* (New York: George Braziller, 1971), p. 354.

18 I take this case from Christopher Ricks, 'Literature and the Matter of Fact', in his *Essays in Appreciation* (Oxford: Clarendon Press, 1996), pp. 280–310, at p. 282. The whole of this brilliant essay is essential reading for anyone interested in these topics.

19 For more detail about this case, see Ricks, 'Literature,' pp. 306–9.

20 Philip Larkin, *Collected Poems* (London: Faber & Faber, 1988), p. 49.

21 Larkin, *Selected Letters of Philip Larkin*, ed. Anthony Thwaite (London: Faber & Faber, 1992), p. 332.

22 Larkin, *Selected Letters*, p. 332.

23 This is also the view endorsed by Ricks, 'Literature', p. 283.

24 F.R. Leavis, *The Great Tradition* (London: Chatto & Windus, 1979), p. 165.

25 Lionel Trilling, 'Sherwood Anderson', in his *The Liberal Imagination* (Oxford: Oxford University Press, 1981), pp. 21–32, at pp. 26–7.

26 The following are further characteristic examples of essays attacking the untruth, perversity and inadequacy of an author's vision of reality: George Eliot, 'Silly Novels by Lady Novelists', in A.S. Byatt and N. Warren (eds), *George Eliot: Selected Essays, Poems and Other Writings* (Harmondsworth: Pengun, 1990), pp. 140–63: Henry James, 'The

Limitations of Dickens', in M.D. Zabel and L.H.P. Powers (eds), *The Portable Henry James* (Harmondsworth: Penguin, 1977), pp. 429–35: D.S. Savage, 'The Fatalism of George Orwell', in B. Ford (ed.), *The New Pelican Guide to English Literature*, Vol. VIII, *The Present* (Harmondsworth: Penguin, 1983), pp. 29–46.

27 This point is also made in Greg Currie's review of *Truth, Fiction and Literature*, in *Mind*, 104 (1995), pp. 911–13.

28 Anthony Savile, *The Test of Time* (Oxford: Clarendon Press, 1982), p. 341.

29 This point is made persuasively by Currie, *Mind* 104, 1995, p. 912.

30 This is pointed out by Ricks, 'Literature,' p. 285.

31 I take this information from Ricks, 'Literature,' p. 305.

32 Quoted in 'How Hollywood Blurs the Facts on Ireland', *Daily Telegraph*, 21 October 1996, p. 7.

33 B. Sheppard, 'Digging up the Past', *The Times Literary Supplement*, 22 March 1996, pp. 12–13.

34 I would like to thank Peter Lamarque and Marie McGinn for extensive discussions of this chapter, and anonymous referees of *The Philosophical Quarterly* for their written comments. I would also like to thank the members of the audience who commented on the paper when it was read as a guest lecture at an Open University Summer School in August 1996, particularly Nigel Warburton, Chris Belshaw, Derek Matravers and Nick McAdoo.

Chapter 7

The Definition of 'Art'

Postwar attempts to give a general account of art have tried to move away from the traditional approaches of Kant and Schopenhauer.[1] The most widely discussed theories have tried to show either that a work of art is a symbol, or forms part of a symbol system (Langer, Goodman); or that it can be identified by its place in a social institution (Danto, Dickie); or that no general account of art's nature and purpose is possible (Weitz, Kennick).[2] Since the early 1970s, however, Roger Scruton[3] has attempted to sharpen the traditional account of art in terms of an aesthetic attitude, and the appearance of two books – one by Michael Mitias and one edited by him[4] – indicate a general revival of interest in the notion. In this paper I try to refine the idea of an aesthetic attitude still further by paying particular attention to one of the central difficulties that have beset aesthetic attitude theories hitherto: the role which propositional beliefs and personal experience can play in our appreciation of art.

The aesthetic attitude is not a feeling or an emotion (although it might give rise to either of these) but is rather a mode of attention or contemplation of an object of sight, hearing or – to a lesser extent – touch. We regard these as the 'aesthetic senses' because their objects have *parts* and an element of internal complexity.[5] Because of this, the imagination is directly involved in the perception of such objects from the very first, and the role it plays in patterning and arranging what is seen becomes evident when we consider ambiguous figures.

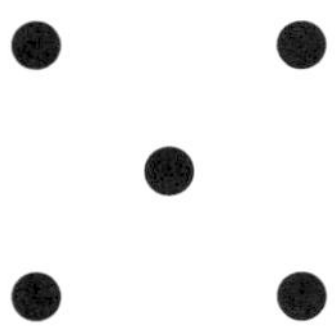

Figure 7.1

This pattern can either be seen as an upright pyramid looked down on from above, or as an inverted pyramid seen from the same position. When we switch aspects, the dots themselves do not undergo physical alteration, and it seems natural to assume that what does change is the interpretation our own imagination projects onto them. It is quite clear that the phenomenon of 'seeing as' or 'hearing as' requires a certain degree of complexity in the object perceived.[6]

From these points, two important consequences follow. First, the possibility that works of art can have the power to express and to depict. One dot alone cannot make a map, and it can only become part of a map when it comes to hold a spatial relationship with at least one other dot.[7] It is for this reason that one unextended, amorphous sensation, such as something's taste or smell, cannot depict anything.[8] Second, because an aesthetic object's parts are organized into patterns by the intellect, these patterns can be affected by what is said or shown to us. Consequently, a well-placed critical remark or gesture can actually alter the structure of what we see and hear: where once we heard this note as the last note in the first phrase we now hear it as the first note in the second; where once we saw this picture as a duck we now see it as a rabbit, and so on. It is this feature that ensures it is possible to argue rationally about the quality and nature of even a non-representational work of art, with at least the possibility of winning-over an interlocutor. Where representational art is at issue, it would be natural to expect critical discussion also to concern itself with the relation between the work and the state of affairs it depicts.

Perhaps it would be an exaggeration to say that smells and tastes do not have aspects, or that the locutions 'tasting as' and 'smelling as' do not have a use. After all, there are such things as acquired tastes and professional tea-tasters, and we do ask whether people cannot discern the cheesecake's musty aftertaste or the metallic edge to the wine. But it is undoubtedly true that the scope for persuasion and interpretation is vastly more limited. Moore reports Wittgenstein as saying, '"You can say more" in discussing whether the arrangement of flowers in a bed is "beautiful" than in discussing whether the smell of lilac is so',[9] and it seems most unlikely that a critical remark could bring about a *Gestalt* restructuring of a smell or taste in the way that it could restructure something seen or heard. Consequently, disputes about such simple properties tend to centre not on their intrinsic qualities – their *whatness*, as it were – but on something else we can control by argument, namely the imaginative realization of their associations and origins. Discussions of favourite colours and the like tend to revolve around what they remind us of – this is the colour of the Mediterranean, that is the smell of autumn bonfires – rather than on the intentional objects themselves, which seem too formless for normal critical rhetoric to get a grip on.[10]

The concept of attention also requires some analysis. There are two basic varieties. The first is brought about by an act of will, so it is something I *do*;

the second is something that *happens to me* when I am caught up in the interest of an object. It is attention of the second sort – which I shall call absorption that concerns us in aesthetics. The ideal work of art is something that can absorb us absolutely, so that the mind never wanders and we do not have to remind ourselves to pay attention. This is not to say that the finest works are those which absorb us immediately, or that those which absorb us immediately are the best. On the contrary, Shakespeare and late Beethoven often require much preliminary attention of the first sort, besides the sometimes laborious business of acquiring the correct critical understanding, before they begin to repay our efforts by sustaining attention of the second sort. Cheap music and light fiction on the other hand, being compounded from fragments of an entirely familiar idiom, are immediately accessible to the majority of us, but unlike better works of art they cannot sustain our attention when repeated. The quality of a work of art is decided by the *durability* as well as the intensity of the experience it offers, with durability decidedly the more important factor.

Absorption must be distinguished from involuntary absorption, a condition which arises, for example, when we cannot tear ourselves away from a simply sickening photograph. 'Involuntary' suggests I am absorbed *against* my will – it is pathological, irrational, compulsive – whereas in the aesthetic case my absorption is unwilled but the will is not against it. In the photograph case my will may be too weakened with horror for me to be able to act as I wish, but asked the questions 'Would you rather have looked away? Would you rather not look at it again?', my answer would be 'Yes' on both counts. In the aesthetic case my answer on both occasions would be 'No', for the excellent reason that absorption of this kind does not give rise to, but actually is, one form of enjoyment. Scruton therefore makes an acute point when he observes that pleasure and the aesthetic attitude are internally related, and that we would not understand a man who claimed that he had often experienced this attitude and yet taken no pleasure in it.[11]

Empiricists tended to conceive of pleasure as a form of sensation, but the position is riddled with difficulties: would not such feelings distract us from the activity we were enjoying? If pleasure is a form of sensation or feeling would it not make perfectly good sense to ask whether we were enjoying it or not? Is it merely a contingent fact that the pleasures of golf could not be reproduced by draughts? And so on. Ryle's attention analysis (which I have outlined[12]) not only answers these difficulties, but also answers the question which Anscombe says reduced Aristotle to a babble, namely, 'How can pleasure be identical with and be different from the activity in which pleasure is taken?'[13] Absorption *is* something over and above the activity enjoyed, and yet its transparency guarantees both that it will not distract us from the thing enjoyed, and that enjoying one kind of activity is, as a matter of logic, a different psychological state from enjoying every other.

I can certainly bring the first kind of attention, willed attention, to bear on any kind of object, but since this attitude is not enjoyable in itself, it would only be a rational thing to do if it were used as a means to some future satisfaction. I cannot, however, become engrossed in just anything, any more than I can decide to be fond of someone or to love them. The mark of creative success, therefore, which makes the intentional production of art objects intelligible, is the production of an object which could hold somebody's attention in the appropriate way.[14] As Cavell puts it:

> [You cannot] contemplate or appreciate or become absorbed in just anything: that an art object is an object which is fit for holding attention, allowing contemplation ... as much determines the nature of art, the criteria of art (what we are going to *call* 'art' and 'criticism of art') as what is fit to sit on determines what we are going to call a 'chair' and 'mending a chair' ... That in certain contexts 'anything and everything' can be ... contemplated ... may be true (although we might try to contemplate a crumpled handkerchief, or become absorbed in a pin – I don't say you *can't*). My point is only that where some special contest required, it must be supposed, imagined.[15]

I assume that what Cavell means here is that it is possible to become absorbed in a pin or a crumpled handkerchief but only as part of a larger aesthetic context or for other than aesthetic reasons. But what distinguishes an aesthetic interest from all others? Traditionally, our contemplation of an object is aesthetic if the object is treated as an 'end in itself'. Let me begin to clarify this notion by considering six sets of reasons for contemplating a picture which do not treat the object aesthetically; my suspicion being that we have trouble understanding aesthetic motivation because we have not brought non-aesthetic reasons into sharp enough focus. Here is the first set.

(I) (a) I am writing the history of the castle represented here, and I want to know if it had a portcullis at the time when this was painted.
(b) I am writing a book about Michelangelo's homosexuality and this is one of his pictures.

In (a) the object of my interest is *the castle itself* and the picture is simply one means amongst others for discovering information about my real interest. As a military historian I will be equally interested in plans, documents, letters and other items of no aesthetic importance which contain information about the castle, in a way that someone who is held by the aesthetic quality of the picture need not be. 'Good source of information about such and such a castle' and 'good picture' *tout court* clearly not the same thing at all. In (b) I am interested in the picture only in so far as it is a source of information about Michelangelo; it is therefore only a *means* to discovering about my real object, although this case will demand some fairly dubious inferences from the content of a work of art to the psychology of the artist which (a) does not require. It is quite possible that the best source of information about Michelangelo's homosexuality will be one of his worst paintings or not a painting at all, and we would expect the biographer *qua* biographer to be more interested in that than in the masterpieces, although presumably it was Michelangelo's fame as an artist that first brought him to the biographer's attention. In both (a) and (b) contemplation of the pictures is a poor substitute for a look at a real castle some centuries back, or for extended contact with Michelangelo, his work, and his *milieu.*

Here are four further reasons which could justify non-aesthetic contemplation.

(II) (c) It was damaged by a suffragette (and I am interested in suffragettes etc.).
(d) It is worth a fortune.
(e) The artist painted it while blindfolded.
(f) It was an exhibit at a famous murder trial.

It is notable that these four share a common feature with (a) and (b), namely that if it were proved beyond a shadow of doubt that it was not *this* picture which the suffragette damaged, or that the picture is not worth a fortune, then the people looking would immediately lose interest. Similarly, if the historian discovers that the castle in the picture is not the one he is writing about, or the biographer discovers that Michelangelo did not paint the picture, then we would expect them to stop looking.

However, imagine someone who is under the impression that *Edmund Ironside* was written by Shakespeare, and who had told us of his profound admiration for that play on account of its depth of characterization, dramatic unity, amplitude of conception etc. If this person immediately stops reading on being shown that it was actually written by one of Shakespeare's contemporaries, then we would have good grounds for supposing that he was lying or self-deceived about his admiration. Normally, we would expect him to carry on reading the play unruffled by the information ('Well, it's good anyway ...'), and we would expect at least some degree of disorientation and perplexity before giving up, but resignedly pushing aside the text without further ado would suggest something fishy. Having the misattribution brought to his attention *may* have alerted him to a certain thinness of imagery and so on, but such explanations are normally seen as feeble rationalizations after the event.

Of course, my initial desire to experience a work may well be stimulated by acquiring a belief about its origin. If, for example, an authority assures me that Shakespeare wrote *The Two Noble Kinsmen*, then that may well be all I need to fetch this volume down from the library shelf. This action would be motivated by some reasonable inductive beliefs having to do with the fact that most of the Shakespeare I have read is interesting and absorbing, and that most of the authority's previous recommendations have turned out to be well grounded. But, in order for these beliefs to be borne out, I must, at a certain stage of my reading, cease to be motivated by them and have my attention held *by the text.* If this comes about then my earlier beliefs will be confirmed, and my industry rewarded with aesthetic pleasure. If this does not happen, then I may decide – because Shakespeare is also usually difficult as well as good – that I have not 'seen what's in it', failed to get a proper grasp on the plot, overlooked some important allusions, misunderstood the tone of some central speeches, and so on. If I work hard at the text by rereading it several times, talking to experts about it, watching a series of performances, and *still* fail to find it rewarding, then I shall probably give up, feeling that it never will be of aesthetic interest to me.

'I am reading this because it is by Shakespeare', could also indicate several other motives. It could mean that I have been told to read all of Shakespeare, or that I want to boast (truthfully) that I have read all of him, or that I want to write his biography, or pass an exam on his work tomorrow. As they stand, such motives are not aesthetic, although the intelligibility of such projects depends on other people valuing aesthetic experience. If, on the other hand, I am reading a play because of my belief that Shakespeare is usually good or because my friends have recommended it, then such a preliminary mode of attention anticipates, and is parasitic upon, genuine aesthetic interest on my part. This willed attention is not yet aesthetic interest, first, because it is quite compatible with being bored stiff, and second, because this kind of attention, unlike genuine aesthetic interest, is only intelligible as a means to some future satisfaction. True aesthetic interest I take to be entirely rational and self-explanatory in its own right.

Clearly, some considerations of aesthetic quality are implicit in (c)–(f); the main interest in looking at a picture which is worth a fortune is to try to see for oneself *why* it is worth a fortune; nobody would be interested in a picture an artist painted blindfolded if it were simply a sludgy daub of meaningless colour; and the better the picture the suffragette damaged the greater would be one's ghoulish desire to look at the results.

Interest in an object simply because it has a weird or unusual story attached to it is not aesthetic, but interest motivated by a strange or unusual appearance is. Indeed, as Bacon observed, 'There is no excellent beauty that hath not some strangeness in the proportion.'[16] Part of the attraction of the *sul ponticello* section at the end of the scherzo of Beethoven's C$^{\#}$ minor quartet, and of the trio section of the minuet of Haydn's 'Sunrise' quartet op. 76 no.4, is their peculiarity, and I return to them frequently with undiminished pleasure. But, notoriously, novelty palls very quickly, and it is because freakishness or weirdness are frequently incapable of *sustaining* interest, that they tend to be held in low esteem. Having seen some of Arcimbardo's paintings composed from fruit and vegetables, and heard Albrechtberger's concerto for Jew's harp and mandora, my curiosity is satisfied, and I have no particular desire to experience them or their ilk again.

A third set of reasons:

(III) (g) I am wondering if it is large enough to cover my wall safe.
(h) I am trying to decide whether the frame is valuable.

Like (a) and (b), this contemplation is motivated by a desire for information, but in this case about the physical object and for practical purposes, rather than about what is represented to satisfy academic curiosity. The reason for looking at the picture (instead of looking up, for example, how much was originally paid for the frame) is that I believe just looking to be the best and most convenient method to hand for discovering the information I want to know. As with all actions designed to discover information, the motive ceases to operate once the information has been secured. Once I have seen what the damaged picture looks like, or seen that the castle has a portcullis, or that the painting is too small to cover my wall safe, I will lose interest in looking at them. A desire for information can explain why you look; it cannot explain why you continue to look once you have it.

The fourth set of reasons:

(IV) (i) Seeing this Rembrandt again takes me back to the time when I first saw it in Paris before the war.
(j) The castle shown here reminds me of the one I stayed in last year.
(k) We saw *Guernica* on our honeymoon; whenever I see it I wonder how things might have turned out if we had not broken up.

As with all the reasons discussed so far, these are quite compatible with aesthetic interest, but if they are my *sole* reason for looking then they are not aesthetic reasons. If the only reason for being interested in a work of art is that it prompts or causes an enjoyable reminiscence then the work is not being treated as an end in itself: once it has served its function, it will be the act of reminiscing that absorbs me and I shall pay only the most minimal attention or no attention at all to the painting itself. The same applies to ruminations or fantasies that are set off by a work but which have little to do with its content. In becoming absorbed in our own thoughts rather than the picture we cease to be aesthetically motivated.

A fifth set of reasons:

(V) (l) When the libido is flagging I always look at this picture.
(m) If I want to work up an appetite I simply look at this picture book's illustrations.
(n) If I do not feel like jogging I look at these pictures of grotesquely fat men to get me going.

Here, as in the previous set, contemplation is merely a prelude to some other activity – sex, exercise or eating. The point of looking at pornography *as* pornography is the arousal of sexual desire, and the natural outcome of sexual desire is sex. If the preliminary act of looking is not followed by sex (as is usually the case), then this will require some explanation in terms of social constraints, personal commitments, the unwillingness of the other party, or whatever. Pornographic photographs or drawings are an inferior *substitute* for real women which effectively prevent sexual desire teaching its normal goal except through masturbation which is itself an inferior substitute. (Preferring real women to pornographic photographs does not require a psychological explanation in a way that a preference for pornography does.) Aesthetic interest, however, does not have a goal over and above looking or listening that is hindered by having to look at representations of objects rather than objects themselves: a look at Van Gogh's *The Potato Eaters* is not an inferior substitute for a look at the group of sullen peasants who sat for it, if there were any such.

The final set:

(VI) (o) An ancestor of mine painted it.
(p) I own it.
(q) It is a picture of my house.

All these reasons concern personal pride, but pride, unlike curiosity or aesthetic interest, is parasitic on some other form of value. In order to understand this feeling we need to know *why* a person takes pride in what he sees. Two conditions are necessary: first, the object must have some connection with the person who feels the emotion; and second, he must *value* it. The usual reason for taking pride in a picture is because of its aesthetic quality, but one could also be proud of it for the kinds of reasons listed in the first two sets. If therefore you discovered that you did not own the picture, or that any of the reasons (a)–(f) were false or founded on falsehoods then interest would lapse unless some other motive (covetousness perhaps) took their place.

These non-aesthetic reasons for looking fall into two groups. (I shall not discuss the sixth set further as that is a special case.) In sets (I) to (III) the person looking was prompted by a desire for knowledge of what the object looked like, of what was represented, of the artist who painted it, or some other facet of its history. In sets (IV) and (V) the person looking was simply engaged in a preliminary to some other activity: fantasizing, reminiscing, eating, sex, jogging. It is clear that in both groups the contemplator treats the picture as a *means* to an end (either practical or purely cognitive), and that at some point he will dispense with the picture having taken from it what he required. But contemplating something as an end in itself entails that the object is never dispensable while interest persists. This is really no more than a tautological truth since if I am interested *in the picture* then, barring special circumstances, my interest in the picture will only lapse when my interest lapses, but if I am only interested in what is represented, the artist, my own practical projects, fantasies etc., then my interest in contemplating the picture can lapse, while continuing to be absorbed by *the very same* practical projects etc. Consequently, two of the points I have mentioned about the aesthetic attitude, viz., that the object contemplated is an end in itself, and that the aesthetic value of the attitude an object supports is determined by that attitude's strength and durability, are not separate, but merely two aspects of the same idea. I shall refer to contemplating something as an end in itself as a 'disinterested' attitude.[17]

Although aesthetic motivation is not concerned with *acquiring* beliefs, beliefs which cannot simply be read off from the aesthetic object play a vital part in ensuring that we experience the object *correctly.* Consider watching a performance of *Hamlet* for instance. In order to understand it properly, you will need to know the meaning of a good number of obsolete words ('romage', 'fardel', 'bodkin', etc.), and also that words like 'let' and 'jump', are not used in their modern senses. Historical information will also be necessary concerning Elizabethan attitudes towards the supernatural, the Great Chain of Being, the contemporary reputation of French falconers, the fortune of theatrical companies at the beginning of the seventeenth century and much else. Even one who commands all the requisite information and abilities could still fail to understand the characters' motivations, the patterns of imagery, the dramatic necessities and ironies, the deeper thematic connections, but enough has already been said to show that *Hamlet* is a great deal more than a pattern of sounds or ink marks – more than the sum of its manifest features – and to establish what it is requires knowledge, skill and imagination.

It is possible to imagine circumstances in which historical information is even more important: where it is necessary even to distinguish one work from another. To adapt one of Kendal Walton's examples, two sculptures may share exactly the same manifest features, but one may be a larger than life portrait bust of a Roman senator, while the other may be a life-sized model of an albino giant cruelly severed below the shoulders.[18] It is only with the help of historical evidence that we shall be able to tell which has the look of serene stoicism and which the expression of comic lugubriousness; which work is novel, witty and grotesque and which is bland, staid, and thoroughly conventional. Clearly, which is which is going to have an enormous effect on our attitude, experience and evaluation, and this ensures that the rather pat device of assuming our external beliefs about a work's origins to be false in order to see if our attitude is disinterested will have to be modified. It may be true that a historian will lose interest in the picture of a castle if it proves to be inaccurate or a picture of another castle altogether, but equally a man who values modern grotesquerie over Roman statuary will lose interest in what he sees if it is shown he is looking at the wrong statue. Similarly, if the reader of *Edmund Ironside* were shown that it was just another Victorian attempt at poetic drama, then we could not be sure that his ceasing to read suggested fakery or self deception, because he would now feel, quite rightly, that the play was an unoriginal, wilfully archaic pastiche.

To say that historical factors will determine what a work *is*, is quite different from saying that appreciating something as a work of art cannot be clearly distinguished from appreciating it as a work of history or as a piece of historical evidence. Let us take *Hamlet* again, considered as a primary source about Tudor history, rather than a secondary source about Dark Ages Denmark. If a historian's sole interest is events around 1600,[19] then he will need to know certain facts about *Hamlet* before he will be able to take an interest in that work. He will need to believe that it was written around 1600 (or have some other fairly direct connection with that date) and that it contains further useful information about that period which he does not already know. Before the text is of any use to him he will have to understand the play, both at the basic level (the vocabulary, the syntax, the allusions etc.), and in some depth (for example, knowing who the patently unreliable characters are, which assertions are ironic and so on). Clearly the literary reader needs to understand these things too, and he will also need to know the date the play was written in order to appreciate its originality, but it is the second half of the historian's motivation – the belief that the play is a source of *further* information about 1600 – that the literary reader does not have to share. Understanding, with the aid of historical information, is a *prerequisite* for interest in both cases, but whereas the historian is motivated by the desire for *more* knowledge, to be obtained via the play, the literary reader is motivated simply by the pleasure he takes in *experiencing the play correctly*.

In neither case will mentioning *necessary* conditions for understanding – I speak English, 'let' means 'hinder', it was written about 1600 – *explain* the person's interest because neither party is interested in just *any* text that fits those specifications. In the historical case, interest can only be completely explained by describing what you hope to find out; in the literary case (ultimately) it can only be conveyed by pointing out and emphasizing aspects of the text or performance. At some point the historian will finish with the play, having assimilated all he needs from it, and turn to different sources relating to the early seventeenth century. The man who appreciates *Hamlet* aesthetically on the other hand, may decide that he has gathered all the historical information he needs to understand the play and either decide to dispense with further background studies altogether, or turn to some other discipline – psychoanalysis perhaps – to explicate the text further. While *Hamlet* is the object of his interest the play can never be redundant, although in the course of time his interest may lapse.[20]

Empiricism[21] – of which the New Critics were a particularly extreme manifestation – has always been wary of the notion that historical beliefs are necessary for aesthetic understanding, fearing that this would collapse literary criticism into history, or sociology, or biography, and distract us from the 'words on the page'. But such suspicion is misplaced, and the idea that one should not talk about originality, or intention, or use contemporary philosophical or political thought to obtain insight into character is quite absurd. As long as historical beliefs allow us to gain access to, to *realize* the experience a work offers, they are an indispensable part of aesthetic understanding. It is only when the acquisition of factual beliefs becomes the *point* of reading, so that we are led away from the text never to return, towards its origin, subject matter, or subsequent history, that motivation becomes non-aesthetic. We have no need to claim that *only* a work's manifest features are aesthetically relevant, merely that they must always be *part* of the aesthetic experience of that work. Beliefs are not always necessary; experience always is.

In the same way, personal reminiscences, fantasies, and general knowledge of the world, are perfectly legitimate and frequently vital aspects of aesthetic experience. If a personal reminiscence about the atmosphere of Scottish castles, an understanding of eroticism, a reverie about how such and such a character must feel increases your appreciation of and desire to return to a work, enriching your aesthetic experience and allowing you to enter more fully into its imaginative world, then that is all to the good. Similarly, some artists are going to appeal to some kinds of personalities but not to others: it required no great prescience to see that Brahms would venerate Bach or that Leavis would not resonate to Sterne. But to assimilate such personal responses to bias would be to deaden and denature the concept of artistic judgement, since it is precisely the fact that these judgements reach down into the unconscious depth of our sensibilities that makes them so significant. Some old-fashioned books of aesthetics give the impression that our personalities, our beliefs and knowledge of life should fall from us when we are raised above self in the act of contemplation, but this view, which is closely related to the theories of the New Critics, is equally implausible, and virtually guarantees the demotion of artistic interests to something akin to wine tasting. *Of course* our personalities and knowledge of life should enter into our appreciation of *Hamlet*, and it is equally right and proper that our aesthetic taste should change and mature as we do. The one truth that the antiquated view recognizes is that normally we look at things either to acquire factual knowledge or as a conscious preliminary to some practical project, but that in aesthetic contexts knowledge and belief have a different role to play.

Clearly, our reminiscences and fantasies must be controlled, moulded and inspired by the work as object, meshing with our experience and subtly enriching our whole manner of perceiving: they are only objectionable if they are extraneous and imposed from the outside, treating the work as a cause to be dispensed with once the fantasy or reminiscence gets under way. Frequently, it will be knowledge of the artist, his culture and subject matter that will enhance our appreciation of a work, although I see little possibility of being able to lay down any principles for determining what is and is not relevant. That can only be done by an individual critic in front of a particular work. The problem is analogous to the question: what can any schematic diagram be seen as? I can certainly say of a particular diagram, such as Wittgenstein's duck/rabbit,[22] 'To see it as a duck or a rabbit is clearly correct; to see it as a hare or a goose is rather strained; to see it as a harp or a football is obviously mad and impossible.' But asked to reply to the question at a wholly general level, it only seems possible to say that a diagram can be seen as anything which any reasonable, sensitive person could see or be persuaded to see it as.

The insight that New Criticism exaggerates is that after all the preconditions for realizing and enriching a work have been met, it is my own experience of the text – its intensity and durability – that will decide whether the poem, for example, is good or had. If discovering the excellence of a poem were analogous to discovering that it was written in six-line stanzas then it would be possible to rely on another, provenly reliable person's authority, and simply take over his report. If I reported – correctly – that a poem I had not read was written in six-line stanzas, and cited my excellent authorities for believing this, then I could hardly be taken to task for making an ungrounded assertion. If, however, I held forth at length about Milton's excellence and it later transpired that I had never actually *read* any Milton, then this would be tantamount to being discovered in the act of lying. It would be no defence to say, 'But look, I've read Tillyard and the later Eliot and they say it's good', because even if everybody were in unanimous agreement that the critics I mentioned were indeed the best, and that what they said was *absolutely true*, my behaviour would be thought no less dishonest or reprehensible. The point is, that if I say, 'Milton is excellent', then a necessary condition for being in a position to make that remark is that I have *knowledge by acquaintance* with at least some of his work, whereas I do not need actually to have seen the Empire State Building in order to say that it is more than 100 feet high. Aesthetic judgement is *aesthetic*; whatever beliefs and abilities it requires, it ultimately rests on my own perceptual experience, which means that pointing out features, prompting new aspects, redescribing, comparing this work with another – which is how we argue about experience – will *always* be relevant to questions of aesthetic valuation.

If we compare aesthetic motivation with the six sets of non-aesthetic reasons we can see that in one sense aesthetic absorption is not *explained* by reasons even though it is possible to give reasons for our absorption. The only complete explanation of my liking for a particular piece of music is to say that it is the way it is, but we never do say such things (except perhaps in a moment of exasperation) because they are rhetorically useless. The purpose of giving aesthetic reasons is to prompt somebody else into hearing or seeing the work as we hear or see it. To do this, we pick out some detail or aspect which we hope will restructure the experience of the other person. I may, for example, draw someone's attention to some grace-notes in a first violin phrase, or the way the oboe plays triplets against the straightforward quavers in the violas. This may be all that is necessary for another to pick up on the feeling of delicate unease that so appeals to me. But clearly, I am not committed to holding that all pieces of music which give grace-notes to the first violins and twos against threes to the violas and oboe are thereby good, or even delicately uneasy. I merely think that highlighting those grace-notes and that rhythmic complexity in that context will be enough to prompt a change of aspect in somebody else; a thought which may or may not be correct.

I hope that what I have said so far shows that the question, 'Are aesthetic judgements subjective or objective?' is unanswerable as it stands. There are certain facts about a work of art which are completely objective (when the work was written, what a particular word means) which you need to know if your judgement is to be considered at all; but even if we agree on all the facts, there is still enormous scope for disagreement. Whether *Hamlet* is structurally satisfactory, whether its hero is morally unappealing, whether the players' scenes are far too long, are not questions that historical or scientific research is going to answer, but they can be *argued* about in the way I outlined in the preceding paragraph. Although some interpretations will be obviously right or obviously wrong, most of us are happy with the idea that such questions allow a certain latitude for informed disagreement, and that your choice of interpretation will be influenced by some of the subjective factors already discussed. Consequently, it is inevitable that any decent discussion of *Hamlet*'s quality will ramify, not only into your response to other works of art, but also into areas of moral and personal experience. Finally, there are elements of works of art about which argument is much more difficult: if you simply adore a certain colour, or find the *timbre* of a particular voice peculiarly exciting then, because these are responses to content rather than form, there does not seem to be a great deal you can say in order to win over people who do not share your opinion. Here, it seems, aesthetic judgement is at its most subjective.

How does a work of art differ from an object which just happens to be of aesthetic interest? One intuitively plausible suggestion is that works of art must be artefacts, but 'found art' – where one piece of unadorned and unworked driftwood is put on display, for example – clearly presents a problem for this idea. The reason why we classify found art as art is that some rational creature *intended* us to look at this object, and that every part is as it is because it is *meant* to be that way. If the artist did not approve of the shape or texture then he could have tried to find some other piece that was more to his liking; if he could not find such a piece then presumably he could have worked or constructed one. Consequently, a piece of driftwood which is put on display invites an entirely different response from any similar piece of driftwood which just happens to lie on the beach. In the latter case we can discuss the driftwood's shape, colour and texture, but in the former we can also discuss its allusiveness, humour, pathos, vigour and originality. In its most basic form creativity is not working or even placing, but *selecting* – and it is precisely for this reason that most people have no difficulty in thinking of photography as an artform. The idea that every part of a work has to be meant seems to articulate the reason lying behind the suggestion that all works of art are artefacts, while avoiding this suggestion's unacceptable restriction of scope.

Previous writers on this subject have tended to make the aesthetic attitude equivalent to the contemplation of appearances. Not only can this view not do justice to the fact that historical evidence may be relevant to judgements concerning a work's interpretation and originality, but it also cannot begin to explain why so many other non-manifest features of a work are obviously relevant to its assessment. For example, the eye alone may not be able to tell that a sculpture is plastic rather than marble, or that a pillar is hollow rather than solid, and yet discovery of these facts can profoundly alter our attitude towards a work. One way round this problem is to start drawing distinctions between the aesthetic and the artistic,[23] or between appreciation of the works of man and appreciation of the works of nature. A major advantage of the version of the aesthetic attitude theory I have defended is that it preserves the unity of aesthetic experience across all objects. By examining non-aesthetic reasons for looking I hope I showed that the aesthetic attitude does not have to be half so restricted as some have supposed, and that aesthetic contemplation can be *informed* by propositional belief, personality and experience while maintaining its aesthetic integrity.

I should therefore define a work of art as either a physical object or a type[24] which can, and is intended[25] to support absorbed, disinterested contemplation by either sight, hearing or touch (or some combination of these) on the basis of correctly apprehending it. I believe this does capture the common features that all works of art – a novel by Forster, a collage by Schwitters, a rhapsody by Brahms – share, while allowing us to exclude all closely related objects and activities.

Notes

1 I would like to thank the following for making helpful criticisms of earlier drafts of this chapter: Marie McGinn, the late Flint Schier, an anonymous referee for *The Philosophical Quarterly*, and the members of the York University Philosophy Department Staff/Graduate Seminar.
2 S.K. Langer, *Philosophy in a New Key* (Cambridge, MA: Harvard University Press, 1976); N. Goodman, *The Languages of Art* (Indianapolis: Hackett, 1969); A.C. Danto, 'The Artworld', *Journal of Philosophy*, 61 (1964), pp. 571–84; G. Dickie, *Art and The Aesthetic: An Institutional Analysis* (Ithaca: Cornell University Press, 1974); M. Weitz, 'The Role of Theory in Aesthetics', *Journal of Aesthetics and Art Criticism*, XV (1956), pp. 27–35; W.E. Kennick, 'Does Traditional Aesthetics Rest on a Mistake?', *Mind*, LXVII (1958), pp. 317–34.
3 R. Scruton, *Art and Imagination* (London: Methuen, 1974), esp. pp. 134–57.
4 Michael H. Mitias, *What Makes an Experience Aesthetic?* (Wurzburg: 1988); and Michael H. Mitias (ed.), *Aesthetic Quality and Aesthetic Experience* (Wurzburg: 1988). There is, of course, a vast literature on this topic, see Bohdan Dziemidok, 'Controversy About the Aesthetic Nature of Art', *British Journal of Aesthetics*, 28 (1988), for a full bibliography.
5 Scruton begins to sketch an account on these lines in *Art and Imagination*, p. 156.
6 The example given in this paragraph is spatially extended, but not everything which possesses the kind of complexity I have in mind is spatial; for example, works of oral literature, mental images, music and equations. For a defence of the idea that music does embody a genuine concept of space see, R. Scruton, *The Aesthetics of Architecture* (London: Methuen, 1979), pp. 81–2.
7 This way of showing that depiction requires parts I owe to J.P. Heawood.
8 In the original version of this chapter I argued that parts were necessary for non-natural representation. John Hyman persuaded me I meant 'depiction'.
9 G.E. Moore, 'Wittgenstein's Lectures in 1930–1933', in *Aesthetics*, ed. H. Osborne (Oxford: Oxford University Press, 1978), p. 86.
10 The unavoidable three-dimensional connotations of the word 'object' at this point are particularly unfortunate. In some ways smells and tastes seem much closer to straightforward sensations than they do to the intentional objects of the aesthetic senses.
11 Scruton, *The Aesthetics of Architecture*, p. 112.
12 See G. Ryle, 'Pleasure', in *Moral Concepts*, ed. J. Feinberg (Oxford: Oxford University Press, 1969), pp. 19–28. I am also indebted to, T. Penelhum, 'The Logic of Pleasure', in H. Gustafson (ed.), *Essays in Philosophical Psychology* (London: Macmillan, 1964), pp. 227–47.
13 G.E.M. Anscombe, *Intention* (Oxford: Blackwell, 1958), p. 77.
14 For an argument which shows that making something is only intelligible if there is a possibility of failure, see M.W. Rowe, 'Why "Art" Doesn't Have Two Senses', *British Journal of Aesthetics*, 31 (1991), pp. 214–21.

15 S. Cavell, *The Claim of Reason* (Oxford: Oxford University Press,1979), pp. 210–11.

16 Francis Bacon, 'Of Beauty', in *The Essays or Counsels Civill and Morall of Frances Bacon Lord Verulam,* ed. O. Smeaton (London: Dent, 1906), p. 129.

17 'Disinterestedness' is, of course, one of the Kantian requirements for aesthetic judgement. See, *The Critique of Judgement*, trans. J.C. Meredith (Oxford: Oxford University Press, 1973), pp. 43–4.

18 Kendal Walton, 'Categories of Art', *Philosophical Review*, LXX1X (1970), p. 345.

19 The date of *Hamlet*'s composition is uncertain and contested. I have assumed 1600 but nothing important turns on this date's correctness.

20 The idea that there is no point at which a work of art is dispensable if our interest in it is aesthetic, although our aesthetic interest itself may cease, is emphasized by Scruton, *Art and Imagination*, pp. 145–6.

21 'Empiricism' is used in this sense throughout G. Currie, *An Ontology of Art* (Basingstoke: Macmillan, 1989).

22 L. Wittgenstein, *Philosophical Investigations* (Oxford: Blackwell, 1976), p. 194e.

23 For an interesting discussion of the way aesthetic and artistic judgement are related see D. Best, 'The Aesthetic and the Artistic', *Philosophy*, 57 (1982), pp. 357–72.

24 I have not discussed ontology in this paper so I hope the physical object/type distinction is relatively uncontentious. The definition could be further streamlined by arguing that all works of art are basically types, and that there only appears to be a distinction because our methods of reproducing sculptures, etc., are, as yet, primitive.

25 The relationship between intention and success is discussed in Rowe, 'Why Art Doesn't Have Two Senses'.

Chapter 8

Poetry and Abstraction

There is a long-running debate as to whether poetry should concern itself with abstract thought. Burke[1] and Winters[2] are emphatically of the opinion that it should, while Yeats,[3] Hulme[4] and Schreiber[5] are equally adamant that it should not. In this essay I shall argue that poetry can deal with abstractions, while acknowledging that there is something right in the intuition that poetry, even at its most abstract, deals with thought in a more sensuous and personal way than, for instance, philosophy.

The reason most commonly adduced for supposing that poetry cannot deal with abstractions is the belief that poetry should summon up mental images of the things it describes. As abstract thought is, by its very, nature, unimageable, it cannot therefore have a place in poetry. Hulme, for example, writes:

> In prose as in algebra concrete things are embodied in signs or counters which are moved about according to rules, without being visualized at all in the process ... Poetry, in one aspect at any rate, may be considered as an effort to avoid this characteristic of prose. It is a compromise for a language of intuition [used in the Kantian sense of 'perception'] which would hand over sensations bodily. It always endeavours to make you see a physical thing, to prevent you gliding through an abstract process.[6]

Before any useful attempt can be made to evaluate this idea, we must consider which version of the image theory is most plausible. It is encountered in at least three forms.

i) *The meaning theory.* The meaning of a word is the image associated with it. Literature is composed of words and therefore, like all other forms of meaningful language, it will evoke images.
ii) *The aesthetic theory.* The meaning of a word is not an image, and we can understand scientific and philosophical works perfectly well without imaging at all. It is, however, the special prerogative of literature to bring images before the reader's mind; the reader who is properly engaged with a literary text will have images of what is described.

iii) *The figure theory.* Simile, metaphor, etc., are generally referred to as 'images' because they are intended to summon up especially vivid *mental* images of the things described. Hulme[7] clearly thought that poetry was a uniquely concrete and visual language because of its high density of such figures.

Frequently, several of the theories are held by one person. The meaning theory is an eighteenth-century commonplace,[8] one consequence of which is that there is no particular problem about the evocative power of literature. Because of this, Burke never distinguishes properly between the aesthetic and meaning theories, and does not see that the second theory avoids many of his criticisms. Hulme, as stated above, holds both the aesthetic and figure theories, although once again the two come apart quite easily. For the purposes of this essay, I shall assume that both the meaning theory and the figure theory are false. The first part of Wittgenstein's *Philosophical Investigations* turned the first into a historical curiosity, and brief consideration of conceits, and the images in 'Prufrock' should disabuse us of the second. In addition, I shall assume that only a weak version of the aesthetic theory need be taken seriously. According to this, we should not expect an image to correspond to each word or to each completed thought (as the meaning theory usually demands), merely that images should form naturally and spontaneously at some point in our reading.

Given that adherence to even this weak version of the aesthetic theory is going to require the heroic step of declaring large tracts of *The Prelude* and *An Essay on Man* to be 'unpoetical', why should anyone be attracted to such a theory in the first place? I think the answer is fourfold.

First, there is the intuition generated by this question: 'If music appeals to the ear, and art, sculpture and dance to the eye, to which of our senses is literature addressed?' Of course, any work of literature can either be read or listened to, and a large element of our experience of drama will be straightforwardly perceptual, but few, I imagine, would wish to claim that enjoying a poem is equivalent to enjoying the *sound* of its words (a pleasure you can experience even – perhaps especially – in a language you cannot understand) or that enjoying a novel is the same as appreciating the *look* of its sentences. This is not to deny that the sound of a poem's words or the way they are set out on the page may be highly significant, but if our interest is focused on the meaning of the words (as surely it must be) then we seem to have lost contact with the perceptual object – Wittgenstein's arguments show that the meaning of a word is not any kind of object, inner or otherwise.

Second, the frequent intensity of our response to literature gives a reason for supporting the aesthetic theory. The fact that fiction makes people cry, or grow angry and agitated, is supported by more than introspective evidence. How is this intensity to be explained? A promising beginning is to observe that what is close, personal and immediate (like sense experience) has a much more profound and lasting effect on our emotional and affective systems than what is distant, impersonal and abstract (like generalized propositional knowledge).

Third, it is possible to become so involved with a work that one can, while reading, find the fictional world to be as concrete, real and visual as the actual world; indeed, sometimes this experience is so intense that the two can almost be confused.[9] (*Contra* Hulme, this experience seems more frequent with novels than with poetry.) While it seems impossible to confuse the word 'sea', or the abstract concept that the word expresses, with the sea itself, there are good experimental reasons for supposing that even faint, voluntarily induced images can be confused with actuality.[10]

The fourth reason, however, is the most important. For reasons to be explained below, the *Verstehen* view of literature requires the reader to form images of what he reads about, and it is also immensely attractive for at least the following reasons. Firstly, it explains how literature and the humanities in general can be centrally concerned with truth and knowledge and yet be complementary to, rather than in conflict with, science. Secondly, it explains why aesthetic knowledge is personal, nontransferable and incapable of being summed up in propositional form. Thirdly, it explains why the link between pleasure and literary knowledge is much more intimate than that between pleasure and scientific knowledge. Fourthly, it shows why literature is not simply a specialist pursuit nor a relaxation for the tired administrator, but provides a form of knowledge which is essential to us as human beings, irrespective of the kind of life we have chosen for ourselves.

Baldly, the *Verstehen* idea runs as follows. Science attempts to show how the world is in itself and not as it appears to any observer. Thus, its explanations do not mention secondary qualities, values or any other properties which might reasonably be thought to depend on the observer's constitution. Literature, however, is concerned not with inanimate objects (or objects treated as if they were inanimate) but with the experiences of conscious creatures who have a point of view on the world. The *Verstehen* technique requires that we construct a person's experience within our own minds in order to appreciate how the world seems from his point of view, and consequently to understand why he behaves as he does. This ability is strengthened and extended by exposure to great literature, because the writer's skill allows us to live – in imagination

– through a variety of situations which we could not have imagined unaided. The knowledge that we derive from literature is not propositional information but knowledge of what some experience is like, and it is internally related to pleasure because the writer can only *prompt* us to have an experience, the experience itself must be the spontaneous product of our own imaginations. Because of these facts, literary knowledge cannot be summarized and passed on to another (he has to read the work himself), and it has a profound and lasting effect on our attitudes and emotions.

If we accept that literature gives knowledge by *Verstehen* then we can see that in reading a poem we need to reconstruct what the narrator perceived. To imagine seeing what someone or something looks like – your mother, for instance – is to have a visual image of that person or object.[11] The same applies to other sense modalities: to imagine what something sounds like is to have an auditory image, to imagine what something feels like is to have a tactile image, and so on. To put ourselves in someone's position, therefore, will require the formation of images. The idea of *Verstehen* thus provides some justification for the aesthetic theory of mental imagery although in an even weaker form than that hitherto considered. It makes it reasonable to expect poetry to evoke imagery when the things that it describes are of a kind which can be perceived or felt.

However, people do not just perceive and feel, they also *think*, and this may affect them just as profoundly, may induce emotional reactions which are just as deep-seated or violent, as anything seen or felt. Thus, to enter into somebody's experience (either an author's or one of his character's) we need to reconstruct not only what they perceived but also *what it was like to think what they thought.*[12] Imagery and abstract thought do not, therefore, stand in opposition to one another: if we stand back and consider the central theoretical rationale for the image theory we see that it also legitimizes the place of abstract thought in poetry.

Frege's 'The Thought'[13] provides some clues as to the role and nature of abstract thought in poetry. This is not because of anything he says in his discussion of poetry in the opening pages – his reflections on the tone of 'steed' differing from that of 'horse' is a direct forbear of the unhelpful distinction between referential and emotive language – but because he draws a sharp demarcation between a *thought* and the psychological process of *thinking.* He drew this distinction for two reasons. Firstly, he wanted to avoid any suggestion that the laws of logic – if A then A, either A or not A, etc. – were dependent on the contingent facts of human psychology; and secondly, because he wanted to emphasize that thoughts, unlike images, are essentially public and shareable. For Frege, a thought is something immaterial, atemporal and abstract, and cannot therefore be any kind of object for the senses; but *thinking* is something which does take place over time and frequently has a very rich phenomenology. This distinction highlights an ambiguity in our ordinary use of 'thought': sometimes we use it to refer to a private *process*, as in 'he was lost in thought', and sometimes we use it to refer to the public, sharable *product* of the process, as in 'The Thought of Max Weber'. Philosophy and science I take to be primarily interested in thought in the second sense, whereas literature, because it is concerned with the entire subjective *Lebenswelt*, is primarily interested in reconstructing the whole psychology of the thinking process, approaching it from the point of view of narrative and the part it plays in the individual's biography. Not that this precludes either logic or the abstract thought itself. Logic, of course, enters into the psychological process, and articulating a Fregean thought will be the natural product of that process.

I now want to test and clarify this idea against some concrete examples. I shall begin by quoting one of Philip Larkin's major poems in full, because it seems a superb example of how the experience of thought can be integrated into experience generally. I shall then isolate several features which explain, at least in part, its emotional impact. Around this paradigm I shall place four passages from other poets which successively lose one or more of these features. I do not aim to produce a set of necessary and sufficient conditions for the correct use of thought in poetry; rather, my concern is to understand why a certain kind of thought, and a certain manner of treating it, feels natural, and fitting and appropriate. There are greater poems than this one of Larkin's, but few I think which so effectively use all the resources of particularity and abstraction which are available to the poet.

Dockery and Son[14]

'Dockery was junior to you,
Wasn't he?' said the Dean. 'His son's here now.'
Death-suited, visitant, I nod. 'And do
You keep in touch with –' Or remember how
Black-gowned, unbreakfasted, and still half-tight
We used to stand before that desk, to give
'Our version' of 'these incidents last night'?
I try the door of where I used to live:

Locked. The lawn spreads dazzlingly wide.
A known bell chimes. I catch my train, ignored.

Canal and clouds and colleges subside
Slowly from view. But Dockery, good Lord,
Anyone up today must have been born
In '43 when I was twenty-one.
If he was younger, did he get this son
At nineteen, twenty? Was he that withdrawn

High-collared public-schoolboy, sharing rooms
With Cartwright who was killed? Well, it just shows
How much … How little … Yawning, I suppose
I fell asleep, waking at the fumes
And furnace-glares of Sheffield, where I changed,
And ate an awful pie, and walked along
The platform to its end to see the ranged
Joining and parting lines reflect a strong

Unhindered moon. To have no son, no wife,
No house or land still seemed quite natural.
Only a numbness registered the shock
Of finding out how much had gone of life,
How widely from the others. Dockery, now:
Only nineteen, he must have taken stock
Of what he wanted, and been capable
Of … No, that's not the difference: rather, how

Convinced he was he should be added to!
Why did he think adding meant increase?
To me it was dilution. Where do these
Innate assumptions come from? Not from what
We think truest, or most want to do:
Those warp tight-shut, like doors. They're more a style
Our lives bring with them: habit for a while,
Suddenly they harden into all we've got

And how we got it; looked back on, they rear
Like sand-clouds thick and close, embodying
For Dockery a son, for me nothing,
Nothing with all a son's harsh patronage.
Life is first boredom, then fear.
Whether or not we use it, it goes,
And leaves what something hidden from us chose,
And age, and then the only end of age.

Here we need to note five factors that typify the successful handling of thought in poetry. First, the poem presents us with a perfectly familiar and evocatively described series of events that everybody can imagine undergoing. It is a poem firmly rooted in concrete human experience, and when we respond to its force and sincerity, it is with a sense of *recognition* – 'Yes, that's exactly how it would be' – rather than with a feeling of being informed.

Second, the central thought of the poem is *about* the particular experience we have lived through with the poet. The abstract idea stated in the last four lines of the poem is, to a certain extent, supported by the episode in the poet's life described in the earlier stanzas.

Third, and most importantly, the thought *develops*. The case of Dockery, introduced by the Dean in line one, is immediately submerged by further memories, conversations, the business of leaving Oxford, and only re-emerges again in the middle of stanza two. The exclamation ('good Lord') and the two unanswered questions suggest that it is only now that the Dean's words have begun to sink in, and their importance to be realized. But this line of thought, although initially animated, fails to develop, and gutters out into something vague and indefinite ('How much ... How little ...'). When the narrator wakes, however, his thoughts about Dockery have crystallized, and assert themselves in notably unhesitant syntax:

> ... To have no son, no wife,
> No house or land still seemed quite natural.
>
> Only a numbness registered the shock
> Of finding out how much had gone of life,
> How widely from the others ...

The thought is still centred on himself, and it is only when we reach the final lines that Larkin risks the universal:

> Life is first boredom, then fear.
> Whether or not we use it, it goes,
> And leaves what something hidden from us chose.
> And age, and then the only end of age.

This thought has gradually emerged – at first haltingly but then with greater readiness and vigour – from a vague sense of dissatisfaction and the contemplation of his immediate surroundings. As Larkin becomes progressively more absorbed in his rapidly clarifying thought, so the final stanzas grow more abstract and less concerned with the external world; but even here it is the empirical-psychological processes rather than the normative-logical ones which predominate, and we follow him up at least one wrong turning, 'No, that's not the difference ...'. In the main body of the poem, however, it is things seen, heard, experienced, which prompt his thoughts and mould their form and direction; and this mixture of perception and reflection would seem to be an accurate reflection of our inner life's content. But the same combination is not to be found in his later 'This Be The Verse', which also deals with the problem of inherited characteristics:

> They fuck you up your mum and dad.
> They may not mean to but they do.
> And fill you with the faults they had
> And add some extra just for you.[15]

To compare this with 'Dockery and Son' is to become conscious of the fact that whereas 'Dockery' allows us to live *through* something, 'This Be The Verse' merely *tells* us something. The dour 12-line squib is a concluded thought versified, while the infinitely richer 'Dockery and Son' not only allows us to see and hear and feel, but charts the psychological process of thinking. It finally ends, as is natural, with the product of the process.

Fourth, the context in which he thinks not only prompts his thoughts but also symbolizes them: there is a sense in which the perceived events are just as much *about* his thoughts as his thoughts are about the events. To return to Oxford is to revisit a scene of his youth, and to revive within himself a sense of youthful freedom and possibility ('The lawn spreads dazzlingly wide') to which he cannot return ('I try the door of where I used to live: / Locked.'). Oxford is familiar, but he no longer belongs ('A known bell chimes. I catch my train, ignored') and he repeats the journey north, the direction his life took on leaving the university. Compared to the earlier 'Canal and clouds and colleges' the reality he wakes to is harsh and unforgiving: '... the fumes / And furnace glares of Sheffield', and the pie he eats is 'awful'. He pauses to reflect on his journey while he walks to the end of the platform, just as the poem itself is a moment of reflection on his life, and notices how the rails – those emblems of determinism, and in marked contrast to the dazzlingly wide lawn of stanza two – join and part, mirroring lives which have intersected briefly only to be pulled apart again. As if to throw the determining forces and constraints on human life into dramatic relief, the moon is 'unhindered'.[16]

This is not the place for a full-dress analysis of symbolism, but it is worth noting that no object has intrinsic symbolic value: it only means something *to somebody*. Sometimes the symbolic power of an object or set of events can be recognized by virtually anyone in any context; Freud's observation that 'Birth is symbolized by water … for dying we have setting out on a *journey* or *travelling* by train …'[17] applies just as much to Larkin's poem as it does to the dreams of Freud's Viennese patients. More frequently, however, everyday objects such as pies, rails, lawns, only have a symbolic value to a particular person in a particular state of mind, as is the case with Larkin's narrator. In some cases, it is, of course, possible for a poet to convey his preoccupations to his readers by this method alone, and without explicitly stating his thoughts at all.

Fifth, the last four lines draw us into their mood of moving resignation. To a large extent, this is due to their position in the poem: had it begun with 'Life is first boredom then fear …' and carried on in a similar vein, then our perceptual imagination would be a blank and we would experience, as opposed to merely comprehend, nothing. However, the rhythm and diction of the verse also plays a significant role: the movement is halting and constrained, and lengthy pauses are demanded at the punctuation marks. It is a truism of practical criticism that the language of a poem should enact its sense, and that a good reading of even the most abstract poetic thought requires that the reader project himself into its mood and atmosphere, but I hope the wider theoretical context sketched above provides a perspicuous rationale for these claims.

The importance of linguistic texture can be demonstrated more clearly by looking at two passages from Wordsworth's 'Tintern Abbey'.[18] Having described the scene, and given thanks for the morally beneficent influence recollection has had on him, he continues:

> … Nor less, I trust,
> To them I may have owed another gift,
> Of aspect more sublime: that blessed mood,
> In which the burthen of the mystery,
> In which the heavy and the weary weight
>
> Of all this unintelligible world,
> Is lightened ….

In this extract, unlike in Larkin's poem, we are shown nothing of the narrator's circumstances and physical environment, and yet we are still able to share in the mood in which the thought was conceived, so it has an effect on our emotions as well as our intellect. This success can only be due to the way the linguistic structure parallels the feelings expressed. The cumbersome repetitions ('In which … / In which …', '… *the* heavy and *the* weary weight'[19]) clog the movement of the verse, and added emphasis is achieved by the alliteration of 'weary weight'. The metre requires us to grant 'unintelligible' its full six syllables in a line where all the other words have only one, and consequently we have the sense of prolonging the word, dragging ourselves through its apparently endless length. By contrast, the light feminine ending of 'Is lightened' echoes our feeling of ease and felicity, and life's burdens, which have taken twenty deliberately clumsy words to describe, evaporate in two. In a later passage too, the sound and structure of the language acts as a physical analogue to its meaning:

… And I have felt
A presence that disturbs me with the joy
Of elevated thoughts; a sense sublime
Of something far more deeply interfused,
Whose dwelling is the light of setting suns,
And the round ocean, and the living air,
And the blue sky, and in the mind of man:
A motion and a spirit, that impels
All thinking things, all objects of all thought,
And rolls through all things. Therefore am I still
A lover of the meadows and the woods
And the mountains …

Rhythm plays an important part in the overall effect here. While it is quite possible, if slightly insensitive, to read the opening lines of the extract as a strict pentameter, the exercise becomes absurd as soon as we reach 'And the round ocean …'. At this point the rhythm takes on a hounding, exultant quality, so that a heavy emphasis comes on 'round', 'living', 'blue', 'mind', 'man', etc., and then falls with really extraordinary weight on 'rolls' – the rhetorical climax to which the whole sentence has been leading.

Some of the sweep of this passage is also to be explained by the repetition of 'and': '*And* the round ocean, *and* the living air / *And* the blue sky, *and* in the mind of man'. In conventional prose 'and' would normally signal the end of a list, but here, no sooner has Wordsworth thought to end it than some other facet of nature's multitudinousness occurs to him. The list is apparently endless, and Wordsworth's profligate way with connectives all adds to the sense of amplitude and prodigality. This impression is strengthened by a similarly extravagant use of 'all': '*All* thinking things, *all* objects of *all* thoughts / And rolls through *all* things.' The omnipresence of the 'a'-sound is also worth noting: seven consecutive lines in this section begin with it, and all the singular, elemental words – 'man', 'and', 'am', 'all', 'a' – contain it. When this ubiquitous sound is coupled with the way every aspect of the universe is merged together with connectives and embraced by repeated 'all's, we have the impression that man, language and the universe are merging together in a paean of ecstatic oneness.

Thought is less effectively handled in this passage from Pope's *An Essay on Man*:

> Fortune her gifts may variously dispose,
> And these be happy called, unhappy those;
> But Heav'n just balance equal will appear,
> While those are plac'd in Hope, and these in Fear:
> Not present good or ill, the joy or curse
> But future views of better, or of worse.[20]

There seem to be two things wrong with this. Firstly, the abstract thoughts of Wordsworth and Larkin grew out of lived, immediate experience. This means that the reader both experienced the context in which the thought arose, and also saw it tested against, and supported by, the concrete. This passage, on the other hand, comes from a poem which consists of nothing but generalized, atemporal statement. However, this cannot be its sole fault since both the passages from Wordsworth (and also many other longer abstract passages in his writings, such as the 'spots of time' section in Book XI of *The Prelude*) can make their impact, even when read in isolation. The real problem is that in reading this passage we gain no sense at all of what it was like to think these thoughts.

The extracts from 'Tintern Abbey', because of the sensuousness of their language, succeeded in being living and personal as well as cogent, whereas the passage from Pope is bereft of emotional charge and impact. Pope *tells* us things and our task is exhausted when we comprehend; we are never invited inside the narrator's consciousness or given material to act as a cue to our own reconstruction of experience. The versification is neat, tepid and a little heartless – quite unsuitable, one would have thought, for a subject as traumatic as human fortune – and the language does not work with the sense to engage our emotions. The form of the poem does not grow out of the subject matter but is a piece of alien elegance imposed from the outside, so that (to employ a handy turn of phrase from Cavell) one has the impression that the passage is not so much written as *written up*[21] – as if Pope first allowed his thoughts to reach completion and then put them into metrical form. Pope has placed a Fregean thought before us – eminently public, sharable, debatable – but shorn of the subjectivity which conceived it. The alchemy by which we are drawn into the thinking process of another is not achieved; nor is it attempted.

My final example is drawn from Sir Richard Blackmore's *Creation*, one of a vast mass of eighteenth-century verse – now largely unread – which celebrates all aspects of human expertise and knowledge. At this point, Blackmore is discussing the digestive system:

> Nature has various tender muscles placed,
> By which the artful gullet is embraced;
> Some the long funnel's curious mouth extend,
> Through which ingested meats with ease descend;
> Other confederate pairs for nature's use
> Contract the fibres, and the twitch produce,
> Which gently pushes on the grateful food
> To the wise stomach, by its hollow road.

The process is followed through for another 40 lines until we reach:

> Th' intestine spiral fibres these protrude,
> And from the winding tubes at length exclude.[22]

This, like Diaper on fish, Thompson and Dyer on agriculture, Philips on glass-blowing, Garth on medicine, Yalden on coal-mining and Moore on fen drainage, strikes us as ridiculous. Why? Well, like the extract from Pope, neither the context (which is very much the same kind of thing) nor the movement and diction of the verse gives any indication of mood or feeling. Above all, however, it is the grotesque incongruity between the elegant poetic surface and Blackmore's chosen subject matter that make this 'poem' risible. Although Pope gives us no concrete particulars, his generalities are at least *based* on what Wordsworth called 'the discipline of our daily life … the knowledge that all men carry about with them',[23] and to discover the correctness of what Pope says requires us only to reflect on possible or actual instances of lived experience. Had Pope set his lines amidst such dramatized instances of life, his lines' effectiveness would have been greatly enhanced. The oddity of Blackmore's poem can be ascribed to the fact that it has no connection whatsoever with *Verstehen*: it does not – in Leavis' words

– invite us to 'feel into and become',[24] but only to *assent*, without a change of perspective. Accordingly, it displays three of the characteristics associated with propositional as opposed to experiential knowledge.

First, if you already know about the digestive system then it would be very hard to understand why you should wish to read the poem. If you did want to learn about the digestive system, and therefore read the poem and assimilated all it had to tell you, it would be equally difficult to motivate a second and third reading. On the other hand, even if you know the Lake District thoroughly, you would still have every reason for reading Wordsworth, and having read some of his work once, to read it again. We do not read his poetry to discover geographical facts, but to share *his experience* of that landscape. Propositional knowledge is an all-or-nothing affair. You either know that the stomach digests food or you do not, whereas our experiential memories of sharing Wordsworth's experiences can be more or less intense, more or less vivid or faded, and a desire to relive them is readily comprehensible.

Second, and closely connected with the foregoing, if Wordsworth has discovered a pattern in experience which we have hitherto overlooked, then it will strike us with the force of recognition ('almost a remembrance', said Keats[25]) because all the materials for intellectual advance are already to hand. But the technical hints and information contained in Blackmore, Yalden, Diaper *et al.* go beyond our normal knowledge of life and do not strike us in this way. They do not re-order or point-up what we already know, but tell us something we did not know at all. At best we are *informed*, and if we are already in possession of this information then there is no point in reading them.

Third, experiential knowledge is always from a *point of view.* When we look at a picture, we stand in the same relation to pictured space as we imagine the artist stood to actual space.[26] In a novel we are told, 'She appeared at the window', implying that the narrative point of view was outside the building rather than in the room with her, or that 'When the others left, he remained at the table playing with the bread-crumbs on the cloth', implying that the point of view has stayed in the room rather than following the others out into the street. In such a context, we will assume that even long passages of abstract thought are from the narrator's viewpoint; the surrounding concrete experience having identified the locus of consciousness where the thinking takes place. This is not the case in contexts where only general propositional knowledge is presented. 'Water flows down hill', 'M.W.R. is less than six feet tall', 'food is digested in the stomach', are not simply reports of how things look or seem from the right-hand side of the room or *for me*, they are true for anybody anywhere.

Although Blackmore speaks of 'the gullet', he is not talking about some particular gullet which he sees in front of him, but of the normal functioning of all human gullets, hence the sense of abstraction we get from his poem, even though it appears to be about a perfectly specific and concrete process. This is what we would expect in a scientific work, since science attempts to *transcend* the individual viewpoint by couching its explanations in terms of primary qualities (size, shape, speed, etc.) that do not depend on the observer's psychology. It attempts to show not how things *seem* to someone's 'senses and passions',[27] but how they objectively *are.* One cannot have an image from everywhere or from nowhere, and consequently knowledge of this degree of generality has to be propositional in form. Although poetry is written in propositions it does not *use* its propositions in the normal way, but to prompt and guide our own reconstructions of experience. As Wittgenstein says: 'Do not forget that a poem, even though it is composed in the language of information, is not used in the language-game of giving information.'[28] Propositions as general as Blackmore's cannot be realized into experiences, and therefore, even though they are in metrical form, they cannot function in the properly poetic manner. His work remains at the level of competent verse, ingenious but frigid and inert. As with medieval animal trials, we struggle to understand the motivation for writing these vast scientific poems, and the language-game for which they were intended remains obscure to us.

It is possible to imagine a good poem on a scientific or even mathematical topic but it would not approach its subject matter in Blackmore's manner. A genuinely moving poem on fen drainage would have to be about how it affected the lives of those who knew or lived on the fell: the sense of bewildering change, the different appearance of the countryside, the loss of wildlife – in other words, the impact such an event would have on the subjective *Lebenswelt.* Similarly, a good poem about glass-blowing could not just be a versified compendium of glass-blowing techniques. It could, however, find larger significances in the glitter and pellucid fragility of the material, or the chiaroscuro of the apparently miraculous processes by which glass is brought into being and fashioned. In fact, Jacobean plays, particularly those of John Webster, are full of striking images drawn from glass and glass-blowing.[29]

In analysing the Larkin poem, I isolated five features which I took to be virtues in its poetic treatment of an abstract thought. These were: (i) the thought grew out of a particular experiential context; (ii) to a large extent the thought was about that context, which also supported the general statement made at the end of the poem; (iii) the thought developed; (iv) the context symbolized the thought; (v) the language in which the final thought (and indeed the whole poem) was expressed enacted its sense. All of these features highlight the experiential nature of the thinking process which, for a logician like Frege, is simply an irrelevance when it is not being a positive nuisance. But a poet is not primarily concerned with proving something true or false, his aim is to allow us to know what some experience – including the experience of thinking – is *like*, and in this, Larkin seems to have been entirely successful. When we read his poem, because of its organic wholeness, we feel we have lived in imagination through an experience whose emotional impact is far greater than either a bare description of his journey or a Fregean presentation of his general conclusion could possibly be.

The experience our mind reconstructs when we read through the poem is, of course, an idealization. The poem is not a direct transcript of what passed through Larkin's head, but is a supremely artful construct that is designed to give that impression. This impression, however, is something that we want to avoid in scientific and philosophical writing. In a philosophical paper the content is too propositional and abstract to establish an experiential point of view, and while it certainly has a writer, it does not have a *narrator*. Because of this, the subject matter need not be restricted to 'the discipline of our daily life', or record a number of connected events in temporal sequence. There is no sense in which the end of a philosophical paper is about something either later or earlier than the beginning. The lack of experiential content rules out symbolism, and if we have the impression that the ideas clarified and developed for the writer as he approached his conclusion, then that is a sign that he should have gone back and rewritten the whole paper. Lastly, and obviously, the quality of a philosophical essay depends on the quality of the thoughts it contains, and these can be assessed from an accurate paraphrase.[30] But the quality of a poem is not solely dependent on the quality of its thought, if only because its language is one of the most vital cues the reader has in reconstructing the emotion in which the thought is embedded. Someone who has only read an accurate paraphrase of 'Tintern Abbey' is not in a position to evaluate the poem. In literature, of course, the language as well as the thought it expresses, is part of the work to be assessed.

From this examination I conclude that abstract thought is a legitimate topic for poetry, but the whole manner of approach must be utterly different from that of the philosopher or logician.

Notes

1 Edmund Burke, *A Philosophical Enquiry into our Ideas of the Sublime and Beautiful* (London: Cassell, 1891), p. 185.
2 Yvor Winters, *The Function of Criticism* (London: Routledge and Kegan Paul, 1962), p. 61.
3 W.B. Yeats, *Essays*, p. 362. Quoted in L.C. Knights, 'Poetry, Politics and Religion', in *Further Explorations* (London: Chatto and Windus, 1965), p. 73.
4 T.E. Hulme, 'Romanticism and Classicism', in H. Reed (ed.), *Speculations: Essays on Humanism and the Philosophy of Art* (London: Routledge and Kegan Paul, 1987), p. 134.
5 S.M. Schreiber, *An Introduction to Literary Criticism* (Oxford: Oxford University Press, 1965), p. 44.
6 Hulme, *Speculations*, p. 134.
7 Hulme, *Speculations*, p. 135.
8 See, for example, Hume, *A Treatise of Human Nature*, ed. L.A. Selby-Bigge, revised P.H. Nidditch (Oxford: Oxford University Press, 1978), p. 1.
9 See Richard Church, *Over the Bridge* (London: Heinemann, 1956), p. 78, for a particularly good account of such an experience.
10 Some experimental findings are contained in C.W. Perky, 'An Experimental Study of Imagination', *American Journal of Psychology*, 21 (1910).
11 This point is made by R. Scruton, *Art and Imagination* (London: Methuen, 1974), p. 100.
12 The fact that a thought in a poem will be expressed in words does not imply that the original thought was in words (although it might have been). A descriptive passage should give the reader a sense of perception, but here there is clearly no implication that perception is verbal. In addition, the phrase, 'the original thought' should not be taken necessarily to suggest something autobiographical – the experience recorded could be entirely fictional.
13 Translated by A.M. Quinton and M. Quinton as 'The Thought: A Logical Inquiry', in P.F. Strawson (ed.), *Philosophical Logic*, Oxford Readings in Philosophy (Oxford: Oxford University Press, 1973).
14 Larkin, *Collected Poems*, ed. A. Thwaite (London: Faber and Faber and the Marvell Press, 1988), pp. 152–3. I would like to thank Anthony Thwaite for granting permission to reprint this poem.
15 Stanza one, in Larkin, *Collected Poems*, p. 180.
16 The last two observations in this paragraph I owe to Timms, *Philip Larkin* (Edinburgh: Oliver and Boyd, 1973), pp. 100–2.
17 S. Freud, *A General Introduction to Psychoanalysis*, trans. J. Riviere (New York, 1967). p. 160.
18 R.S. Thomas (ed.), *A Choice of Wordsworth's Verse* (London: Faber and Faber, 1977), p. 22.
19 This point is also made in R.O.C. Winkler, 'Wordsworth's Poetry', in B. Ford (ed.), *The Pelican Guide to English Literature*, vol. 5 (Harmondsworth: 1975), p. 100.
20 Pope, *An Essay on Man*, Epistle III, lines 67–2, in H. Davis (ed.), *Pope: Poetical Works* (Oxford, 1985), p. 270.
21 S. Cavell, 'The Availability of Wittgenstein's Later Philosophy', in *Must We Mean What We Say?* (Cambridge: Cambridge University Press, 1976), p. 70.

22 This extract is from D. Davidson (ed.), *The Penguin Book of Eighteenth Century Verse* (Harmondsworth: Penguin, 1983), pp. 229–31.
23 Wordsworth, 'Preface to "Lyrical Ballads" (1802)', in S. Gill (ed.), *William Wordsworth*, The Oxford Authors Series (Oxford: Oxford University Press, 1984), p. 606.
24 Leavis, 'Literary Criticism and Philosophy', in *The Common Pursuit* (Harmondsworth: Penguin, 1983), p. 212.
25 Keats. letter to John Taylor, 27 February 1918, in R. Gittings (ed.), *Letters of John Keats* (Oxford: Oxford University Press, 1985), pp. 69–70.
26 The point is made by John Searle in '*Las Meninas* and Representation', in W.J.T. Mitchell (ed.), *The Language of Images* (Chicago: University of Chicago Press, 1980), p. 251.
27 Wordsworth, 'Essay, Supplementary to the Preface (1815)', in Gill, *William Wordsworth*, p. 641.
28 L. Wittgenstein, *Zettel*, trans. G.E.M. Anscombe (Oxford: Blackwell, 1967), section 160, p. 28e.
29 See Roy Booth, 'John Webster's Heart of Glass', *English*, 40 (1991), pp. 97–113.
30 At this point, I am only concerned to distinguish the role of thought in poetry from its role in the standard conception of philosophy described on p. viii. To distinguish it from the conception of philosophy outlined in the first five chapters would require another article.

Chapter 9

Larkin's 'Aubade'

Aubade

I work all day, and get half-drunk at night.
Waking at four to soundless dark, I stare.
In time the curtain-edges will grow light.
Till then I see what's really always there:
Unresting death, a whole day nearer now,
Making all thought impossible but how
And where and when I shall myself die.
Arid interrogation: yet the dread
Of dying, and being dead,
Flashes afresh to hold and horrify.

The mind blanks at the glare. Not in remorse
– The good not done, the love not given, time
Torn off unused – nor wretchedly because
An only life can take so long to climb
Clear of its wrong beginnings, and may never;
But at the total emptiness for ever,
The sure extinction that we travel to
And shall be lost in always. Not to be here,
Not to be anywhere,
And soon; nothing more terrible, nothing more true.

This is a special way of being afraid
No trick dispels. Religion used to try,
That vast moth-eaten musical brocade
Created to pretend we never die,
And specious stuff that says *No rational being*
Can fear a thing it will not feel, not seeing
That this is what we fear – no sight, no sound,
No touch or taste or smell, nothing to think with,
Nothing to love or link with,
The anaesthetic from which none come round.

And so it stays just on the edge of vision,
A small unfocused blur, a standing chill
That slows each impulse down to indecision.
Most things may never happen: this one will,
And realisation of it rages out
In furnace-fear when we are caught without
People or drink. Courage is no good:
It means not scaring others. Being brave
Lets no one off the grave.
Death is no different whined at than withstood.

Slowly light strengthens, and the room takes shape.
It stands plain as a wardrobe, what we know,
Have always known, know that we can't escape,
Yet can't accept. One side will have to go.
Meanwhile telephones crouch, getting ready to ring
In locked-up offices, and all the uncaring
Intricate rented world begins to rouse.
The sky is white as clay, with no sun.
Work has to be done.
Postmen like doctors go from house to house.

Philip Larkin

I

Mine is the first and only life. (Wittgenstein, *Notebooks 1914–16*)

When the commonplace 'We must all die' transforms itself suddenly into the acute consciousness 'I must die – and soon', then death grapples us and his fingers are cruel. (George Eliot, *Middlemarch*)

Larkin invariably uses French words and French titles ironically. For him, French is the language of style, sophistication, sensuality, urbanity, passion, and worldliness: it is the language of *la politesse* [CP:179],[1] *sens d'occasion*, and *savoir vivre* [SL:629] – all qualities he felt he and his world conspicuously lacked. Appropriately therefore, in the only poems with French titles from the forties – 'Femmes Damnées' [CP:270] and 'Ballade des Dames du Temps Jadis' [TWG:247–8] – Larkin takes two rather elevated French poems and affectionately reduces them to something more quotidian. Baudelaire's lesbians – Hippolyte and Delphine – become Rosemary and Rachel, and they are set amongst builders' estates and cabbage patches rather than 'languishing lamps' and scented cushions. Villon's majestic elegy for great women in history – Thaïs, Heloïse, Joan of Arc – and his refrain of 'But where are the snows of yester-year?', becomes a lament for now dispersed school friends – Valerie, Julia, Elspeth – with a last line that rings the changes on 'So many summer terms away'.

There are no French titles in the 1950s and 1960s, possibly because Larkin took the official Movement line on foreign cultures. However, in the 1970s he wrote two, and we can here note a subtle change of approach. In the 1940s he takes particular poems by particular poets as his models, and is largely interested in deflating their contents. (Even his one poem with a German title, 'Träumerai' [CP:12], mocks the quiet rapture of Schumann's famous piano piece,[2] a work found in many pre-war piano stools.) In the 1970s, his titles allude to the *forms* of general *kinds* of poetry, although, to a certain extent, the nature of the form determines the nature of the content. Perhaps he was still enough of a Movement poet to feel that poems whose enjoyment depended on a knowledge of specific foreign models could only be arty and affected.

The irony has also grown more complex. Consider 'Vers de Société' [CP: 181], the first of these 1970s poems. In a way, the poem is *vers de société* (the versification's light and accomplished); in another way it isn't (it glories in crudities quite unsuited to the drawing room.) On the other hand it isn't light in either sense – smooth or coarse – since it contains some of Larkin's most memorable images and soul-searchings. But the complexities do not end there. 'Vers de Société' could also mean verse *about* society. And this seems true; until we reflect that it's more about solitariness.

Before we can approach the ironies in 'Aubade' we need to know what Larkin thought the word's straightforward meaning was. This is by no means easy to determine as the word has never quite taken root in English: many competent native speakers have never heard it, and those that do know it frequently admit to an uncertain grasp of its meaning. Most informed speakers would probably say that 'aubade' was a French word referring to a kind of open-air dawn serenade, and that it had something to do with the troubadours.

There is some truth in this. The word's first recorded use in English was in 1678 when one Phillips – presumably a musician or music publisher – advertised: '*Aubades* (French) songs, or instrumentall music, sung, or playd under any ones Chamber window in the morning.'[3] Despite its age, the word does not appear in Johnson's dictionary of 1756, and modern dictionaries, even those produced by the same publisher, diverge in their definitions. The *Oxford English Dictionary* (*OED*) has 'A musical announcement of dawn, a sunrise song or open-air concert'. The *New Shorter Oxford English Dictionary* has 'A piece of music or a poem written to be heard at or appropriate to dawn'. The first is unsatisfactory because it omits all reference to poetry; the second because it omits all reference to the open air and the occasion of performance. A more satisfactory (if rather more cumbersome) definition than either might be 'A piece of music, song or poem either about, or to be sung, recited or played at, dawn. Usually, it is played in the open air outside a house, often in honour of the woman inside it. The word can also refer to the occasion of performance as well as the piece or poem performed or recited.' The etymological sections of all dictionaries agree, however, that the word derives from an old troubadour lyric song called the *alba*, and that later forms of this lyric, in Old French rather than Old Provençal, began to be referred to as 'aubades' at the beginning of the fifteenth century.

Give or take a few details, it's natural to assume that this was Larkin's understanding of the term, and he certainly knew several aubades that conform to the definition sketched above. From its first appearance in 1900, until it was replaced in 1972, the standard poetry anthology in schools and universities was Sir Aurthur Quiller-Couch's, *The Oxford Book of English Verse 1250–1900*. It was a book Larkin knew well. This contains two poems entitled 'Aubade': Shakespeare's 'Hark! Hark! The Lark' from *Cymbeline*, and Sir William Davenant's, 'The lark now leaves his watery nest'. Both songs are sung to a young woman in bed by a young man outside her window. These works were written prior to the *OED*'s first citation of the word; and in both men's collected works they are merely called songs. The title 'Aubade' would therefore seem to be an editorial initiative, but there is no reason for thinking Larkin knew this.

Louis MacNeice, whom Larkin much admired, wrote two aubades in the thirties: 'Aubade for Infants',[4] and one titled simply 'Aubade' [MCP:86], which is one of his best known poems. These are about the beginning of life rather than the beginning of day, and they are slightly ominous, threatening works. They belong to the category of ironic or subverted aubades: the one warns of the harsh adult world, the other of tedium and war. If Larkin thought of the aubades of Shakespeare and Davenant – as well as MacNeice's inversions – as paradigmatic aubades, then he would think of an aubade as an erotic and joyful dawn song.

However, several commentators have assumed that Larkin's understanding of 'aubade' was *not* that outlined above. Andrew Swarbrick writes that Larkin's 'Aubade' alludes to 'the traditional dawn which *separates* lovers' [OOR:151] (my italics). Lawrence Lerner is more specific:

> The *aubade* or *alba* was a well-known and popular lyric genre in the Middle Ages, ... Larkin's poem makes no explicit reference to this tradition, but the title invites us to notice the contrast: this speaker is not with his beloved but alone, he grieves when dawn comes not because of the joys of love and companionship are over, but because he is terrified of death. [L:38]

They think that Larkin's 'Aubade' does not use the word in its standard modern sense (insofar as there is one) but that he uses the word to refer back to the troubadours' *alba*.

The *alba* is not a lover's dawn serenade[5] to a woman in bed. Of the 19 surviving *albas*, six are religious and describe how the dawn brings an enhanced awareness of sin. The others are erotic, and generally involve a knight in bed with a lady whose jealous husband is away. The couple have enjoyed a night of illicit sexual passion but know the dawn means the end of their bliss. When they are woken by the birds or the cry of the castle watchman the lady denies that dawn has arrived. When the lover affirms it has, both of them curse the rising sun. The knight departs, leaving the lady prostrated by misery and longing. The lyric is always dramatized: sometimes the knight speaks, sometimes the lady, sometimes the watchman, although straightforward dialogue is avoided.[6]

It is quite likely that Larkin knew about this. He had studied medieval and renaissance literature at Oxford, where he had been lectured by Neville Coghill and C.S. Lewis. Even if the *alba* was not an object of study, it is quite possible that one of them mentioned that it was a profound influence on the morning after the wedding in *Romeo and Juliet* or the dawn scene in Chaucer's *Troilus and Cresyede.* Larkin had studied both works, and frequently remarked how bored he was with the latter [SL:38]. In July 1942, he read Lewis's *The Allegory of Love* [SL:37], a book which makes extravagant claims for the troubadours' importance ('Compared with the [effect of the troubadours on literature] the Renaissance is merely a ripple on the surface ...' [AOL:4]) and Lewis explicitly mentions the *alba* in his discussion of the morning scene in *Troilus* [AOL:196].

Even better evidence for Larkin's familiarity with the *alba* comes from his knowledge of modern aubades, because several of these were conscious attempts to revive the *alba* tradition.[7] Larkin knew William Empson's 'Aubade' because he selected it for his anthology, the *Oxford Book of Twentieth Century English Verse*, published in 1973; in fact, it is the only poem with that title in the book. He soon came to know it better than he wanted. Shortly after publication, Christopher Ricks pointed out that the anthology missed out the second half of the poem. Larkin found this deeply upsetting, and one can easily imagine the vexed and anxious checking and rereading the news entailed: a letter to Anthony Thwaite [SL:477–8] expresses his mortification, and there is a long correspondence with Oxford University Press as to how the matter could best be put right.[8]

Empson's poem describes being woken early in the morning by an earthquake, and his indecision about whether to leave Japan and his Japanese girlfriend now war is imminent. In a note on the poem he later wrote: 'an aubade is traditionally the song warning lovers to separate before dawn.'[9] His aubade not only has this story, but it is the only modern aubade with a refrain (in fact it has two which alternate), something also shared by its medieval ancestor. Ricks wrote to Larkin about Empson's poem in March 1973. A little over a year later, in April 1974, Larkin began work on his own poem, and the title 'Aubade' first appears in the manuscripts on 1 June 1974.[10]

Another aubade he would have known is by Stevie Smith, one of his favourite poets. If Empson drew his inspiration from the *alba* tradition then Smith's is a conscious reconstruction. Hers is the only modern poem which contains – except for the refrain – every feature of the troubadour lyric: the mode of dramatization is identical, the content is the same, and the language is studiedly antique. In the first stanza the woman denies the dawn has arrived. She says: ''Tis not the day lights yonder sky / It is too soon / I hear the cock's discordant cry, / He doodles to the moon.' The man then replies: 'Alas my love it is the day, / ...Farewell, my love, adieu, it is the dawn.'[11] The revivification of the *alba* tradition has proved so influential that, in our own day, the *Oxford Companion to Literature* now defines 'Aubade' as: '[A] dawn song, usually describing the regret of two lovers at their imminent separation.'[12]

If you do not know about the *alba* tradition then it is easy to read these two poems as ironic or subverted aubades; works designed to undercut the innocence of the joyful dawn song. If you do know the tradition, then one sees that 'aubade' is used in a perfectly straightforward descriptive sense, and that no mockery of any kind is intended. When Larkin wrote his 'Aubade', therefore, he could well have had these two models in mind rather than an aubade in its more usual modern sense. If this were so, then an aubade for Larkin would be a poignant, dramatized poem about lovers who curse the dawn and have to separate.

When Larkin called his poem 'Aubade' was he making reference to the *alba* tradition or was he using the term to mean a morning serenade? Contrary to Swarbrick and Lerner's opinion, the latter seems the more likely alternative. Larkin may have known about the *alba*, but he was very aware of, and wrote for, the ordinary reader who could not be assumed to know about it. It could be replied that the same consideration ought to apply to Empson and Smith, but they seem very different kinds of poets. Empson is deeply obscure and academic – his work positively demands exegesis – while a good deal of Smith's charm depends on being quirky and oblique. In addition, assuming an aubade is an erotic dawn song from a lover outside to the beloved inside makes the ironies of Larkin's own 'Aubade' less muted and equivocal. If the *alba* interpretation is correct, then the only major irony in Larkin's title would be the one Lerner identifies – the narrator has no lover to part from. Most of the other features of the *alba* – the dread and pain of dawn, for example – would just be straightforwardly true. The erotic serenade interpretation thus gives the title much more poignancy and point.

Finally, it is worth pointing out that 'aubade' became a regular title for pieces of music after the 1860s. French composers in this period were eager to escape the influence of Wagner and German Romanticism generally, and turned for inspiration to the more finely etched archaic forms of their native land – a trend which culminated in works like Ravel's *Le Tombeau de Couperin*. As part of this endeavour, they returned to the word 'aubade' and made a concerted attempt to remove the military and ironic accretions the word had acquired in the nineteenth century: Bizet's 'Aubade' for piano, and Lalo's 'Aubade' for strings and five wind instruments, are well-known early examples.[13] These musical aubades are invariably small-scale, fresh, joyful pieces that carry no taint of loss or departure. 'Aubade' became a popular title for pieces of music – particularly for wind instruments – in the early to middle twentieth century, and Larkin, who knew more about classical music than he often pretended, could well have come across a few examples.[14]

Having clarified Larkin's intention, we can see that the ironies Larkin finds in 'Aubade' are less multivalent than those in 'Vers de Société', but the word's larger stock of historical associations makes them richer. Had he chosen to entitle the poem 'Morning Song' (like Sylvia Plath) or 'Dawn Song' there would be no Gallic gloss to roughen. It would also sever our link with the troubadours. With them comes the hint of the warm south and Provençal mirth; nobility and refinement; courtly love and the devotion to an exalted woman; chivalry and the celebration of heroes and crusades; the clarity and gravity of the pre-Raphaelite world; a life of wandering and artistic freedom; a life devoted to the refining of music and lyric; a young, richly costumed, amorous performer; a life set amongst castles, winding staircases, woods, the glint of dark wine in goblets, rich tapestries, feasts, and most speaking looks. In fact, it is quite likely that no troubadour ever sang a joyful dawn song outside his lover's window. The *alba* is not joyful or sung from outside, and troubadours tended to leave performance to *jongleurs*. But the myth is firmly rooted in our imaginations, and continues to be nourished by children's history books and prewar costume dramas. This is the mental landscape in which a poem's title is intended to resonate; not in that of esoteric, hard-won, historical facts.

Larkin systematically subverts all these associations. His 'Aubade' is not a song, and is the kind of poem which could not be sung; nor is it set outside but in a stuffy bedroom ('hot as a bakery' as he later described it [CP:215]). The poem is set in the north; the outskirts of Hull. The weather is cold; there is no sun; the sky is white as clay. It does not celebrate the life of freedom but endures the routines of administration. There is nothing rich or antique about the life portrayed; it is savourlessly bland and contemporary. Its narrator is ageing, hung-over and staled. It does not greet the dawn but dreads it. As an aubade is a dawn greeting, usually to a man from outside to a woman within, Larkin's ironic implication may be that he is alone, and that all thought of love and romance are simply bitter memories. Alternatively, we could recall that in 'Essential Beauty', Larkin portrays death as a woman: 'that unfocused she / No match lit up ...' [CP:144]. The irony in 'Aubade' may be that a man inside a house offers horrified acknowledgement of the woman who approaches. Finally, we must not forget that, after the Empson debacle, the title 'Aubade' would have been a cause of discomfort and anxiety to Larkin. Far from being innocent and fresh, it was already sicklied o'er with the pale cast of irritation and embarrassment.

A further striking inversion in Larkin's 'Aubade' is its sensory blankness. The traditional aubade, as Larkin knew it, celebrates awakening nature, and the sharpness and precision of the senses. For example, Davenant's: 'The lark now leaves his wat'ry nest / And climbing shakes his dewy wings' [OBEV: 308], or Shakespeare's, 'Hark! Hark! The lark at heaven's gate sings, / And Phoebus 'gins arise, / His steeds to water at those springs / On chaliced flowers that lies' [OBEV:184]. Even in later aubades that want to ironize and subvert this aspect, there is an awareness that this quality needs to be emphasized in order for the forthcoming misfortune to be heightened. MacNeice's 'Aubade', begins with the striking sensory immediacy of: 'Having bitten on life like a sharp apple / Or, playing it like a fish, been happy, / Having felt with fingers that the sky is blue / What have we after that to look forward to?' [MCP: 86]. Before throwing this into contrast by saying that all which lies ahead is boredom and conflict.

Larkin's does not begin with the first stirrings of life, but with soundless dark; he is alone with his thoughts. The lack of sight, sound, and movement, already make him seem partially anaesthetized; they act as a portent and analogue for the oblivion to come. Even when some light does appear, the fear of death is so overwhelming and paralysing that it has bleached all life and colour from the sensory world: no sounds, textures, tastes or smells are noticed; no colours are mentioned but 'dark' and 'white'. In the entire poem, the only objects he certainly perceives are the curtain edges in the first stanza, and the strengthening light and the room's shape in the last. The wardrobe in the last stanza may just be part of a simile, the telephones and offices are merely things he knows about, and it's not even clear whether the sky, postmen and non-sun are seen or only posited. He fears death because it will eliminate his senses; and yet the fear of death has virtually done this already. Similarly, he wants the coming day, but he is quite incapable of enjoying it because the fear of death has so shrunken and reduced it that it now serves only as a sign that death is one day closer.

II

Trevor Tolley describes the language of 'Aubade' as 'resolutely declarative, unwavering in its intent',[15] and Larkin's last workbook shows this tone was hard won. There are three early intimations of the poem. The first sign is a short squib jotted down at the end of 1972:

> Spare Time
>
> In the old days
> I used to come home
> And settle to write
> In the famous evenings.
>
> Now I hit the jug
> And go out like a light.
> Waking, go to bed
> With a hangover. [13.11.72]

The second sign is contained in a letter written to Judy Egerton on 11 January 1974. Here we find him returning to the topic of his routine: 'As I say it's late, & I am rather worn out: my life at present resembles that of the French plongeurs in *Down & Out in Paris and London* – work all day, drink at night to forget it' [SL:498].

The third sign is a short imagistic fragment noted down eight days later on 19 January 1974. This sketch – reminiscent of a de Chirico landscape – takes up at least four major symbols from Larkin's previous collections:

> Daily the deaths like a scatter of unemphatic waves
> Breaks in the personal columns.
>
> I turn and look at my life
> There is little to see
> Except the blue sky and sand-coloured sand
> And here and there white buildings.
>
> I think of love.

Larkin's first formal attempt at 'Aubade' can be found about three months later on 11 April 1974. On the one hand he uses the idea of death and looking back over his life from the wave-fragment; on the other, he takes phrases and the description of his routine from the squib and the letter:

> I work all day and hit the jug at night.
> Waking at five, I stare into the dark,
> And watch the curtain edges to grow light.
> The hours of thought, when daily I remark
> Life is three-quarters done. If I look back
> Some twenty years it's nothing. Yet with luck
> That's all that's left. Not good years either.

Matters did not progress smoothly. On 2 May he writes to Robert Conquest, almost certainly referring to 'Aubade': 'An hour spent at a poem without adding a single (sodding) word … One never gets any better at this lark. Perhaps I shouldn't be sipping an expensive bottle of cheap port …' [SL:505]. Over the next two months, he made at least 14 attempts to get this stanza right, and eventually gave it up on 7 June.

One of the main difficulties was that he would not abandon facetious phrases from the squib which destabilize the tone. Consider this, his last attempt at the first verse before setting it aside for three years:

> I work all day and hit the jug at night.
> Waking at five, I stare into the dark.
> In time the curtain edges will grow light.
> Till then I have leisure to remark
> That more than half of life has elapsed by now
> (two thirds, three-quarters), and I lie wondering how

And where and at what season I shall die.
Routine/Ancient preoccupation, yet the dread
Of dying and being dead
Flashes afresh to hold and horrify. [1.6.74][16]

The diction, and consequently the tone, is uncertain and incongruous. 'Hit the jug' is slightly dated, semi-humorous taproom slang. It is the kind of masculine jocosity which Larkin likes to use in his short comic pieces but proves too weakly slangy for this context. It also mixes poorly with 'at what season I shall die' (which has a slightly eighteenth-century ring) and 'I have leisure to remark …' (which suggests a pose of languid connoisseurship). The staleness of the narrator's circumstance demands flat, quotidian speech, but it was difficult to do this and at the same time to attain the right kind of poetic weight. Achieving this was a matter which extended far beyond revising the diction alone; it also meant rethinking the way he approached structure, imagery, subject matter, metre and narration. It was because resolving these difficulties meant abandoning several stylistic habits of long standing that the poem proved so troublesome to write. In consequence, the finished 'Aubade' is a substantially different kind of poem from the other long serious pieces in the Larkin canon, and it is worth giving detailed consideration as to why this is so.

III

In his longer poems, Larkin frequently likes to hint at the character of the narrator and send him up a little. He wears cycle clips, he eats awful pies, he disdains to notice what is happening in the shade, he had parents who listened to the same seaside quack. But in 'Aubade', fear, inaction, the dark, and the universality of the foreseen end, strip the narrator of personality. The only hints about his life and age that might distinguish him from anybody else are the remark that he gets half drunk at night, and the indication that death is coming 'soon' – although the latter term is so elastic that it could include more or less anyone. Larkin fears loss of his individuality in death, and yet the poem is already profoundly depersonalized. Just as the thought of losing sensation appears to deprive him of sensation, so fear of losing his personality appears to diminish his sense of self. Dread of death has begun to accomplish what death will finish, and the narrator already appears to exist in a panic-stricken limbo.

Early drafts of the poem show that it originally contained more details of his personal circumstances, in particular, his age. He spent some time calculating how much of his time was already over: '...I have leisure to remark / That more than half of life has elapsed by now / (Two-thirds, three-quarters) ...', and 'If I look back / Some twenty years it's nothing. Yet with luck / That's all that's left. Not good years either.' But these details are quickly dispensed with. Larkin must have realized one advantage of a narrator whose personality has been erased: he becomes a kind of Everyman.

Just as the narrator does not present a figure to be sent up, so Larkin avoids humour and facetiousness generally. There are no quirky and amusing observations: no girls in hair-do's fetching their separates from the cleaners; uncles shouting smut; mustachioed women shaking in flowered frocks; pound-note men decamping. Once again terror, inaction and the dark prevent the achievement of any kind of observation or ironic distance.

The sudden changes of speech register found throughout *High Windows* are also absent. The reason is plain enough. In this poem, Larkin is obsessed with himself, and the presence of others is utterly minimal. He is also too terrified to take on another persona or mimic the tone and diction of another voice. *High Windows* contains many feats of ventriloquism: 'A decent chap, a real good sort' [CP:168]; 'Just let me put this bastard on the skids, / I'll get a couple of semesters leave / To work on Protest Theatre' [CP:170]; 'Next year we are to bring the soldiers home / For lack of money, and that is all right' [CP: 171]. 'Aubade' contains no such parodies. Similarly, in this poem, Larkin does not tease us by veering between disparate vocabularies. We find no 'crowd of craps' alongside 'the moon thinned / to an air-sharpened blade' [CP:181]; no 'Groping back to bed after a piss', followed by 'clouds that blow loosely as cannon-smoke' [CP:169]. Moreover, in earlier work, Larkin occasionally likes to heighten awareness of himself by using the odd rare word ('prinked' [CP:52], 'cicatrized' [CP:184], 'blort' [CP:126]), but the diction of 'Aubade' is plain, self-denying, and unfussy throughout.

High Windows contains many sudden shifts from statements to images that try to move beyond words: from thinking about contraceptive precautions to 'The sun-comprehending glass, / And beyond it, the deep blue air ...' [CP:165]; from contemplating money, to 'looking down / From long french windows at a provincial town ...' [CP:198]. Occasionally, as in 'Solar' [CP:159], one gets the pure unmediated image. The wave fragment would have fitted into such a pattern, but after several attempts to incorporate it into 'Aubade', Larkin gave up. This is because the latter is primarily a poem of abstract statement, and the occasional illustrative images indicate psychological exhaustion and damage.

The images are worth looking at in more detail. They fall into two groups. Those in the first are used to convey the reality of death and the fear of death. They are fleeting and immaterial, lacking in definition and outline. Into this category fall the flashes, glares, blurs, and chills. Those in the second establish connections with more recognisable material objects, but they exist in remarkable proximity to the ideas they are supposed to illuminate. The narrator's mind does not have the energy to travel far, and the images have difficulty raising themselves above the level of the literal. Something of the same pathos is found in 'The Building' [CP:191–3], a work that goes through the motions of being a puzzle although it no longer has the heart to be one. Fear of death saps this poem too.

Describing death as 'the anaesthetic from which none come round' is barely a metaphor but rather a direct statement of the truth: a permanent anaesthetic would, from the point of view of consciousness, be equivalent to death. 'That vast moth-eaten, musical brocade' seems more like a synecdoche than a metaphor; after all, churches do contain music and moth-eaten brocade. In '[Death] stands plain as a wardrobe' the object compared with death is (probably) literally seen; all the imagination does is establish the connection. 'The sky is white as clay' is deliberately plain and drab; anything more exuberant and flashy would be wholly out of character with the established mood – washed-out, energyless. Finally, a simile is supposed to be a non-literal comparison, and yet postmen going from house to house could well genuinely look like doctors, in the same way that someone could look like his own brother. The vagueness and inertia of 'Aubade''s imagery is quite as telling – because it is subliminal – in its impact on the reader's emotional response as any of the poem's direct and gloomy statements.

Generally, Larkin's long, serious poems begin hesitantly: he starts with detailed descriptions of a place and then gradually teases the thought from the reality around him. As the thought emerges, Larkin conveys a genuine sense of self-discovery, and frequently takes several wrong turnings.[17] Towards the end, the poems grow more reflective and abstract until they arrive at a transcendent image or philosophical conclusion.

'Aubade' is certainly not a voyage of self-discovery. Rather than the fear of eternal oblivion coalescing and clarifying from details of the material world, it is horribly clear to begin with. The idea presents itself in the middle of the first verse fully formed and unusually quickly: it has clearly been thought through countless times before. Although the main argument of stanzas two and three is *why* the narrator fears death, this cannot disguise the fact that the poem's main problematic is the natural *fact* of death and how to cope with it.

Any alternative explanations offered for his feelings of horror are to prevent misunderstanding on the part of the reader; they do not allow *Larkin* to discover what he really feels; he knows quite well already.

At first glance 'Aubade' seems to be written the wrong way round. All the philosophical conclusions and reflections seem to occur at the beginning and in the middle, and all the detailed observations of the world occur at the end; only in the last stanza does the thought fray and dissipate back into objects. But this is not strictly accurate. The beginning of 'Aubade' does have a physical context, but, apart from the anticipated light around the curtain edges, it is characterized negatively: no sound and no light. Just as the journey in 'Dockery and Son' [CP:152] both symbolizes and prompts the thought of ageing, so the soundless dark symbolizes and prompts the thought of blank non-existence. (The same is true of the blanked mind at the beginning of stanza two: this mirrors its object and anticipates the state it will soon arrive at.) It is in the middle section that the poem broadens out into philosophical reflection. The poem begins with 'I', but at the beginning of the second verse Larkin speaks of '[the] mind' rather than 'my mind'. This prepares the way for the first person plural in line seven: 'The sure extinction that *we* travel to' (my italics) and the pronoun is retained until the end of the poem.[18] This broadening often occurs in Larkin's longer poems, but here the shift is unusually early and suggests how frequently this path has been travelled. It is true that most of the objects occur in the last stanza and with the coming of daylight, but this brings no comfort. On the contrary, any sense of tentative solidarity achieved in the middle verses appears to evaporate as each of us is squeezed back into the narrow channel of our own lives.

Most of the other long poems tend to be about day-trips: either the journeys themselves or the things seen when away. (Even 'Vers de Société' considers the *prospect* of going out, and implies that the narrator probably will.) 'Aubade' is quite other. One cannot get closer to home or more static than being in your bedroom in bed. Larkin shows that the thought of death is like death itself in Kingsley Amis's quip: 'Death has got something to be said for it: / There's no need to get out of bed for it; / Wherever you may be, / They bring it to you, free' [OBD:17].

Metrically, 'Aubade' is also slightly different from the other longer poems. The opening line of the poem is the only one of Larkin's major pieces to begin with a strict pentameter, and the opening verse as a whole is strikingly regular: in four lines the opening foot is a formally inverted, but apart from this there are only five additional unstressed syllables.[19] I think there are two basic reasons for this. First, he makes the stale ordinary speech registration he selects for the poem memorable and weighty by setting it to a sombre, classical, undeflectable rhythm. Second, observations about places, people and events in the other long poems tend to break in on a poem's metre, producing a lively, choppy, slightly unpredictable line. The most rhythmic irregularity, for example, is found in 'Show Saturday' [CP:199–201], the poem most heavily freighted with observation. Soundless dark and inaction are uniform, even and uneventful.

IV

In 'Aubade''s final version, no traces of the squib or the wave fragment are visible. The jocosities of the one, and the images of the other, finally proved to be incompatible with the poem's mood. Significantly, it is only the plain language of the letter that remains:

> I work all day, and get half-drunk at night.
> Waking at four to soundless dark, I stare.
> In time the curtain-edges will grow light.
> Till then I see what's really always there:
> Unresting death, a whole day nearer now,
> Making all thought impossible but how
> And where and when I shall myself die.
> Arid interrogation: yet the dread
>   Of dying, and being dead,
> Flashes afresh to hold and horrify.

The language of the opening line is now appropriately stale, flavourless, and without humour; these, we feel, are dull, grey words. Although, as I observed above, the line is a strict iambic pentameter, you can imagine it passing unnoticed between virtual strangers in a bar: 'Me? I work all day, and get half-drunk at night.' The diction is deliberately drab, but Larkin ensures memorability by being careful with his vowel sounds. By laying the stress on 'work', 'day', 'get', 'drunk', and 'night', he manages to emphasize every major vowel in the language – o, a, e, u, i.

This first line consists of ten monosyllables. Sometimes this device can convey trenchancy and vigour, but frequently it can be used to drain energy from a line altogether: one thinks of Pope's 'And ten low Words oft creep in one dull Line',[20] or Wordsworth's 'The things which I have seen I now can see no more'.[21] Compared with Larkin's statement, however, these lines positively pulse with meaning: Pope's words, besides self-referential wit, have a certain beady purposiveness; and Wordsworth's convey a powerful sense of stunned introspection – like the character in Proust who looks into his hat as though it were twenty feet deep. Larkin's words never aspire to such evocative power. The unnecessary comma after 'day' makes the line flatter still. Syntax would only require this if the sentence were long, or if it changed its grammatical subject, but neither holds true in this context, and the comma serves only to break the back of an already flaccid utterance.

Lack of movement is striking in the next two lines: 'Waking at four to soundless dark, I stare. / In time the curtain-edges will grow light.' Like the first line, they too end in full stops. Larkin's thoughts, we feel, are cold and depressed. We remember his remark about 'the drink gone dead' [CP:215]; nothing grows or develops. It's only when the thought of death makes its inevitable entry that his thoughts begin to gather momentum and start to take on a disagreeable life of their own. The colon after 'always there' suggests more to come. Now there are only commas, and suddenly the sentence begins to run away with no punctuation at all: '... / Making all thought impossible but how / And where and when I shall myself die' with powerful rhythmic impetus being supplied by emphases on 'how', 'where' and 'when'. At least three commas could have been used here, but Larkin wants to give the sense that one thought about death brings all the others rushing unstoppably in its train. We also notice the slight literary swell as the idea of death begins to take hold, his mind begins to function, and unwanted passions are engaged. The diction becomes more polysyllabic and Latinate – 'impossible', 'interrogation' – and words begin to alliterate: 'dread ... dying ... dead', 'Flash ... afresh', 'hold ... horrify'.

The diction takes on additional force when we notice, as Seamus Heaney notices [TRP:155–6], that several key words in the stanza glance backwards at and subvert their earlier employment in Larkin's poetry. The first stanza of 'Aubade' echoes the last stanza of 'The Trees'.

> Yet still the unresting castles thresh
> In fullgrown thickness every May.
> Last year is dead, they seem to say,
> Begin afresh, afresh, afresh.

In the later poem, what once brought solace now enhances despair. In 'The Trees', the adjective 'unresting' characterizes the soothing sway of ample trees; in 'Aubade' it is used to release the all too goal-directed enmity of unresting death. Similarly, 'afresh' which signals new hope and new life in 'The Trees' enhances the terror of dying and being dead in 'Aubade'. These self-allusions and self-reversals are not surprising, since there is a sense in which 'The Trees' is a dishonest or at least sentimental poem. The central verse acknowledges that trees cannot provide a message or example of immortality – 'Is it that they are born again / And we grow old / No, they die to.' But the last stanza forgets this and affirms what the trees *seem* to say – it is the years which die, we always begin anew – and no line in Larkin relies so heavily on its sheer *sound* as the last line of this poem. On the manuscript Larkin wrote 'Bloody awful tripe' [M:372]; 'Aubade' provides more conclusive criticism.

V

Part of the first stanza's weight and authority of utterance derives from the way sentences, and the natural pauses within sentences, are correlated with line length. This natural relationship is not found in the second stanza. Sentences spill across line endings or end in mid-line; parentheses run across line breaks. The general effect is altogether more torturous; the restless turnings of a man facing the unfaceable:

> The mind blanks at the glare. Not in remorse
> – the good not done, the love not given, time
> Torn off unused – nor wretchedly because
> An only life can take so long to climb
> Clear of its wrong beginnings, and may never;
> But at the total emptiness for ever,
> The sure extinction that we travel to
> And shall be lost in always. Not to be here,
> Not to be anywhere,
> And soon; nothing more terrible, nothing more true.

Many readers have found 'Aubade' to be a cancellation, an annulment, of the Christian message; a further negation of the troubadour world from which aubades sprang. Of course, this is largely because religion is disparaged as a 'trick', something 'created to pretend we never die', but it also has to do with the whole sensory tone and atmosphere of the poem. Heaney notes the ironic significance of its first being published – in the *Times Literary Supplement* – on 23 December 1977, so that many people first read it on Christmas Eve or Christmas Day. He continues:

> It would be hard to think of a poem more opposed than this one to the life enhancing symbolism of the Christ child in the Christmas crib. It is as if the mid-winter gleam and promise of medieval carols had been obliterated completely by the dread and dolour of a medieval morality play like Everyman. [TRP:155]

The 'mid-winter gleam and promise of medieval carols' was an aspect of Christmas to which Larkin proved responsive. Explaining why he liked the 'Coventry Carol' in 1976, he remarked: 'This suggests to me Christmas, not the Christmas of Dingly Dell, more the Christmas of the illuminated manuscripts and the book of hours with the red and blue robes and the gold crowns and the gold haloes and the snow ...' [FR:109]. Medieval carols suggest Christmas to Larkin, and Christmas suggests the rich colours of illuminated manuscripts: red robes, blue robes, gold crowns, gold haloes, white snow. How utterly these are obliterated by 'Aubade''s colourless, anaesthetized, blank.

We can see just how deeply 'Aubade''s negation penetrates Christianity if we consider the sentence: 'The mind blanks at the glare.' This is the second time that dread of 'the coming dark' [CP:193] is characterized in terms of light: it gives off a glare; earlier it 'flashes'. Perhaps this is less paradoxical than it seems: you can see total blackness either by looking at blackness or by looking at brilliant light too long. Larkin noticed this when he wrote: 'Light spreads darkly downwards' in 'Friday Night in the Royal Station Hotel' [CP:163]; Milton noticed it when he wrote of God: 'dark with excessive bright thy skirts appear' [PL:III:380]. For Larkin, fear of death has the properties of light which blind, frighten, and hurt, but not those which illuminate. It is this painful negation of light which extinguishes the midwinter gleam of medieval Christianity.

If we think of glare, dazzle, and a light source which is painful to look at, we are likely to think of the sun. Usually this is a life force in Larkin's poetry, most notably in 'Solar': 'Single, stalkless flower / You pour unrecompensed' [CP:159]. When sunlight is moving and human, so that it congregates [CP:93] or throngs [CP:110], it is usually benign and joyous; but when it is fierce or direct it can be damaging and destructive: in 'Deceptions', for instance, we read that '... light, unanswerable and tall and wide, / Forbids the scars to heal' [CP:32]. Larkin acknowledges a connection between the destructive power of sunlight and death when he approvingly quotes La Rochfoucauld's famous remark: 'Death and the sun are not to be looked at steadily' in his review of Enright's the *Oxford Book of Death* [FR:333]. Significantly, it is an aphorism which does not occur in the book.

Light, particularly the light of the sun, and religion are closely associated in Larkin's mind. 'If I were called in / To construct a religion...' he says in 'Water', then the climax of its liturgy would be raising '... in the east / A glass of water / Where any-angled light / Would congregate endlessly' [CP: 93]. Similarly, 'Solar', his hymn to the sun, summons Christian imagery to express his sense of the sun's bountifulness: 'Our needs hourly / Climb and return like angels' [CP:159].

This association of light and Christianity is, of course, traditional: we remember that God is clothed in light [Psalm 104.2], Christ is the light of the world [John: 3.18 and 8.12], and that those who discover God see the light [Eph.5.11–3].[22] Milton, at the beginning of Book III of *Paradise Lost*, says 'God is light' [PL:III:3], something that the Bible does not say directly. But for Milton, and for other traditional Christians, God and death are utterly opposed; indeed, in Book II of *Paradise Lost*, Satan, Death and Sin form a kind of grotesque anti-Trinity which stand in opposition to God the Father, God the Son, and God the Holy Ghost [PL:II:629–889]. For Larkin, unprepared to meet his unmaker, the 'coming dark' which flashes and glares, has taken the place of God. All is now hellish 'darkness visible' [PL:I:63]; Milton's 'universe of death' [PL:II:662] has become the universe.

Alternatively, we can think of Larkin's glaring dark as a ghastly inversion and parody of the Christian God. This is because, for some Christians, God himself is a kind of darkness: 'The Divine Darkness is unapproachable light, in which God is said to dwell' [VCP: 629], wrote Dionysius the Areopagite, a thought brought into the mainstream of English literature by Henry Vaughan:

> There is in God (some say),
> A deep, but dazzling darkness... [VCP:290]

A further negation of Christianity can also be found in 'Aubade''s next lines: 'Not in remorse / The good not done, the love not given ....' Lawrence Lerner argues that these thoughts echo, but take issue with, T.S. Eliot's morning agonizings in 'Little Gidding'. Here, Eliot faces the ghost of his literary ancestors, and is forced to confront 'the gifts reserved for age': '... the shame / Of motives late revealed, and the awareness / Of things ill done, and done to others' harm / Which once you took for exercise of virtue' [L:38].[23] For the Christian Eliot, regret rather than death is the problem of age.[24] For the agnostic Larkin, the implacable blankness of death utterly occludes the significance of regret and remorse.

Such solemnity of phrasing, however, is undercut in the next phrase: 'time / Torn off unused', a remark which is itself slightly puzzling. It could simply signify the waste of something which seems abundant: tissue paper, for example, might be torn off and not used. But this isn't helpful because it's hard to see why Larkin should use an example where the product is so *cheap*, and it's difficult to think of something which is both characteristically torn off and valuable. Much more likely is the idea that Larkin is thinking of a particular kind of calendar. Here each leaf represents a day, and you begin each morning by ripping off the old page. Usually, these are cheap, plain calendars found in offices, and this also fits with the bureaucratic world imagined at the end of the poem.

About 'nor wretchedly because / An only life can take so long to climb / Clear of its wrong beginnings, and may never', it's worth remarking that, as Larkin grew older, he seems to have become more conscious that there was something seriously amiss with his childhood and to blame it for his failures. In the early published poetry, his childhood is simply 'unspent' [CP: 81] 'a forgotten boredom' [CP:33] 'opaque' [CP:184]. But in one of his last poems, he hopes his failing memory and lack of perspective will 'blank out whatever it is that is doing the damage' [CP:211], and by the time we arrive at his last significant poem he hints that his failure in love is 'Something to do with violence / A long way back …' [CP:215]. So far as I know, nobody has given a good account of what Larkin means by this. Is he referring to his childhood? Is he talking about physical violence? By whom on whom? Why did this conviction grow as he aged? Perhaps he simply felt freer to articulate it. His mother died in 1977, and he may have felt less inhibited about making his feelings public.

The last line is metrically interesting. The last lines of stanzas one, three, four and five are more or less perfect ten syllable iambic pentameters. The phase 'And soon' introduces a significant and unexpected irregularity. The line retains five stressed beats, but the syllable count would lead one to expect:

> … Not to be here,
> Not to be anywhere,
> … nothing more terrible, nothing more true.

The same pattern is hinted at by the symmetrical rhetorical structure:

> Not to be …
> Not to be …
> [N]othing more … nothing more …

The step-like lineation also makes us expect, as would make perfect grammatical sense, a full stop after 'Not to be anywhere'. For at least three reasons, therefore, the extra two syllables of 'And soon' come as a nasty and unexpected jolt. The phrase interposes itself; it shoulders all our expectations aside and supplies an ugly, brusque reminder that these things will not only happen but happen shortly.

For Larkin, the word 'true' has close affinities with death, as if nothing could be more real or truer. In 'Ambulances', as in 'Aubade', he emphasizes this by end-stopping a line with the word:

> [They] sense the solving emptiness
> That lies just under all we do,
> And for a second get it whole,
> So permanent and blank and true. [CP:132]

However, in 'Aubade' he is readier to confront his fears, and the poem represents two kinds of advance over 'Ambulances'. Firstly, 'Ambulances' is one of a number of poems about ageing and dying, all of which have death in view but none of which quite confronts the topic squarely. Thus we have poems about heads in women's wards, hospital visits, hospitals, ambulances, old people, helplessness and senility. But 'Aubade' is not about ageing or even dying; it is unequivocally about death itself, shorn of its usual preliminaries. Secondly, 'Ambulances' does not call death by its usual name, but refers to it as 'the solving emptiness'; indeed, part of the poem's unique tone is the undertaker's tact with which death is dealt with. Cities at midday are noisy, ambulances are noisy, and yet the poem is full of verbs of silent discretion: the ambulances 'thread', they 'come to rest', 'recede', patients are 'borne away', traffic 'parts'.

In this indirectness at least, 'Ambulances' is of a piece with most of Larkin's earlier poems in *The Less Deceived* and *The Whitsun Weddings*. Here, death is not mentioned by name, but referred to by rather beautiful euphemisms. It is 'oblivion' [CP:42], 'a black- / Sailed unfamiliar' [CP:52], it 'Brings, the priest and the doctor … Running over the fields' [CP:67], it is found 'down Cemetery Road' [CP:148], 'the only end of age' [CP:153] 'the coming dark' [CP:193].

By the time of *High Windows*, Larkin is able to mention death more directly. In 'The Building' he says, 'All know they are going to die. / Not yet, perhaps not here, but in the end …' [CP:192] while in 'The Old Fools', we find: 'At death you break up …' [CP:196], but these only mention death in the third and second person, and it is part of a general misfortune. But 'Aubade' is the first occasion when death and the first person encounter one another; where Larkin says, 'Yes, I'm going to die soon' and the ramifications of this fact are explored not glancingly, but for five gruelling stanzas.

VI

This is a special way of being afraid
No trick dispels. Religion used to try,
That vast moth-eaten musical brocade
Created to pretend we never die,
And specious stuff that says *No rational being*
Can fear a thing it will not feel, not seeing
That is what we fear – no sight, no sound,
No touch or taste or smell, nothing to think with,
Nothing to love or link with,
The anaesthetic from which none come round.

The image of a 'vast moth-eaten musical brocade' is puzzling. It is true, as I pointed out above, that churches frequently contain music and brocade, and 'moth-eaten brocade' is clear enough. Larkin often used elaborate clothes and materials as emblems of fuss and excess, as when he remarks that women are always finding excuses to show you their emotional haberdashery [SL:158], or that Art Tatum is like someone who has discovered that if one frill looks nice, then 99 would be better still [AWJ:173]. But what exactly is a *musical* brocade? One way to answer this is to assume that Larkin is using a deliberately incoherent image to describe an incoherent thing, or possibly something that he cannot be bothered to think about coherently, like the 'brass and stuff up at the holy end' from 'Church-Going' [CP:97–8].

Another, complementary answer is provided by some recently published biographical material. In *The Philip Larkin I Knew*, Maeve Brennan says that some years before 'Aubade' was written, she and Larkin had read Cardinal Newman's *The Dream of Gerontius* together, and that Larkin had subsequently asked to borrow Elgar's setting from her father's record collection. Shortly after his mother's death, when she first heard 'Aubade', Brennan suggested to him that the poem was an agnostic's response to Newman's poem. 'He did not dispute this view', she says, 'but turned away, overcome by his recent bereavement and the thoughts of his own end' [PLIK:64]. The notion of a brocade, a rich and elaborate material, is clearly more fitted to (Newman and

Elgar's) Catholicism than to any of the Protestant churches; 'moth-eaten' could well apply to the vanished Edwardian and Victorian eras; 'vast' captures the epic scale of Elgar's setting; and the adjective 'musical' is surely applied to religion because one of Larkin's most prolonged recent exposures to religious eschatology was through Elgar's music.[25]

The idea that Larkin was thinking of religion through the twin filters of Newman and Elgar is supported by a number of parallels between 'Aubade' and *The Dream of Gerontius*. In the latter, these occur at the beginning of the second part. Here, the soul of Gerontius, like Larkin at the beginning of his poem, wakes from sleep, but in Gerontius's case it is the sleep which precedes eternal life and the emotional tenor is wholly different: 'I went to sleep: and now I am refresh'd, / A strange refreshment: for I feel in me / An inexpressive lightness ... [DG:817]. The emotional reversal between Gerontius waking to Life-in-Death, and Larkin waking to Death-in-Life, ramifies later: Larkin dreads experiencing '... – no sight, no sound, / No touch or taste or smell ....' The middle of this list is foreshadowed by a similar list, in the same order, in Newman's poem, but whereas Larkin's senses are nonexistent and consequently blank, Gerontius's are redeemed, perfected, and glutted by glorious music: 'And hark! I hear a singing; yet in sooth / I cannot of that music rightly say / Whether I hear, or touch, or taste the tones ... [DG:819]. Finally, the Angel tells Gerontius two lines later, 'My work is done', whereas for Larkin, 'Work has to be done'. The thought that 'Aubade' is a partial unwriting of *The Dream of Gerontius* is hard to resist.

If religion is conveyed by a deliberately inflated, over-elaborate, unworkable image, then philosophy – specifically the view of the Epicureans – is dispatched in a phrase: it is 'specious stuff'. These images are the only points in the poem where there is a hint of levity, presumably because the topic is now hopeless human theorizing about death, or more accurately human wish-fulfilment fantasies, rather than the natural, grim actuality of death itself.

The eighth and ninth lines are some of the most contentious in the poem:

> ... this is what we fear – no sight, no sound,
> No touch, or taste, or smell, nothing to think with,
> Nothing to love or link with,
> The anaesthetic from which none come round.

In his *Memoirs*, Kingsley Amis says that the rhyme '... with / ...with' shows that Larkin's skill deserted him for a moment.[26] William Pritchard, on the other hand, feels the doubled 'with' has a point:

> The specious stuff of religion and philosophy is dismissed, but there is nothing specious about the rhyming, especially the double one of 'think with' and 'link with' which touchingly links itself with the reader who both sees and hears a life-affirming connection made in the midst of death.[27]

Neither explanation really works. Amis's fails to carry conviction because Larkin was a most fastidious and observant poet, he was clearly very proud of this poem, and it was slowly polished over a period of three years. If the two lines were a blemish, he could easily have rewritten them. Pritchard's interpretation does not make clear why this kind of doubled rhyme reaches out to the reader more effectively than any other kind of rhyme. In addition, to hear 'a life-affirming connection made in the midst of death' seems far too cosy in the context of a poem which insists that death is the end of all connections.

The real reason for the doubled 'with' is surely that the rhyme scheme enacts and dramatizes the failure of linkage. There are two ways lines can fail to rhyme: either the final syllable of the word at the end of the second line has no sound in common with the final syllable of the word at the end of the first line; or the word at the end of the second line is the same as the word at the end of the first line. After all, if I ask you for a rhyme for 'lost' and you reply with either 'chipmunk' or 'lost' then I will think you are being uncooperative in both cases. In Larkin's lines, 'or link with' looks for the previous line to link with and discovers only 'to think with'; the hand reaching out fails to find another and slides off. Lines about failing to link fail to link. The idea of the doubled 'with' gives Larkin the paradoxical ability both to maintain and not maintain his rhyme-scheme, because the point at which a rhyme becomes perfect is exactly the point where it ceases to be a rhyme. The rhyme of the penultimate words in each line – 'link' and 'think' – proves a wholly misleading anticipation and encouragement; it sets us up for disappointment. The use of a doubled rhyme in 'Aubade' is no more accidental or dissonant with the poem's message than the doubled rhymes used in 'Homage to a Government' [CP:171]. Here, such rhymes are used throughout to indicate the brain-death and spiritless conformity of the speaker.

The grammatical mistake in the last line, however, *does* appear to be an oversight, as Larkin later admitted. Writing to C.B. Cox he asks: 'Tell me, as a professor of English, are you offended by 'None come round'? Would you be happier with 'None comes round'? As a natural illiterate, I never think of these things until it is too late. But it could be changed if the poem is ever collected' [SL:669].

VII

At one stage in the workbook, he tries to work the obituary idea from the wave fragment into stanza three: '… was it [religion] put / Aside when death was driven into age, / And shrunk to the obituary page?' [7.6.74]. Three years later, he decides to begin the fourth stanza with a more complete version of the fragment: 'Death breaks each morning like a tiny wave / In newspapers' [11.6.77].

If the remarks about his own age were too personal, then these remarks about obituaries were too public to survive into the poem's final version. Somehow the thought of reading about other people's deaths – as well as the comfy domestic regimes of reading newspapers and having them delivered – democratizes and thereby defuses the terror that confronts Larkin. This is because he confronts *his own* death, and no poet ever felt the difference between a misfortune happening to him, and a misfortune occurring to somebody else, more keenly. Looked at in the third person, and from the point of view of society, a plurality of deaths, like a plurality of births, is part of a natural process. But Larkin is not interested in a plurality of deaths; he is interested in one – his own – which is quite different from all the others. Not only does Larkin dismiss the possibility of immortality, he does not show any interest in what happens after his death at all. One striking absence in 'Aubade' is that, unlike many poems about death, no mention is made of funerals, mourning relatives, the gap in colleagues' lives, the evaluations of posterity. In a certain sense, argued Schopenhauer, the world comes to an end at my death; this is the only sense of 'the world' in which Larkin was interested. Obituaries, being part of the social world and published *post mortem*, are wholly alien to 'Aubade''s grimly solipsistic focus.

In the poem, Larkin is hideously aware that his is an 'only life' and that nothing that happens before it, after it, or to others, is of any account. It is for this reason that he denies himself the comfort of the routines, rituals, ceremonies and traditions he so frequently contemplates elsewhere – county shows, Remembrance Days, annual seaside holidays, and so forth. This is especially noticeable in his treatment of Christianity. Although he was an agnostic, he was deeply attached to the Anglican Church, and derived much comfort from the history and continuities it represented. This is evident at the end of 'Church Going'. Here the narrator 'tends to this cross of ground' because 'it held unspilt / So long and equably what since is found / Only in separation – marriage, and birth, / And death, and thoughts of these.' And he discovers in himself 'a hunger … to be more serious' and gravitates to the ground 'If only that so many dead lie round' [CP: 98]. But Larkin's feelings for the building, the institution and its history, are only comforting because they are based on incoherence. He knows that many dead lie round and *notionally* assents to the idea that he will one day join them. In this way he can think of his death as part of a pattern sustained and sanctified by tradition. But when he awakes panic-stricken at four in the morning, he *really* assents to the fact of his own death, and in doing this realizes it is quite unlike any of the others.[28] His death will bring the world to an end. Christianity as institution is irrelevant; only Christianity as doctrine is of any account here – and he bitterly dismisses that as so many tawdry rags.

The other notable lacuna in 'Aubade' is nature – and not only the sun, trees, and larks, characteristic of aubades. This is slightly surprising because *High Windows* differs from his two previous mature collections in the number of times that nature and its continuities are evoked. As Larkin aged, these cycles provided a source of solace and comfort: the apparent rebirth of trees, the passing of day into night, 'Celestial recurrences, / The day the flowers come, / And when the birds go' [CP:184]. But contemplation of their permanence and his impermanence would make his situation worse rather than better; and he realizes that nature is responsible for the dark that will shortly greet him. Consequently, he says nothing about the nature in 'Aubade', and when his mind begins to turn towards the outside world, he focuses on its least meaningful and most ephemeral aspects. He does not think about churches, or seasons, or people's homes; instead he conjures up the 'uncaring / Intricate rented world' of locked offices and crouching telephones. This world is impersonal and impermanent; those who use it do not own it; it is sanctified by no religion, ritual or history; it is denatured and artificial; it is deliberately ephemeral, bland, and flavourless. This is the world which conforms most precisely to his state of mind now; like him it is temporary, and no one who loses it could care for it.

In its final version, the fourth stanza runs:

> And so it stays just on the edge of vision,
> A small unfocused blur, a standing chill,
> That slows each impulse down to indecision.
> Most things will never happen: this one will,
> And realization of it rages out
> In furnace-fear when we are caught without
> People or drink. Courage is no good:
> It means not scaring others. Being brave
> Lets no one off the grave.
> Death is no different whined at than withstood.

It is as if, just for a moment, all the philosophical thought of the previous two stanzas – largely moral in the second, largely metaphysical in the third – has allowed him to distance his fear of death and get it under some control. He remembers that in everyday life death is omnipresent but on the *edge* of vision, and it is indistinct and cold rather than ragingly central. But the respite is shortlived because in his current state he lacks the distractions of normal life. At 'this one will' the fear of death floods back, and he is again plunged into the tortured imaginings of the opening verse. The similarity of state is mirrored by similarity of language. Here again the energy of dread is expressed by alliteration: 'realisation… rages', 'furnace-fear', 'being brave', 'death … different … whined at … withstood'.

The stanza then moves on to consider the uselessness of courage, and Larkin's analysis is deeply questionable. In an early draft of the stanza, he is inclined to argue that it is an archaic military virtue that he simply doesn't have. The verse of the draft also illustrates the desperate uncertainty of tone and diction which characterizes the early drafts as a whole:

> Courage, that dated helmet-head
> Among the virtues: When you've found
> You haven't got it, what d'you do?
> Stay away from where it's needed –
> Love and war and wanting, all
> The rot that makes the world go round … [17.1.75]

In the final version, in line with its generally greater impersonality, he removes the reference to his personal lack of courage, and instead attempts to devalue the concept altogether; a move which has the effect of making his own lack less significant. He does this, not by developing the idea that it's dated, but by saying that all courage amounts to is not scaring others. If courage only has to do with outer expression, and not inward motivation, then it looks a very minor virtue.[29]

However, the analysis of courage only looks plausible because of the particular kind of danger Larkin is facing. If we consider some other examples than we can see that courage amounts to much more than this. A soldier who walks calmly off the battlefield, without scaring anyone has not shown courage. There also seem to be circumstances where you *do* scare others by your emotional state but still show courage. For example, a man in a burning building may be beside himself with fear, and may convey this fear to those around him, but if he goes in deeper to rescue someone we would still say he'd shown courage – we might even be more impressed by his courage because he was evidently so scared. These cases make us see that courage involves acting appropriately and for the good, even though you have a full imaginative realization of the dangers you are facing.

The difficulty with trying to say what courage is when faced – as we all are – by the inevitability of death, is that it is not at all clear what the appropriate and beneficial action is. (Hence the initial convincingness of Larkin's analysis.) The only option is not to lie gibbering in bed, but go about your normal business, live up to your station and its duties, care for those who depend on you, get on with your daily life. This, it seems to me is exactly what Larkin does in the last stanza; a stanza Motion correctly characterizes as 'stoic' [M: 468]. There, his behaviour demonstrates both that the analysis offered in the fourth stanza is false and trivializing, and that he actually does have the real courage which, in the early version of the stanza, he claimed to lack. Larkin *says* in the early draft that he doesn't have courage, and then in the later draft that courage is trivial or irrelevant; his behaviour in the last stanza *shows* he does have it and it isn't either trivial or irrelevant. I think Larkin does get up to draw the curtains, look at the sky, and watch the postmen. I also think that, when he arrives at the library, he will go about his work stoically, efficiently and courteously.

VIII

The last stanza is masterly. If you try to reading the poem and stop at the end of any of the other verses there is a palpable diminution of the poem's power. It is in this stanza that Larkin's consciousness begins to move beyond its private tormented thoughts and starts to spread out into the world again.[30] This ought to make it seem heartening; indeed, many have found the last verse more optimistic than the others. To me, it seems utterly desolate. This is largely because one sees how his struggle has bleakened waking; how it has saddened and stunned the coming day. His nocturnal terrors have not been left behind in the darkness: they imbue the early world, suffuse it, seep into its detail and texture, rendering every aspect void and savourless.

> Slowly light strengthens, and the room takes shape.
> It stands plain as a wardrobe, what we know,
> Have always known, know that we can't escape,
> Yet can't accept. One side will have to go.

> Meanwhile telephones crouch, getting ready to ring
> In locked-up offices, and all the uncaring
> Intricate rented world begins to rouse.
> The sky is white as clay, with no sun.
> Work has to be done.
> Postmen like doctors go from house to house.

This, as Motion points out, is a verse full of *things* [M:468], but in line with the poem's lack of observation, and the depersonalization of the narrator, we should observe how unindividual these things are. The curtains in the first verse do not fall within five inches of the sill [CP:102], they are simply curtains, anybody's curtains; they tell us nothing. Similarly, fear has washed away all identity from the room: the wardrobe (if there is one), the locked office, the telephone are bleached-out and generic. On the one hand this makes them unsettlingly numb and blank; on the other it makes them more universal. It requires an act of imagination to be with Larkin on his rail trips and his seaside holidays; but nearly every reader woke this morning to a room, curtains, and a wardrobe. Here only memory is required.

Why do Larkin's thoughts turn to the world of work? One reason may be that the end of the poem negates and undercuts two kinds of poem that were at the forefront of Larkin's mind as he wrote: Christian meditations on death and aubades in general. Christian poems about the afterlife often end with visions of rest and peace. At the beginning of part two of *The Dream of Gerontius*, for example, Gerontius awakes to experience '… the deep rest, so soothing and so sweet' [DG:817]. For Larkin, on the contrary, there is no rest, only the grim reality of toil and drudgery. However, work can have its cheering and enlivening aspects. Aubades frequently end with a vision of work, as the day comes to life and others stir. Davenant's last verse, for example, begins with merchants and ploughmen who are already about their business: 'The Merchant bowes unto the Seamens Star, / The Ploughman from the Sun his Season takes' [OBEV:308]. Davenant's characters appear to find joy and invigoration in work, whereas Larkin finds only a grim and painful duty.

Andrew Swarbrick detects a hint of cheer in Larkin's vision of work. He recommends that we think of the scenes Larkin sketches as aspects of 'that workaday world which sustains itself by individuals' mutual reliance' [OOR:152], but this sounds a little too communal and healthy-minded to be wholly persuasive. As he comes close to admitting, for his suggestion to carry conviction, two of the three adjectives in 'uncaring / Intricate rented world …' would need to be ignored:

> Tucked between two dismissive adjectives but prominent at the beginning of the line, 'Intricate' pays tribute to whatever resists, however temporarily, the encroachments of death. It is the intricacy of 'smells of different dinners' ('Ambulances'), of 'sports finals / stuck / In front doors' ('Show Saturday'), of 'Fathers, brothers, nicknames, laughter' ('The Explosion'). [OOR:152]

What gives Swarbrick's other examples of intricacy their positive affect is the warm social activities and relationships – sports, meals, families, laughter – in which they are embedded. If we remove these, then we are left with bare intricacy, and intricacy *tout court* has nothing to recommend it – surely simplicity is better. If we then apply a few adjectives like 'uncaring' and 'rented', and place the word in a context of locked-up offices and crouching telephones, then it surely gestures away from sustaining communities towards the stressful, indifferent, and impersonal. If Larkin had wanted to illustrate a world that 'sustains itself by individuals' mutual reliance' in these central lines of the stanza he could surely have chosen a better example, since, at best, the people in Larkin's scene are merely implied. He could have imagined people who are already up and at their trades (like the postmen he sees at the end of the stanza); he could have imagined his own workplace once the people had arrived; he could have imagined sitting in the bar with friends.

Late in life, Larkin made a number of remarks about work that could support Swarbrick's interpretation. To Roy Plomley, in 1976, he said: ' ... over the years I've come to think that I rather like work' [FR:103]; and in the same year he had written to Winnifred Bradshaw: 'And of course *work*, paradoxically enough *is* a comfort. One wakes up wanting to cut one's throat; one goes to work, & in 15 minutes one wants to cut someone else's – complete cure!' [SL: 551]. More intimate friends were aware, however, that his attitude was changing. 'As time passed', writes Maeve Brennan, 'it became very noticeable that he was increasingly depressed and dependent on alcohol. I remember how shocked I was when he confessed to regularly drinking half a bottle or more of sherry before going to work, just to enable him to face the day' [PLIK:90]. When the poetic muse deserted him [he described 'Aubade' as 'the death-throes of a talent' SL:574] ... personal sorrow took over and his soul became once more trapped in the dark recesses of his mind. By the mid-1970s, feeling that he had also given of his best professionally, even "the toad work" no longer afforded the challenge and fulfilment it had once done' [PLIK:135]. Work is no longer a comfort. It comes to mind only because he will shortly have to go to his office, and it's an indifferent, uncaring, impersonal place that offers no solace. It is also slightly aggressive; to be locked out is to be deprived of power, and the telephones crouch in readiness to attack rather than in submission,

In the last line, as in MacNeice and Davenant, Larkin turns his attention to the street: the postmen who go like doctors from house to house. His observation seems inconclusive. The sentence has none of the imposing resonance of the previous stanzas' final lines which complete or encapsulate what has been said, but it is all the more powerful for that. This is because the action of the poem is implied to continue long after the poem has finished. The postman will continue their task after the poet's glance has left them, and one has a sense of death gradually spreading itself out through the city and into the countryside beyond. The final stanza's deadly chill seeps out through the membrane of the final line and into our lives.

Of course, for many critics, the image of the postmen is not a pessimistic image at all. According to Anthony Thwaite, it is a symbol of hope: 'the image' he says, 'is one of healing or renewal, of the diurnal comfort of letters through the post' [SL:xi]. Andrew Swarbrick endorses this reading: 'The final 'Postmen like doctors' are emblems of that workaday world which sustains itself by individuals' mutual reliance…' [OOR:152]. Certainly, there are several pieces of evidence that can be offered in support of their view. Larkin was a great letter writer and hugely enjoyed receiving letters. Thwaite quotes the lines 'I know, none better, / The eyelessness of days without a letter' [SL: xi]. Swarbrick, mentions an early optimistic version of the final line found in the relevant workbook: 'Postmen go / from house to house like doctors to persuade / Life to resume' [12.8.77. OOR:152].

On the other hand one can point out that, in Larkin, doctors and medical services are rarely shown as healers but usually anticipate and attend on death. 'Where can we live but days? // Ah, solving that question / Brings the priest and the doctor / In their long coats / Running across the fields' [CP:67]. Hospitals are places that you die in ('not yet, perhaps not here, but in the end' [CP:192]); and ambulances bring to mind that solving emptiness rather than a return to rude health. Like 'Aubade''s doctors, these ambulances spare no one: 'all streets in time are visited' [CP:132]. Medical services are as cheerfully quotidian and democratic as death.

Against Thwaite's endorsement of the optimistic reading, it can be pointed out that if even postmen – those emblems of optimism and renewal – can come to look like doctors, then this shows how far death has negated all hope. Swarbrick's citation of the cancelled version of the last line is not conclusive either. The very fact that Larkin cancelled it and replaced it by something altogether gloomier shows that he realized the earlier version was too facile: it didn't fit the poem; it wasn't what he wanted to say.

Although I have argued that the abstract thoughts of the earlier part of the poem dissipate into things in the final stanza, fade into the common light of day, death still permeates the whole of this last verse. Consider the 'it' at the beginning of the second line: 'It stands plain as a wardrobe.' When we read this line, we naturally assume that the 'it' refers to one of the nouns in the previous line – either 'light' or 'room'. This assumption is strengthened by the fact that both the light and the room probably have some relationship with the wardrobe – one illuminates it, one contains it. Surprisingly, this is not what the word denotes. The 'it' at the beginning of the second line actually refers back to death, and the narrator's assumption that we will take this for granted, in spite of the sentence before and the new topic of the illuminated room, shows the depth of his preoccupation. The weight of his knowledge is emphasized by the concatenation of '… know/ … known, know …'. The arrival of day does not disperse his fears; they still stand in front of him more clearly than what he actually sees. This makes the meaning of the slightly obscure 'One side will have to go', plain enough: we can't accept death but death will happen; it is we who will go.

We then have a sketch of the world of lifeless impersonal offices, before reaching the next image: 'The sky is white as clay.' One reason why the image might have come to mind is that clay is the very substance of our mortality; it is what we are made from; it is what we will return to. The mortality suggested by this clay is enhanced by its colour: clay is normally brown or grey; this particular clay has been bled white. This clay may suggest death in another way. It may be that the narrator anticipates looking at the interior of his own grave,[31] and the words 'with no sun' reinforce this idea. In many poems the idea of removal from sunlight indicates death. In the song from *Cymbeline*, Fidele's death is memorialized by the line 'Fear no more the heat o' the sun' [NOBEV:141]; and one line in Browning's 'A Toccata of Galuppi's', runs, 'Death stepped tacitly and took them where they never see the sun' [NOBEV: 667]. If this interpretation is correct then the line fits a frequently noted pattern in this poem: the thought of death prefigures what death itself will bring. Fittingly, the phrase '…with no sun' consists entirely of stressed syllables; spondees. All life has been taken from it. In one more line we arrive at the final image of the postmen, and we should hear it as the culmination of a number of images and rhythms about the idea of death which, although dissolved in things, is still omnipresent.

Rhythmically, the poem ends as it began: each of the four lines is end-stopped; each is a complete sentence. But here the emotional effect is different. At the opening the full stops reinforced the sense of staleness and inertia; here they indicate the gritted teeth of stoicism: work has to be done.

IX

There are, no doubt, many reasons why 'Aubade' was Larkin's last significant published poem, even though he lived for another eight years. Some of these are external reasons: reasons concerning his life and circumstances. His new house – to which he could never properly adjust – may have had something to do with it, as might growing responsibilities, drink, depression, illness, cohabitation, even success. Alternatively, there may be internal reasons for his lack of productivity: reasons to do with the development and shape of his oeuvre. One of these has already been hinted at. 'Aubade' is the poem where death is clearly and unequivocally confronted for the first time: death is not screened by the process of dying, or merely glanced at, or called by soft names. But why should this affect his creativity? It could be that the significance of this topic, and the conclusiveness of the poem, dwarfed all other subject matters, making them seem trivial or peripheral. It could be that a repressed horror of death coloured and animated his poetry, in a way that the same horror confronted, dissected and analysed could not.

But the most significant clue is to be found in his review of Enright's, *Oxford Book of Death*. This is largely a prose reprise of many things he had said in 'Aubade' although he adds a few twists and details, but there is one point which he does not, with good reason, make in the poem. He begins the second paragraph of the review discussing the hopelessness of using religion as a palliative, and continues:

> But there is also literature, where death is still the only possible end to the story, except marriage. Unfortunately nothing is quite real in literature, not even death; we are either left feeling that in some indefinable way it is *all right*, or that the characters will get up unharmed and advance bowing to the footlights. This is not how death affects us in reality. … [FR:331]
>
> The intrusion of death into our lives is so ruthless, so irreversible, so rarely unaccompanied by pain, terror and remorse, that to 'anthologize' it, however calmly, quizzically and compassionately, seems at best irrelevant, at worst an error of taste. … [By] their natures anthologies do not look steadily, nor

> do they explain or console: they entertain. And death is not entertaining. The chapter on 'Care of the Dying' in any nursing manual makes this point more clearly. [FR:333]

Larkin never abandoned the principle that 'poetry, like all art, is inextricably bound up with giving pleasure, and if a poet loses his pleasure-seeking audience he has lost the only audience worth having ... [No] pleasure ... no poetry' [RW: 81–2]. And yet now he discovers that a truthful treatment of death cannot give pleasure; the topic that now dwarfs all others in his consciousness is therefore beyond the powers of literature to depict. For all its unflinching, wintery bleakness, 'Aubade' is still a poem, it is still literature,[32] and that means it falsifies to entertain. The unproductive years ahead would be reserved for the attitude embodied in 'Care of the Dying'. And death itself, of course.[33]

Notes

1 I use the following abbreviations. Works by Larkin: AWJ: Philip Larkin, *All What Jazz: A Record Diary* (London: Faber and Faber, 1970); CP: *Philip Larkin: Collected Poems*, ed. Anthony Thwaite (London: The Marvell Press and Faber and Faber, 1988); FR: Philip Larkin, *Further Requirements*, ed. Anthony Thwaite (London: Faber and Faber, 2001); RW: Philip Larkin, *Required Writing* (London: Faber and Faber, 1983). SL: *Selected Letters of Philip Larkin* (ed) Anthony Thwaite (London: Faber and Faber, 1992); TWG: *Philip Larkin, 'Trouble at Willow Gables' and Other Fictions*, ed. James Booth (London: Faber and Faber, 2002). Works about Larkin mentioned more than once: L: Lawrence Lerner, *Philip Larkin* (Plymouth: Northcote House, 1997); M: Andrew Motion, *Philip Larkin: A Writer's Life* (London: Faber and Faber, 1993); OOR: Andrew Swarbrick, *Out of Reach: The Poetry of Philip Larkin* (London: Macmillan, 1995); PLIK: Maeve Brennan, *The Philip Larkin I Knew* (Manchester: Manchester University Press, 2002); TRP: Seamus Heaney, 'Joy or Night: Last Things in the Poetry of W.B. Yeats and Philip Larkin', in *The Redress of Poetry* (London: Faber and Faber, 1995), pp. 146–63. Other works mentioned more than once: AOL: C.S. Lewis, *The Allegory of Love: A Study in Medieval Tradition* (Oxford: Oxford University Press, 1953); DG: John Henry Cardinal Newman: *The Dream of Gerontius*, in Geoffrey Tillotson (ed.), *Newman: Poetry and Prose* (London: Hart-Davies, 1957), pp. 812–42; HVCP: *Henry Vaughan: The Complete Poems*, ed. Alan Rudrum (Harmondsworth: Penguin, 1983); MCP: *Louis MacNeice: Collected Poems 1925–1948* (London: Faber and Faber, 1949); NOBEV: *New Oxford Book of English Verse 1250–1950*, ed. Helen Gardner (Oxford: Clarendon Press, 1973); OBD: *The Oxford Book of Death*, ed. D.J. Enright (Oxford: Oxford University Press, 1983); OBEV: *The Oxford Book of English Verse*, ed. Sir Arthur Quiller-Couch (Oxford: Oxford University Press, 1900); PL: Milton, *Paradise Lost*, ed. Alistair Fowler (London: Longman, 1989).

2 Schumann, *Kinderszenen*, Op. 15, No. 7.

3 J.A. Simpson and E.S.C. Weiner (eds), *The Oxford English Dictionary*, 2nd edn (Oxford: Clarendon Press, 1991), Vol. 1, p. 777.

4 W.H. Auden (ed.), *Selected Poems of Louis MacNeice* (London: Faber and Faber, 1977), p. 85.

5 'Serenade' – which derives from the troubadours' *serena* – literally means 'evening song', just as 'aubade' literally means 'dawn song.' I therefore apologize for the slightly oxymoronic flavour of 'dawn serenade', but it seems to be the easiest way to convey my intended meaning. 'Serenade' has been much more happily assimilated into the language than 'aubade'. The former does appear in Johnson's dictionary and its meaning has grown more inclusive over the years. 'Aubade' only refers to single pieces of music, but a serenade can either be a single movement or a suite of pieces. 'Serenade', of course, can also be a verb.

6 I have found the following books and articles particularly helpful in researching the history of the *alba* and the troubadours: Jonathan Saville, *The Medieval Erotic Alba: Structure as Meaning* (New York: Columbia University Press, 1972); Peter Dronke, *The Medieval Lyric* (Cambridge: D.S. Brewer, 1996); Robert P. Miller (ed.), *Chaucer: Sources and Backgrounds* (New York, Oxford University Press, 1977); Jefrey Dean, 'The Alba', in *The New Grove Dictionary of Music and Musicians*, 2nd edn, Vol. I, ed. Stanley Sadie and John Tyrrell (London: Grove, 1998); Percy Scholes, 'Minstrels, Troubadours, Trouveres, Minnesingers, Mastersingers', in his *The Oxford Companion to Music* (London: Oxford University Press, 1938).

7 Besides the aubades mentioned in the text, I have found poems with this title by the following authors: Frederick Bock, Madison Cawein, Marylin Chin, Nuala Ni Dhomhnaill (trans. from Irish by Michael Longley), Ibn Hani (trans. from the Arabic by A.J. Arberry), Richard Howard, Richard Keney, Thomas Merton,Vassar Miller, Karl Schapiro, Timothy Steele, Robert Wallace and Robert Penn Warren. There are also two anonymous aubades: 'O Lady, awake, the azure moon', and 'Stay, O sweet, and do not rise'. The latter is sometimes attributed to John Donne. Some of these works were written after Larkin's death, and it seems unlikely he knew the others. On the other hand, he may have known the aubades by Agnes Robinson, Edith Sitwell, Sir Osbert Sitwell and Sylvia Plath. The last of these is a juvenile poem collected in Hughes's 1981 edition which Larkin reviewed in 1982; Edith Sitwell's poem appears set to music in William Walton's *Façade II.*

8 The 43 letters concerning the *Oxford Book of Twentieth Century English Verse* are unpublished, and are deposited in the Brynmor Jones Library in Hull.

9 John Haffenden (ed.), *William Empson: The Collected Poems* (Harmondsworth: Penguin, 2001), p. 316.

10 Larkin's drafts for 'Aubade' are found in his last workbook, Workbook No. 8, deposited in file DPL 1/8 (formerly DPL/11) in the Larkin archive of the Brynmor Jones Library. I identify each entry by Larkin's own datings.

11 *The Collected Poems of Stevie Smith* (London: Allen Lane, 1978), p. 46.

12 Margaret Drabble (ed.), *The Oxford Companion to English Literature*, rev. edn (Oxford: Oxford University Press, 1995), p. 50.

13 'Aubade' is a much more familiar word in French than English. We can see this from its occurrence in idioms, whereas there are no English expressions which make use of it. Thus 'donner une aubade à une jeune fille' means to have early morning sex with a girl; 'recevoir une aubade' means to be thoroughly told off; and 'aubade' is frequently used ironically to refer to the clatter of servants or other 'bruits hostiles'. Its connotations are also slightly different in French. The leading sense of the word is to refer to a dawn performance rather than the piece performed, and the latter is just as likely to be a fanfare or full scale military band concert as a song. The *Trésor de la Langue Francaise* (Paris:

Centre Nationale de la Recherche Scientifique, 1974), Tome III, defines an aubade as: 'Concert de voix ou d'instruments donné à l'aube en l'honneur de quelq'un, sous ses fenêtres ou à sa porte; air compose pour ce concert.' The military and ironic connotations of the word are presumably the reason why there are no French poems called 'aubade' in the nineteenth century.

14 His interest and knowledge of classical music are made clear in PLIK, pp. 52–3.

15 A.T. Tolley, *My Proper Ground: A Study of the Work of Philip Larkin and its Development* (Edinburgh: Edinburgh University Press, 1991), p. 135.

16 The stanza Larkin uses in 'Aubade' is prefigured in his early poem about death, 'And the wave sings because it is moving' [CP:6–7; see M:150]. 'The wave sings …' doesn't have a regular rhythm of rhyme scheme, but it too has a ten line stanza with the ninth line shortened. It was characteristic of Larkin in the 1970s to revisit and rework material from the late 1940s and early 1950s. 'Vers de Société' is a recomposition of 'Best Society' probably finished in 1951: 'Livings I' harks back to 'Negative Indicative' from 1953; 'The Card Players' to 'Two Guitar Pieces' from 1946.

It is quite difficult to say why Larkin chose this unusual stanza structure. He may have enjoyed the way the shortened ninth line precipitates one into the generally gloomy and sonorous final line. It's also worth pointing out that 'Aubade' inverts the stanza of Larkin's most affirmative long poem, 'The Whitsun Weddings'. This uses a ten line iambic pentameter except for the *second* line which is truncated.

Appropriately, the ABBA rhyme scheme of the final four lines is reminiscent of Tennyson's *In Memoriam*. And Tennyson – whose collected works Larkin reviewed in 1969 [RW:182–7] – may have been at the back of Larkin's mind at several points in 'Aubade': for example, 'The casement slowly grows a glimmering square' from 'Tears, idle tears …' in *The Princess*.

17 The differences between 'Aubade''s certainty and Larkin's usual poetic hesitations are also noted in Trevor Tolley, *My Proper Ground*, p. 135. For some more detailed remarks about the structure of 'Dockery and Son' see M.W. Rowe, 'Poetry and Abstraction', this volume, pp. 165–81.

18 This point is made on pp. 51–2 of Jack B. Bedell's, 'The Metrics of Connection: Form and Tone in Philip Larkin's "Aubade"', *Hellas: A Journal of Poetry and the Humanities*, 8, Pt 1 (1997), pp. 47–58.

19 'Vers de Société' also has a strictly iambic first line, but the tone and diction of that poem are rather different from Larkin's longer, serious, pieces: 'Church Going', 'Faith Healing', 'Dockery and Son', 'The Whitsun Weddings', 'To the Sea', and so on.

20 John Butt (ed.), *The Poems of Alexander Pope* (London: Methuen, 1984), p. 154.

21 Stephen Gill (ed.), *William Wordsworth: The Oxford Authors* (Oxford: Oxford University Press, 1984), p. 297.

22 If Freud's speculation in *Moses and Monotheism* is true, then the Jews took their monotheism from the Egyptian cult of Aton, the sun god, and the Christians derived their conception of God from the Jews. A common emphasis on light is therefore not surprising.

23 *T.S. Eliot: Collected Poems 1909–1962* (London: Faber and Faber, 1974), p. 218.

24 There are two reasons why a conventional Christian like Eliot might think death less important than sin. First, for a sinless man, or a man purged of sin, death is blissful eternal life; if death is unpleasant, this is a direct result of one's own sinfulness. Second, death only came into the world because of man's sinfulness (see Romans 5.12, and Milton PL, II, 629–889). I am grateful to Harry Orr for drawing the passage in Romans to my

attention.

25 Elgar eventually lost his Catholic faith and came round to Larkin's view. 'There is nothing but oblivion', he remarked towards the end of his life. See Andrew Walton's sleeve notes to *Elgar: The Dream of Gerontius*, Naxos 8.553885–86, p. 3.

26 Kingsley Amis, *Memoirs* (London: Hutchinson, 1994), p 62.

27 William H. Pritchard, 'The Least Deceived: Philip Larkin, Poet of Death', in *About Larkin: The Newsletter of the Philip Larkin Society*, No. 5, April 1998, pp. 8–9, at p. 9.

28 The notions of real and notional assent are taken from Newman. See John Henry Cardinal Newman, *A Grammar of Assent* (New York: Image Books, 1955).

29 There are several other poems where Larkin tries to excuse his own lack of altruism by a contentious reanalysis designed to show that altruism is actually a disguised form of egoism. Indeed, he implies that his own position is more honest, first, because he is more clear sighted, and second, because at least *he* – unlike the altruist – never pretends that his own position is morally superior or even laudable. For example, in 'Self's the Man' (if Larkin is not just assuming an ironic mask) he compares the time and effort Arnold puts into his family with his own self-concern, and comments:

> But wait, not so fast:
> Is there such a contrast?
> He was out for his own ends
> Not just pleasing his friends;
>
> And if it was such a mistake
> He still did it for his own sake,
> Playing his own game.
> So he and I are the same. [CP:117–18]

Similarly, the women (and possibly children) who see someone carried off in an ambulance whisper '*Poor soul … / …* at *their own* [my italics] distress' [CP:132–3] in contrast to the genuinely disinterested sympathy one might expect. Perhaps Larkin is implying disinterested sympathy is and must be a myth. If so, he is mistaken. A surprisingly popular conception of altruism holds that egoists want to satisfy their own desires but altruists don't. Larkin is right to imply that this conception of altruism is incoherent, but it does not follow that *altruism* is incoherent. In reality, both the egoist and the altruist have desires they want satisfied, but in straightforward circumstances this is just a necessary condition for having a desire. A desire you did not want satisfied – even when it was not over-ridden by duty or some higher-order desire – simply wouldn't be a desire. The difference between an egoist and an altruist is therefore found in the different *content* of their desires. The happiness of others plays no part in an egoist's happiness, whereas the happiness of others *is* part of an altruist's happiness. This is all the difference there is between the two. To argue therefore that there is no difference between egoists and altruists because both have desires they want to satisfy, is to overlook the fact that one has *selfish*, and the other, *unselfish* desires. In the same way, sympathy for another's distress need not involve any thought about oneself undergoing the same distress, although this could happen on a particular occasion.

30 This point is not in tension with my remark in Section III about the way the last verse channels Larkin back into his own life. The middle stanzas are private in the sense that they represent the unarticulated thoughts of a particular man. They are public in the sense that the content of the thoughts, being abstract, could be entertained by anyone. The last

stanza is public in that it frequently mentions physical objects which part of the objective realm. It is private in the sense that we know of objects' existence through perception, and perception, unlike thought, always implies a unique point of view. You and I can share the same thought at the same time, but we cannot both look at the same object from the same angle at the same time. Perception consequently emphasizes the separateness of persons in a way that thought does not.

31 I would like to thank Alison Mace for making this point to me.

32 'Aubade' is one of the few poems – Plath's 'Daddy' is another – that seem to provoke a more than literary response. They somehow get through to people who normally think nothing of poetry. Others, who came expecting only to appreciate, turn away stunned and sickened. 'I remember reading it', said one of Larkin's colleagues at the university, 'and it upset me so much it nearly ruined my holiday' [M:468–9]. The reaction is typical.

33 I would very much like to thank Alan Heaven and Marie McGinn for extremely helpful comments on earlier drafts of this paper.

Bibliography

Abrams, M.H., *Natural Supernaturalism: Tradition and Revolution in Romantic Literature* (London: Norton, 1973).

Allot, Kenneth, 'Matthew Arnold's Reading Lists in Three Early Diaries', *Victorian Studies*, 11 (1959).

Amis, Kingsley, *Memoirs* (London: Hutchinson, 1994).

Amrine, F., F.J. Zucker and H. Wheeler (eds), *Goethe and the Sciences: A Reappraisal*, Boston Studies in the Philosophy of Science, vol. 97 (Dordrecht: Reidel, 1987).

Anderson, Warren D., *Matthew Arnold and the Classical Tradition* (Ann Arbor: University of Michigan Press, 1965).

Annas, Julia, *An Introduction to Plato's Republic* (Oxford: Oxford University Press, 1991).

Annas, Julia, *The Morality of Happiness* (New York: Oxford University Press, 1993).

Anscombe, G.E.M., *Intention* (Oxford: Blackwell, 1958).

apRoberts, Ruth, *Arnold and God* (Berkeley: University of California Press, 1983).

Aristotle, *The Ethics of Aristotle. The Nicomachean Ethics*, trans. J.A.K. Thompson, Introduction and notes Jonathan Barnes, revised with notes and appendices by Hugh Tredennick (Harmondsworth: Penguin Books, 1976).

Arnold, Matthew, *Essays Literary and Critical*, ed. G.K. Chesterton (London: Dent, 1919).

Arnold, Matthew, *Unpublished Letters of Matthew Arnold*, ed. Arnold Whitridge (New Haven: Yale University Press, 1923).

Arnold, Matthew, *The Letters of Matthew Arnold to Arthur Hugh Clough*, ed. Howard Foster Lowry (London Oxford University Press, 1932).

Arnold, Matthew, *The Note-Books of Matthew Arnold*, ed. Howard Foster Lowry, Karl Young and Waldo Hilary Dunn (London: Oxford University Press, 1952).

Arnold, Matthew, *The Complete Prose Works of Matthew Arnold*, 11 vols, ed. R.H. Super (Ann Arbor: Michigan University Press, 1960–77).

Arnold, Matthew, *Arnold: The Complete Poems*, ed. K. and M. Allott (London: Longman: 1987).

Auden, W.H., 'The Joker in the Pack', in J. Wain (ed.), *Othello: A Casebook* (London: Macmillan, 1985).

Augustine, Saint, *Confessions*, ed. R.S. Pine-Coffin (Harmondsworth: Penguin, 1971).

Austen, Jane, *Emma* (London: Oxford University Press, 1973).

Bacon, Francis, 'Of Beauty', in *The Essays or Counsels Civill and Morall of Frances Bacon Lord Verulam*, ed. O. Smeaton (London: Dent, 1906).

Baker, G.P. and P.M.S. Hacker, *Wittgenstein: Meaning and Understanding* (Oxford: Blackwell, 1980).

Baldwin, T.W., *William Shakespere's Small Latine & Lesse Greeke* (Urbana: University of Illinois Press, 1944).
Bambrough, R., 'How to Read Wittgenstein', in G. Vesey (ed.), *Understanding Wittgenstein* (London: Macmillan, 1974).
Barlow, William, *The Summe and Substance of the Conference ... at Hampton Court* (1604).
Barnes, Julian, 'Favourite Lines', *Sunday Telegraph Review*, 25 February 1996.
Bate, Jonathan (ed.), *The Romantics on Shakespeare* (Harmondsworth: Penguin Books, 1992).
Bate, J., *Shakespeare and Ovid* (Oxford: Clarendon Press, 1993).
Battenhouse, Roy W., '*Measure for Measure* and the Christian Doctrine of Atonement', *Publications of the Modern Language Association*, 61 (1946).
Beardsley, Monroe C., *Aesthetics: Problems in the Philosophy of Criticism* (New York: Harcourt, Brace, 1958).
Bedell, Jack B., 'The Metrics of Connection: Form and Tone in Philip Larkin's "Aubade"', *Hellas: A Journal of Poetry and the Humanities*, 8, Pt 1 (1997).
Best, D., 'The Aesthetic and the Artistic', *Philosophy*, 57 (1982).
Blake, William, *Complete Writings*, ed. Geoffrey Keynes (Oxford: Oxford University Press, 1989).
Blum, Peter, 'Heidegger and Rorty on "The End of Philosophy"', *Metaphilosophy*, 21, 3 (July 1990).
Booth, Roy, 'John Webster's Heart of Glass', *English*, 40 (1991).
Booth, Wayne C., 'The Peculiar "Logic" of Evaluative Criticism', in his *The Company We Keep: An Ethics of Fiction* (Berkeley: University of California Press, 1988).
Bouveresse, J., 'Wittgenstein and the Modern World', in A. Phillips Griffiths (ed.), *Wittgenstein Centenary Essays* (Cambridge: Cambridge University Press, 1991).
Bradley, A.C., *Shakespearean Tragedy* (London: Macmillan, 1985).
Breithaupt, F. and R. Raatzsch (eds), *Seeing the World's Unity in its Variety: Goethe and Wittgenstein* (Berlin: Peter Lang, 2003).
Brennan, Maeve, *The Philip Larkin I Knew* (Manchester: Manchester University Press, 2002).
Brooks, Cleanth, 'Wordsworth and the Paradox of Imagination', in M.H. Abrams (ed.), *Wordsworth: A Collection of Critical Essays* (Englewood Cliffs, NJ: Prentice-Hall, 1972).
Bortoft, H., *Goethe's Scientific Consciousness* (Tunbridge Wells: Institute for Cultural Research, 1986).
Budd, Malcolm, *Wittgenstein's Philosophy of Psychology* (London: Routledge, 1989).
Bunyan, John, *The Pilgrim's Progress*, ed. H. Elvert Lewis (London: Dent, 1927).
Burke, Edmund, *A Philosophical Enquiry into our Ideas of the Sublime and Beautiful* (London: Cassell, 1891).
Burke, K., 'Symbolic Motion in a Poem by Keats', in C.S. Fraser (ed.), *Keats: Odes* (London: Macmillan, 1971).

Casey, John, *The Language of Criticism* (London: Methuen, 1968).
Cavell, S., *Must We Mean What We Say?* (Cambridge: Cambridge University Press, 1976).
Cavell, S., *The Claim of Reason* (Oxford: Oxford University Press, 1979).
Chambers, R.W., 'Measure for Measure', in *Measure for Measure*, The Signet Classic Shakespeare, ed. S. Nagarajan (New York: New American Library, 1963).
Church, R.W., 'The Essays of Montaigne', in *Oxford Essays*, contributed by Members of the University, vol. 3 (London: John W. Parker and Son, 1857).
Church, Richard, *Over the Bridge* (London: Heinemann, 1956).
Coleridge, Samuel Taylor, *The Table Talk and Omniana of Samuel Taylor Coleridge, with Additional Table Talk from Allsop's Recollections etc.*, ed. H.N. Coleridge (Oxford: Oxford University Press, 1917).
Coleridge, Samuel Taylor, *Selected Poems of S.T. Coleridge*, ed. James Reeves (London: Heinemann, 1988).
Collini, Stephan, *Arnold* (Oxford: Oxford University Press, 1988).
Copenhaver, Brian P. and Charles B. Schmitt, *Renaissance Philosophy, A History of Western Philosophy*, vol. 3 (Oxford: Oxford University Press, 1992).
cummings, e.e., *Collected Poems* (New York: Harcourt, Brace, 1953).
Currie, G., *An Ontology of Art* (Basingstoke: Macmillan, 1989).
Currie, Greg, review of Peter Lamarque and Stein Haugom Olsen, *Truth, Fiction and Literature*, *Mind*, 104 (1995).
Danto, A.C., 'The Artworld', *Journal of Philosophy*, 61 (1964).
Davidson, D. (ed.), *The Penguin Book of Eighteenth Century Verse* (Harmondsworth: Penguin, 1983).
Dawson, Carl (ed.), *Matthew Arnold: The Poetry: The Critical Heritage* (London: Routledge and Kegan Paul, 1973).
Dawson, Carl and John Pfordresher (eds), *Matthew Arnold. Prose Writings: The Critical Heritage* (London: Routledge, 1979).
Dean, Jefrey, 'The Alba', in *The New Grove Dictionary of Music and Musicians*, 2nd edn, Vol. I, ed. Stanley Sadie and John Tyrrell (London: Grove, 1998).
Dickie, George, *Art and The Aesthetic: An Institutional Analysis* (Ithaca: Cornell University Press, 1974).
Dickie, George, *Evaluating Art* (Philadelphia: Temple University Press, 1988).
Dickstein, M., *Keats and his Poetry: a Study in Development* (Chicago: Chicago University Press, 1971).
Donne, John, *The Complete English Poems*, ed. A.J. Smith (Harmondsworth: Penguin, 1980).
Drabble, Margaret (ed.), *The Oxford Companion to English Literature*, rev. edn (Oxford: Oxford University Press, 1995).
Dronke, Peter, *The Medieval Lyric* (Cambridge: D.S. Brewer, 1996).
Durham, W.H., 'What art thou, Angelo?', *University of California Publications in English*, VIII (2) (1951).

Dutton, Denis, 'Why Intentionalism Will Not Go Away', in Anthony J.Cascardi (ed.), *Literature and the Question of Philosophy* (Baltimore: Johns Hopkins University Press, 1989).

Dziemidok, Bohdan, 'Controversy About the Aesthetic Nature of Art', *British Journal of Aesthetics*, 28 (1988).

Emerson, Ralph Waldo, *Selected Essays*, ed. Larzer Ziff (Harmondsworth: Penguin, 1982).

Eliot, George, 'Silly Novels by Lady Novelists', in A.S. Byatt and N. Warren (eds), *George Eliot: Selected Essays, Poems and Other Writings* (Harmondsworth: Penguin, 1990).

Eliot, George, *Middlemarch* (Harmondsworth: Penguin, 1994).

Eliot, T.S., *Collected Poems 1909–1962* (London: Faber and Faber, 1974).

Ellis, J.M., *The Theory of Literary Criticism: A Logical Analysis* (Berkeley: University of California Press, 1974).

Elton, W.R., 'Aristotle's *Nicomachean Ethics* and Shakespeare's *Troilus and Cressida*', *Journal of the History of Ideas*, 58 (1997).

Empson, William, *William Empson: The Collected Poems* ed. John Haffenden (Harmondsworth: Penguin, 2001).

Enright, D.J. (ed.), *The Oxford Book of Death* (Oxford: Oxford University Press, 1983).

Frege, G., 'The Thought: A Logical Inquiry', in P.F. Strawson (ed.), *Philosophical Logic*, Oxford Readings in Philosophy (Oxford: Oxford University Press, 1973).

Freud, S., *A General Introduction to Psychoanalysis*, trans. J. Riviere (New York, 1967).

Fruman, Norman, *Coleridge and the Damaged Archangel* (New York: George Braziller, 1971).

Frye, Northrop, *The Anatomy of Criticism* (Princeton, NJ: Princeton University Press, 1957).

Gardner, Helen (ed.), *New Oxford Book of English Verse 1250–1950* (Oxford: Clarendon Press, 1973).

Gasking, D.A.T. and A.C. Jackson, 'Wittgenstein as Teacher', in K.T. Fann (ed.), *Ludwig Wittgenstein: The Man and His Philosophy* (Brighton: Harvester, 1978).

Glanvill, Joseph, *The Vanity of Dogmatizing* (New York: Columbia University Press, 1931).

Goethe, J.W. von, *Die Schriften Zur Naturwissenschaft*, herausgegeben im Auftrage der Deutschen Akademie der Narurforscher (Leopoldina) (Weimar: 1947).

Goethe, J.W. von, *Theory of Colours (Zur Farbenlehre)*, trans. C.L. Eastlake (Cambridge, MA: MIT Press, 1970).

Goethe, J.W. von, *Wilhelm Meister's Apprenticeship*, ed. and trans. Eric A. Blackall in cooperation with Victor Lange (New York: Suhrkamp Publishers, 1989).

Goodman, N., *The Languages of Art* (Indianapolis: Hackett, 1969).

Grayling, A.C., *Wittgenstein* (Oxford: Oxford University Press, 1988).
Haller, R., *Questions on Wittgenstein* (London: Routledge, 1988).
Harrison, Frederic, 'Culture: A Dialogue', *Fortnightly Review*, 11 (November 1867).
Hartner, W., 'Goethe and the Natural Sciences', in Victor Lange (ed.), *Goethe: A Collection of Critical Essays* (New Jersey: Prentice-Hall, 1968).
Heaney, Seamus, 'Joy or Night: Last Things in the Poetry of W.B. Yeats and Philip Larkin', in *The Redress of Poetry* (London: Faber and Faber, 1995).
Hegel, G.W.F., *Phänomenologie des Geistes*, 6th edn, ed. Johannes Hoffmeister (Hamburg, 1952).
Hegel, G.W.F., Preface to *The Phenomenology of Spirit*, trans. Walter Kaufmann, in *Hegel: Reinterpretation, Texts, and Commentary* (New York, 1965).
Hegel, G.W.F., *Phenomenology of Spirit*, trans. A.V. Miller (Oxford: Oxford University Press, 1977).
Heidegger, M., *On Being and Time* (New York: Harper and Row, 1972).
Heller, E., *The Disinherited Mind* (London: Bowes and Bowes, 1975).
Hilmy, S. Stephen, 'Tormenting Questions in *Philosophical Investigations* Section 133', in *Wittgenstein's Philosophical Investigations: Text and Context*, ed. Robert J. Arlington and Hans-Johann Glock (London: Routledge, 1991).
Hipple, Walter J. Jr, 'Matthew Arnold, Dialectitian', *The University of Toronto Quarterly*, 32 (1963).
Holloway, John, 'Matthew Arnold', in D.J. DeLaura (ed.), *Matthew Arnold: A Collection of Critical Essays* (New Jersey: Prentice-Hall, 1973).
Housman, A.E., *Collected Poems*, ed. J. Sparrow (Harmondsworth: Penguin, 1956).
Hulme, T.E., 'Romanticism and Classicism', in H. Reed (ed.), *Speculations: Essays on Humanism and the Philosophy of Art* (London; Routledge and Kegan Paul, 1987).
Hume, David, *A Treatise of Human Nature*, ed. L.A. Selby-Bigge, revised P.H. Nidditch (Oxford: Oxford University Press, 1978).
Hume, David, 'Of the Standard of Taste', in W. Kennick (ed.), *Art and Philosophy* (New York: St Martin's Press, 1979).
Hume, David, *Dialogues on Natural Religion*, ed. J.M. Bell (Harmondsworth: Penguin Books, 1990).
Isenberg, A., *Aesthetics and the Theory of Criticism*, ed. W. Callaghan et al. (Chicago: University of Chicago Press, 1988).
James VI and I, *Political Writings*, ed. Johann P. Sommerville, Cambridge Texts in the History of Political Thought (Cambridge, New York, Oakleigh, and Melbourne: Cambridge University Press, 1994).
James, Henry, 'Henry James on Arnold's Importance', *English Illustrated Magazine*, 1 (January 1884).
James, Henry, 'The Limitations of Dickens', in M.D. Zabel and L.H.P. Powers (eds), *The Portable Henry James* (Harmondsworth: Penguin, 1977).

Johnson Abercrombie, M.L., *The Anatomy of Judgment* (London: Hutchinson, 1960).

Jones, Emrys, *The Origins of Shakespeare* (Oxford: Clarendon Press, 1977).

Kant, Immanuel, *The Critique of Judgement*, trans. J.C. Meredith (Oxford: Oxford University Press, 1973).

Kant, Immanuel, *The Moral Law* (*Groundwork of the Metaphysic of Morals*), ed. H.J. Paton (London: Hutchinson, 1976).

Keats, John, *The Selected Poetry of Keats*, ed. Paul de Man (New York: New American Library, 1966).

Keats, John, *Letters of John Keats*, ed. R. Gittings (Oxford: Oxford University Press, 1985).

Kennick, W.E., 'Does Traditional Aesthetics Rest on a Mistake?', *Mind*, LXVII (1958).

Kermode, Frank, *The Sense of an Ending: Studies in the Theory of Fiction* (London: Oxford University Press, 1968).

Kerrigan, William, *Hamlet's Perfection* (Baltimore: Johns Hopkins University Press, 1994).

Knights, L.C., *Further Explorations* (London; Chatto and Windus, 1965).

Lamarque, Peter and Stein Haugom Olsen, *Truth, Fiction, and Literature* (Oxford: Oxford University Press, 1994).

Langer, S.K., *Philosophy in a New Key* (Cambridge, MA: Harvard University Press, 1976).

Larkin, Philip, *All What Jazz: A Record Diary* (London: Faber and Faber, 1970).

Larkin, Philip, *Required Writing* (London: Faber and Faber, 1983).

Larkin, Philip, *Collected Poems*, ed. A. Thwaite (London: Faber and Faber and the Marvell Press, 1988).

Larkin, Philip, *Selected Letters of Philip Larkin*, ed. Anthony Thwaite (London: Faber and Faber, 1992).

Larkin, Philip, *Further Requirements*, ed. Anthony Thwaite (London: Faber and Faber, 2001).

Larkin, Philip, *Philip Larkin, 'Trouble at Willow Gables' and Other Fictions*, ed. James Booth (London: Faber and Faber, 2002).

Lawrence, W.W., *Shakepeare's Problem Comedies* (New York: Macmillan, 1931).

Leavis, F.R., *The Great Tradition* (London: Chatto and Windus, 1979).

Leavis, F.R., *The Common Pursuit* (Harmondsworth: Penguin, 1983).

Leech, Clifford, 'The Meaning of *Measure for Measure*', in G.K. Stead (ed.), *Measure for Measure: A Casebook* (London: Macmillan, 1971).

Lerner, Lawrence, *Philip Larkin* (Plymouth: Northcote House, 1997).

Levin, Richard, 'The King James Version of *Measure for Measure*', *Clio*, 3 (1974).

Levinson, M., *Keats' Life of Allegory: the Origin of a Style* (Oxford: Blackwell, 1988).

Lewis, C.S., *The Allegory of Love: A Study in Medieval Tradition* (Oxford: Oxford University Press, 1953).

Lodge, David, *Changing Places* (Harmondsworth: Penguin, 1978).
Luther, Martin, *Werke*, Kritische Gesamtausgabe, vol. 6 (Weimar/Graz: H. Böhlau, 1888).
Luther, Martin, *Luther's Works*, ed. J. Pelikan and H.T. Lehmann, trans. H.E. Jacobs and J. Atkinson, vol. 44 (St Louis, MO: Concordia, 1958).
Lycan, William G. and Peter K. Machamer, 'A Theory of Critical Reasons', in B. Tilghman (ed.), *Language and Aesthetics* (Lawrence: Kansas University Press, 1973).
MacNeice, Louis, *Collected Poems 1925–1948* (London: Faber and Faber, 1949).
MacNeice, Louis, *Selected Poems of Louis MacNeice* ed. W.H. Auden (London: Faber and Faber, 1977).
Malcolm, Norman, *Wittgenstein: A Memoir* (Oxford: Blackwell, 1984).
Martindale, Ch. and M. Martindale, *Shakespeare and the Uses of Antiquity* (London and New York: Routledge, 1990).
McAllister, J.W., *Beauty and Revolution in Science* (Ithaca: Cornell University Press, 1996).
McCarthy, Mary, *The Writing on the Wall* (Harmondsworth: Penguin, 1973).
McEwan, Ian, *The Comfort of Strangers* (London: Cape, 1981).
McGuinness, B., *Wittgenstein: A Life: Young Ludwig* (London: Duckworth, 1988).
Medcalf, Stephen, 'Shakespeare on Beauty, Truth and Transcendence', in A. Baldwin and S. Hutton (eds), *Platonism and the English Imagination* (Cambridge: Cambridge University Press, 1994).
Mendelson, E., *Early Auden* (New York: Viking Press, 1981).
Meron, Theodor, *Henry's Wars and Shakespeare's Laws: Perspectives on the Law of War in the Later Middle Ages* (Oxford: Clarendon Press, 1993).
Middleton Murry, J., *Studies in Keats, New and Old* (Oxford: Oxford University Press, 1939).
Miller, Robert P. (ed.), *Chaucer: Sources and Backgrounds* (New York, Oxford University Press, 1977).
Milton, John, *Paradise Lost*, ed. Alistair Fowler (London: Longman, 1989).
Mitias, Michael H., *What Makes an Experience Aesthetic?* (Wurzburg: 1988).
Mitias, Michael H. (ed.), *Aesthetic Quality and Aesthetic Experience* (Wurzburg: 1988).
Monk, R., *Ludwig Wittgenstein; The Duty of Genius* (London: Cape, 1990).
Montaigne, Michel de, *The Essays of Michael Lord of Montaigne*, trans. John Florio (1603), ed. Henry Morley (London: Routledge, 1886).
Montaigne, Michel de, *Essais*, ed. M. Rat, vol. 2 (Paris: Editions Garnier, 1962).
Montaigne, Michel de, *Montaigne's Essays in Three Volumes*, trans. John Florio, Everyman's Library 440–42 (London: Dent 1910; repr. 1965).
Montaigne, Michel de, *Essays*, ed. and trans. J.M. Cohen (Harmondsworth: Penguin, 1981).
Montaigne, Michel de, *The Essays of Michel De Montaigne*, ed. and trans. M.A. Screech (Harmondsworth: Penguin, 1987).

Moretti, Franco, *The Way of the World: The Bildungsroman in European Culture* (London: Verso, 1987).

Motion, Andrew, *Philip Larkin: A Writer's Life* (London: Faber and Faber, 1993).

Mulhall, S., *On Being in the World: Wittgenstein and Heidegger on Seeing Aspect* (London: Routledge, 1990).

Nagel, Thomas, *Mortal Questions* (Cambridge: Cambridge University Press, 1979).

Nagel, Thomas, *The View from Nowhere* (Oxford: Oxford University Press, 1986).

Nellist, Brian, 'Disconcerting the Reader: *Friendship's Garland* and the True Voices of Mr Arnold', in M. Allott (ed.), *Matthew Arnold: A Centenial Review, Essays and Studies* (London: Murry, 1988).

Nevo, Ruth, '*Measure for Measure:* Mirror for Mirror', *Shakespeare Survey*, 40 (1988).

Newman, John Henry Cardinal, *A Grammar of Assent* (New York: Image Books, 1955).

Newman, John Henry Cardinal, *The Dream of Gerontius*, in Geoffrey Tillotson (ed.), *Newman: Poetry and Prose* (London: Hart-Davies, 1957).

Newsome, David, *Two Classes of Men: Platonism in English Romantic Thought* (London: Murry, 1974).

Nicholson, Harold, *Some People* (Oxford: Oxford University Press, 1983).

Nietzsche, F., *The Genealogy of Morals: An Attack*, trans. Francis Golffing (New York: Doubleday, 1956).

Nietzsche, F., *Zur Genealogie der Moral*, ed. C. Colli and M. Montinari, *Nietzsche Werke*, Kritische Gesamtausgabe, Vol. 6.2 (Berlin: Walter de Gruyter, 1968).

Nietzsche, F., *The Anti-Christ* (Harmondsworth: Penguin, 1978).

Nisbet, H.B., *Goethe and the Scientific Tradition* (London: Institute of Germanic Studies, 1972).

North, Helen, *Sophrosyne: Self-knowledge and Self-restraint in Greek Literature*, Cornell Studies in Classical Philology 35 (Ithaca, NY: Cornell University Press, 1966).

Nussbaum, Martha, *Love's Knowledge. Essays on Philosophy and Literature* (Oxford: Oxford University Press, 1990).

Pears, D., *The False Prison: A Study of the Development of Wittgenstein's Philosophy*, Vol. 1 (Oxford: Clarendon Press, 1987).

Perky, C.W., 'An Experimental Study of Imagination', *American Journal of Psychology*, 21 (1910).

Penelhum, T., 'The Logic of Pleasure', in H. Gustafson (ed.), *Essays in Philosophical Psychology* (London: Macmillan, 1964).

Pfeiffer, R., *History of Classical Scholarship from 1300 to 1850* (Oxford: Clarendon Press, 1976).

Plato, *Plato: The Collected Dialogues*, ed. Edith Hamilton and Huntington Cairns (Princeton, NJ : Princeton University Press, 1973).

Plato, *The Republic*, ed. and trans. Desmond Lee (Harmondsworth: Penguin, 1987).

Pope, Alexander, *The Poems of Alexander Pope*, ed. John Butt (London: Methuen, 1984).

Pope, Alexander, *An Essay on Man*, ed. H. Davis, *Pope: Poetical Works* (Oxford, 1985).

Pope, Elizabeth, 'The Renaissance Background of *Measure for Measure*', *Shakespeare Survey*, 2 (1970), pp. 66–82.

Popkin, Richard H., *The History of Scepticism from Erasmus to Spinoza* (Berkeley: University of California Press, 1979).

Pritchard, William H., 'The Least Deceived: Philip Larkin, Poet of Death', *About Larkin*: *The Newsletter of the Philip Larkin Society*, No. 5, April 1998, pp. 8–9.

Quigley, Austin E., 'Wittgenstein's Philosophizing', *New Literary History*, 19, 2 (Winter, 1988).

Quiller-Couch, Sir Arthur (ed.), *The Oxford Book of English Verse* (Oxford: Oxford University Press, 1900).

Reed, T.J., *Goethe* (Oxford: Oxford University Press, 1984).

Reichert, John, *Making Sense of Literature* (Chicago: Chicago University Press, 1977).

Richards, I.A., *Principles of Literary Criticism* (London: Routledge and Kegan Paul, 1955).

Richards, I.A., *Speculative Instruments* (Routledge and Kegan Paul: London, 1955).

Ricks, Christopher, *Essays in Appreciation* (Oxford: Clarendon Press, 1996).

Roe, John, 'The Poetry of Sidney, Shakespeare, Chapman and Donne', in A. Baldwin and S. Hutton (eds), *Platonism and the English Imagination* (Cambridge: Cambridge University Press, 1994).

Robertson, J.M., *Montaigne and Shakespeare* (London: Adam and Charles Black, 1909).

Rowe, M.W., 'Why "Art" Doesn't Have Two Senses', *British Journal of Aesthetics*, 31 (1991).

Rowe, M.W., 'Arnold, Plato, Socrates', in Anna Baldwin and Sarah Hutton (eds), *Platonism and the English Imagination* (Cambridge: Cambridge University Press, 1994).

Rowe, M.W., 'The Objectivity of Aesthetic Judgements', *British Journal of Aesthetics*, 39 (1999).

Rowe, M.W., 'How do Criticism and Aesthetic Theory Fit Together?', *British Journal of Aesthetics*, special issue, *Aesthetics in Britain*, 40 (2000).

Rowe, M.W., 'Wittgenstein, I.A. Richards, and Psychological Aesthetics', *Wittgenstein-Jahrbuch 2001/2002*.

Russo, John Paul, *I.A. Richards: His Life and Work* (London: Routledge, 1989).

Ryle, G., 'Pleasure', in *Moral Concepts*, ed. J. Feinberg (Oxford: Oxford University Press, 1969).

Savage, D.S., 'The Fatalism of George Orwell', in B. Ford (ed.), *The New Pelican Guide to English Literature*, Vol. VIII, *The Present* (Harmondsworth: Penguin, 1983).

Savile, Anthony, *The Test of Time* (Oxford: Clarendon Press, 1982).

Saville, Jonathan, *The Medieval Erotic Alba: Structure as Meaning* (New York: Columbia University Press, 1972).
Schlegel, August Wilhelm, *Vorlesungen über dramatische Kunst and Literatur*, vol. 2 (1808, publ. 1809–11).
Schlegel, August Wilhelm, *Kritische Schriften und Briefe*, vol. 6, ed. Edgar Lohner, *Sprache und Literatur, 38* (Stuttgart: Kolhhammer Verlag, 1967).
Schmitt, Charles B., *Aristotle and the Renaissance* (Cambridge, Mass.: Harvard University Press, 1983).
Schoenbaum, S., *William Shakespeare: A Compact Documentary Life* (Oxford: Oxford UniversityPress, 1987).
Scholes, Percy, *The Oxford Companion to Music* (London: Oxford University Press, 1938).
Schopenhauer, Arthur, *The World as Will and Representation*, trans. E.F.J. Payne (New York: Dover Books, 1958).
Schreiber, S.M., *An Introduction to Literary Criticism* (Oxford: Oxford University Press, 1965).
Scruton, R., *Art and Imagination* (London: Methuen, 1974).
Scruton, R., *The Aesthetics of Architecture* (London: Methuen, 1979).
Searle, John, '*Las Meninas* and Representation', in W.J.T. Mitchell (ed.), *The Language of Images* (Chicago: University of Chicago Press, 1980).
Shakespeare, William, *Troilus and Cressida*, Arden Edition, ed. Kenneth Palmer (London: Methuen, 1982).
Shakespeare, William, *Measure for Measure*, The Arden Edition, ed. J.W. Lever (London: Routledge, 1988).
Sheppard, B., 'Digging up the Past', *The Times Literary Supplement*, 22 March 1996.
Sibley, Frank, 'General Criteria and Reasons in Aesthetics', in John Fisher (ed.), *Essays in Aesthetics: Perspectives on the Work of Monroe Beardsley* (Philadelphia: Temple University Press, 1983).
Sidgwick, Henry, 'The Prophet of Culture', *MacMillan's Magazine*, 16 August 1867.
Simmons, Ernest J., *Tolstoy* (London: Routledge and Kegan Paul, 1973).
Simpson, J.A. and E.S.C. Weiner (eds), *The Oxford Dictionary*, 2nd edn (Oxford: Clarendon Press, 1991).
Smith, Stevie, *The Collected Poems of Stevie Smith* (London: Allen Lane, 1978).
Stauffer, Donald A., *Shakespeare's World of Images. The Development of his Moral Ideas* (New York: Norton, 1949; repr. Bloomington, IN: Indiana University Press, 1966).
Stephenson, R.H., *Goethe's Conception of Knowledge and Science* (Edinburgh: Edinburgh University Press, 1995).
Stevenson, Donald Lloyd, *The Achievement of Shakespeare's Measure for Measure* (Ithaca: Cornell University Press, 1966).
Stirling, John, *London and Westminster Review*, July 1838.

Swarbrick, Andrew, *Out of Reach: The Poetry of Philip Larkin* (London: Macmillan, 1995).

Tanner, Michael, 'Wittgenstein and Aesthetics', *Oxford Review*, 3 (1966).

Tanner, Michael, 'Objectivity and Aesthetics', *Proceedings of the Aristotelian Society, Supplementary Volume*, XLII, 1968.

Taylor, Charles, *Hegel* (Cambridge: Cambridge University Press, 1975).

Taylor, Daniel, *Explanation and Meaning* (Cambridge: Cambridge University Press, 1970).

Thompson, J.A.K., *Shakespeare and the Classics* (London: George Allen and Unwin, 1952).

Tillotson, Geoffrey, 'Matthew Arnold's Prose: Theory and Practice', in D.J. DeLaura (ed.), *Critical Modern English Usage* (Oxford: Oxford University Press, 1954).

Timms, D., *Philip Larkin* (Edinburgh: Oliver and Boyd, 1973).

Tolley, A.T., *My Proper Ground: A Study of the Work of Philip Larkin and its Development* (Edinburgh: Edinburgh University Press, 1991).

Trésor de la Langue Francaise (Paris: Centre Nationale de la Recherche Scientifique, 1974).

Trevelyan, G.M., 'Goethe as Thinker', in *Essays on Goethe*, ed. W. Rose (London: Cassell, 1949).

Trilling, Lionel, *The Opposing Self* (Oxford: Oxford University Press, 1980).

Trilling, Lionel, *The Liberal Imagination* (Oxford: Oxford University Press, 1981).

Vaughan, Henry, *Henry Vaughan: The Complete Poems*, ed. Alan Rudrum (Harmondsworth: Penguin, 1983).

Velz, J.W., 'The Ovidian Soliloquy in Shakespeare', *Shakespeare Studies*, 18 (1986), pp. 1–24.

Vendler, H., *The Odes of John Keats* (Harvard: Harvard University Press, 1983).

von Wright, G.H., 'A Biographical Sketch', in K.T. Fann (ed.), *Ludwig Wittgenstein: The Man and His Philosophy* (Brighton: Harvester, 1978).

von Wright, G.H., *Wittgenstein* (Oxford: Blackwell, 1982).

Vyvyan, John, *Shakespeare and Platonic Beauty* (London: Chatto and Windus, 1961).

Waisnann, F., *The Principles of Linguistic Philosophy*, ed. R. Harré (New York: St Martin's Press, 1965).

Walton, Kendal, 'Categories of Art', *Philosophical Review*, LXX1X (1970).

Weitz, M., 'The Role of Theory in Aesthetics', *Journal of Aesthetics and Art Criticism*, XV (1956).

Wells, G.A., *Goethe and the Development of Science 1750–1900* (Alpen aan den Rijn: Sijthoff and Noordhoff, 1978).

Westphal, J., *Colour: Some Philosophical Problems From Wittgenstein* (Oxford: Blackwell, 1987).

Wharton, Edith, *The House of Mirth* (Harmondsworth: Penguin, 1986).

Wilkinson, E.M. and L.A. Willoughby (eds), *Goethe: Poet and Thinker* (London: Edward Arnold, 1962).

Williams, Bernard A.O., *Ethics and the Limits of Philosophy* (London: Collins, 1985).

Williams, Bernard A.O., *Shame and Necessity*, Sather Classical Lectures 57 (Berkeley: University of California Press, 1993).

Wilson Knight, G., '*Measure for Measure* and the Gospels', in G.K. Stead (ed.), *Measure for Measure: A Casebook*, (London: Macmillan, 1971).

Winkler, R.O.C., 'Wordsworth's Poetry', in B. Ford (ed.), *The Pelican Guide to English Literature*, vol. 5 (Harmondsworth: Penguin, 1975).

Winstanley, Gerrard, *The New Law of Righteousness*, in G.H. Sabine (ed.), *The Works of Gerrard Winstanley* (Ithaca, New York, 1941).

Winters, Yvor, *The Function of Criticism* (London: Routledge and Kegan Paul, 1962).

Wisdom, John, *Philosophy and Psycho-analysis* (Oxford: Blackwell, 1969).

Wittgenstein, Ludwig, *The Blue Book*, ed. R. Rhees (Oxford: Blackwell, 1964).

Wittgenstein, Ludwig, *Zettel*, ed. G.E.M. Anscombe and G.H. von Wright (Oxford: Blackwell, 1967).

Wittgenstein, Ludwig, *On Certainty*, ed. G.E.M. Anscombe and G.H. von Wright (Oxford: Blackwell, 1969).

Wittgenstein, Ludwig, *Tractatus Logico-Philosophicus* (London: Routledge and Kegan Paul, 1973).

Wittgenstein, Ludwig, *Philosophical Investigations*, ed. G.E.M. Anscombe (Oxford: Blackwell, 1976).

Wittgenstein, Ludwig, *Remarks on Colour*, ed. G.E.M. Anscombe (Blackwell, Oxford, 1977).

Wittgenstein, Ludwig, *Lectures and Conversations on Aesthetics*, ed. C. Barrett (Oxford: Blackwell, 1978).

Wittgenstein, Ludwig, *Remarks on the Foundations of Mathematics*, ed. G.E.M. Anscombe, R. Rhees and G.H. von Wright (Oxford: Blackwell, 1978).

Wittgenstein, Ludwig, 'Wittgenstein's Lectures in 1930–33', ed. G.E. Moore, in H. Osborne (ed.), *Aesthetics* (Oxford: Oxford University Press, 1979).

Wittgenstein, Ludwig, *Wittgenstein's Lectures, Cambridge 1932–1935*, ed. A. Ambrose (Oxford: Blackwell, 1979).

Wittgenstein, Ludwig, 'Remarks on Frazer's *Golden Bough*', trans. John Beverslius, in C.G. Luckhardt (ed.), *Wittgenstein. Sources and Perspectives* (Brighton: Harvester, 1979).

Wittgenstein, Ludwig, *Culture and Value*, ed. G.H. von Wright (Oxford: Blackwell, 1980).

Wittgenstein, Ludwig, *Remarks on the Philosophy of Psychology*, vol. I, ed. G.E.M. Anscombe and G.H. von Wright (Oxford: Blackwell, 1980).

Wordsworth, William, *A Choice of Wordsworth's Verse*, ed. R.S. Thomas (London: Faber and Faber, 1977).

Wordsworth, William, *William Wordsworth*, ed. S. Gill, The Oxford Authors Series (Oxford: Oxford University Press, 1984).

Index